Frames of Southern Mind

For
Richard J. Calhoun, J. Lasley Dameron,
Lewis A. Lawson, Marion Montgomery
and Thomas Daniel Young
Scholars & Friends

Jan Nordby Gretlund

Frames of Southern Mind

*Reflections on the Stoic,
Bi-Racial & Existential South*

Odense University Press 1998

FRAMES OF SOUTHERN MIND

The publication was made possible by grants from
Odense University, on the recommendation of Clara Juncker,
Morten Nøjgaard and Lars Ole Sauerberg,
and from A/S Fehr og Co.'s Legat

© Jan Nordby Gretlund and Odense University Press 1998
Printed by Narayana Press, Gylling, Denmark
Cover design by Ulla Poulsen Precht
ISBN 87-7838-397-8

The author holds the copyright to the cover photos except:

Martin Luther King, Sr. and Jimmy Carter by Associated Press/Nordfoto
K. A. Porter (child) courtesy Special Collections,
University of Maryland College Park Libraries
K. A. Porter and Flannery O'Connor by Thomas Gossett
Josephine Humphreys by Stuart Kidd

Odense University Press
Campusvej 55 · DK-5230 Odense M

Phone +45 66 15 79 99 · Fax +45 66 15 81 26
E-mail: press@forlag.ou.dk
Internet bookstore: http://www.ou.dk/press

Distribution in the United States and Canada:

International Specialized Book Services
5804 NE Hassalo Street
Portland, OR 97213-3644
USA
Phone +1-800-944-6190

Contents

Framing Southern Minds: An Introduction   7

The Stoic South

1 The Man at the Gate: Allen Tate and the Confederate Dead   *19*
2 Katherine Anne Porter and the Old South   *31*
3 Madison Jones's Last Southern Agrarians   *45*
4 The Woman by the Side of the Road: Flannery O'Connor's Social Stoicism   *57*
5 Mint-juleping with Marcus Aurelius: Walker Percy's Stoicism   *73*

The Bi-Racial South

6 The Man in the Tree: Katherine Anne Porter's Lynching Story   *89*
7 In a Run-Away Buggy: Ralph Ellison's Bi-Racial America   *103*
8 "A Good Man with a Good Voice": A Visit with Martin Luther King, Sr.   *117*
9 Eudora Welty's Reaction to the Killing of Medgar Evers   *125*
10 Silencing the Voice of the Past in Southern Fiction   *145*

The Existential South

11 Southern Silence?: A. R. Ammons, James Dickey, and Donald Justice   *159*
12 Eudora Welty's Existential Statement   *171*
13 Walker Percy: A Literary Correspondence   *191*
14 Josephine Humphreys's New Southerner   *217*
15 The Man by the Jukebox: Larry Brown's Haunted Voices   *231*

The Lagniappe

16 New Frames of Southern Mind   *245*
17 Frames of Southern History, Biography, and Fiction: A Provocation   *263*

Index   *279*

Introduction

Framing Southern Minds

Ever since I had begun taking painting lessons, I had made small frames with my fingers, to look out at everything....
All through this summer I had lain on the sand beside the small lake, with my hands squared over my eyes, finger tips touching, looking out by this device to see everything: which appeared as a kind of projection.

Eudora Welty, "A Memory"

Framing Southern Minds

One cool March evening in North Carolina in 1996, as I was leaning against the red-bricked wall of a lecture hall at Wingate University, getting ready to give a talk on Southern literature in the 1990s, it suddenly became abundantly clear to me that for more than twenty years I have written on the same three topics: the stoic, biracial, and existential South.

I see the origin of my monomania in the conservative nature of Southern literature itself, which develops and renews itself, but hardly ever ignores a topic once raised. As it is demonstrated in these reflections, the literature of the American South has for the last sixty some years argued about its revered stoic heritage, lingered on the region's biracial identity, and eventually dealt with universal existential questions. This is not really a description of a development, it is more like a recurring, even cyclical shift in emphasis. The existential searching was never foreign to Southern literature, nor were the stoic ideas or the racial concerns ever absent from Southern writing. The main emphasis is forever shifting, but its concerns about heritage, identity, and everyday malaise reappear with cyclical regularity, as reflected in these chapters, which are necessarily cyclical, at least in this sense.

Stoic ethics is a counterpoint for Allen Tate's, Katherine Anne Porter's, and Madison Jones's portraits of anguished modern individuals with existential problems. Flannery O'Connor's and Walker Percy's characters are equally haunted, and the writers make stoic ethics the foundation of their religious searching and social satire. The prejudiced South is the topic of my conversation with Martin Luther King, Sr., whose thoughts on the biracial situation are full of protest, but also of affirmation. And the unethical treatment of African Americans and the lack of Christian compassion among people of both races were also emphasized by Katherine Anne Porter, Ralph Ellison, Eudora Welty, and Madison Jones. For about ten years I corresponded with Walker Percy, at a slow rate, fortunately I can offer our complete exchange of literary letters in this volume. I learned how Walker Percy had used Søren Kierkegaard's existentialist thought to enable himself to move, without rejecting it, beyond his stoic heritage to a Christian faith and a less prejudiced view. The Southern poets A. R. Ammons, James Dickey, and Donald Justice dealt with similar universal questions from a traditional background. So did Eudora Welty, Josephine Humphreys, Larry Brown, and an impressive number of new Southern writers. And for all of them the stoic and the racial issues are essential and integrated parts of the existential quests. At the end of the collection, as a bonus, I offer my view of the situation in Southern writing today.

Southern novels used to imply the values of the old South, there was a distinctive body of work that was rooted in an enduring sense of community, and people knew what you meant when you mentioned "Southern writing." Have the inherited values survived the modernization of the last decades? Or have they been bulldozed away like the sharecropper shacks? The South is also victimized by interstate highways, chain stores, suburban life, and mass media advertising. And Dixie is, of course, losing its distinctiveness, for the more prosperous South of today participates fully in the vast sameness of the nation. But if all Americans are rapidly losing their regional identity, why is it only Southerners that miss it so much that their reading habits reflect the pain of loss? All the old virtues are supposed to evaporate now that every place and every thing are made to look, taste, feel, and sound like every other place and thing. But at the same time historians have argued for a persistent Southern identity that survived modernization. In his *Place over Time* Carl Degler argued for the continuity of a Southern distinctiveness.[1] And the region has remained poorer, more rural, more religious, more violent, and more African American than the rest of the nation.

The purpose of Southern literature, from Thomas Jefferson until today, was always to convince others, from potential immigrants to foreign readers, and perhaps mainly Southerners themselves, that the South is *the best place*: the best place for you and me to live our lives! Not that the South was ever considered God's own country, and calling it "the best place" is not a spiritual reference. In perfect correspondence with the hopes of the first Southern settlers, it was a material idea: the best place for growing rice, sugar, tobacco, and cotton. Nowadays with the success in attracting industries and their accompanying pollution and destruction of the land, the pride in the natural plenty of the South has only survived in small pockets of the region. In spite of the growth ethic espoused by some politicians, few people consider the new industry a natural boon – it does not quite fill the bill. The important question for politicians and Southern writers is whether it is possible to urbanize and yet preserve and protect basic ethical and aesthetic values. Is it possible to avoid creating devastated areas and alienated people by emphasizing the old stoic values of a sense of place, a sense of community, and an awareness of the history of a place?

As the chapterss show, the function of a contemporary literature is among others to express the meaning of contemporary culture in representations of actuality, i. e. to show what we are doing right now. But often the writing also has an ethical purpose and an existential goal, which are to help arrest the dehumanization inherent in our technological everyday. As readers we are looking to literature for ways to recover, or restore, or reconstruct our selves. Lewis P. Simpson pointed out that "the only meaningful covenant for the latter-day writer is one with the self on terms generally defined as existential."[2]

The Southern writers I have written about confirm this claim. But I disagree with Simpson's assumption that the covenant is *new* and with his claim that our memory is now dispossessed of the covenant with history. This "old bulwark against the dehumanization of man" – is still needed, sought after, and occasionally found in Southern fiction of the 1990s.[3]

Today's creative artist in the South has to look for the landscape behind a repetitive labyrinth of highways, motels, restaurants (that do not serve grits), burger-places, gas stations, shopping malls, etc. A modular world in which we are too easily at home because things are everywhere the same. The new Southerner is certainly more consumer-oriented than past-haunted. But in fiction the South is still "the best place," as contemporary novelists insist on testifying. The pride in natural resources of earlier centuries has been replaced by a great pride in the values demonstrated in everyday Southern life. The myth of the contemporary South insists that it is "the best place" to live, because most Southerners pretend to traditional, cultural, ethical, and even racial standards supposedly unrivaled, and apparently unheard of, in other areas of the country.

Contemporary Southern literature is the cause of much contention among critics. Jefferson Humphries argues: "It seems to me, ... , that Rubin, and the New Criticism of Brooks and Warren, which imbues the thinking of most of the Rubin generation, distort literature most grievously by confusing its achieved, and admitted mediatedness with unmediated Truth. This is only a thinner, watered-down version of the nationalist, ideological organicism of the Old South, ... , which led the first generation of scholars of southern literature to a rather sentimental and celebratory view of the past."[4] Michael Kreyling has been one of the most persistent of critics in his attacks on the literary celebration such as it has been expressed by the good ol' boys[5] of *The History of Southern Literature* (1985) and in various collections by Ben Forkner and Patrick Samway, such as *A Modern Southern Reader* (1986). As Kreyling sees it, they argue for a view of Southern literature that identifies, certifies, and celebrates the South and its culture. What he finds wrong with the orthodox southernist approach is that it defines and judges Southern writing solely in relation to a Southern reality.

In his own books Kreyling has tried to see the Southern Literary Renaissance as a development in the history of ideas of the Western world. He wants us to see "cultural waves originating outside the South wash through its literature and change it."[6] He sees a tradition of this approach to Southern literature going back to Jay B. Hubbell's *The South in American Literature: 1607-1900* (1954), and he finds that Richard King's *A Southern Renaissance* (1980) and Daniel Singal's *The War Within* (1982) are good examples of how principles *not* native to the region might be applied to its writings. It worries me that almost all the books he singles out for praise are by historians who only focus on literature to support their historical, political, psychological, or even sociological theses. In his fight against scholars who establish "one, fixed, academized southern literature," Kreyling has found allies among cultural commentators *not* devoted to the South whose primary interest is *not* Southern literature. I am not convinced that lacking devotion and passing interest are special qualifications for a critic of Southern literature.[7]

In contrast to Kreyling I think that Southern history does not weigh heavily enough upon the consciousness of most contemporary Southerners. They behave as if they had finally escaped the biracial past. During the second phase of the Southern Renaissance (1954-68) much fiction by celebrated writers, such as Faulkner, Styron, and Warren, was marred by a desire to demonstrate political correctness on racial issues. But the pendulum has swung fully in the opposite direction, if we judge by the fiction of the new writers, it is today possible to travel through broad stretches of the South and find scarcely a black face in sight. Most of today's Southern fiction by white authors contains little emphasis on race, and the awareness of the issue of race as a problem is not really reflected in the fiction. In general the Southern writers of both races have little to say on race. The subject is not significant in their fiction, it may be brought up, but it is not explored. In these chapters I argue that it is just wishful thinking that race should be unimportant in today's South.

I also write about another lacking dimension of Southern fiction today: in spite of an increasing awareness of existential problems, life in the many large cities of the South is not a popular topic with Southern writers. Marc K. Stengel in the weekly *Nashville Scene* took exception, in the fall of 1990, to the publishing policy of Algonquin Books of Chapel Hill, who publish Larry Brown, Clyde Edgerton, Kaye Gibbons, Jill McCorkle, and Dori Sanders. Stengel's point was that the great cities of the South and all the people who live in them languish unchronicled, while hucksters of Hee Haw mentality mass-produce literary country music about "some giant tobacco plot tended by besotted mobile home denizens with warty children." We are looking for new writers to elaborate on the ideas behind Walker Percy's and Peter Taylor's city-oriented fiction. But we get very few Southern novels about love affairs between receptionists and store managers, or any other city-people. In general, Southern novelists still reject the city as "no kind of place," as Flannery O'Connor put it.

Josephine Humphreys, on the other hand, thinks the painful transition from the old rural world has been completed. And if we discuss the images of country life, i. e. living on and off the land, and the representations of the town and the city in her three novels, the transition certainly seems to have been completed. Humphreys says that Southern writing is becoming more urban and points out that "Walker Percy was really an urbanization, the first Southern city writer."[8] It has been an old worry in the South that education, modernization, exposure to the outside world, and city life would eradicate traditional values. But Humphreys considers herself a Southern city writer and makes it clear that she does not really know much about rural life or farming. The richness of place she creates is of the city, as I show in a chapter on her fiction. She does not seem concerned that uniqueness may be lost as the South becomes more urbanized. Her concern, and that of other contemporary Southern novelists, is for the people in her area and their existential problems.

The best reaction to Michael Kreyling and Jefferson Humphries's attempts to get out from under the Louis D. Rubin, Jr. generation may be to concentrate on the condition of contemporary Southern fiction, as Fred Hobson did in his Mercer lectures *The Southern Writer in the Postmodern World* and in his essays.[9] Hobson's reply to Kreyling and Humphries is essentially that contemporary Southern fiction is healthy. Except for the lack of attention to racial issues and life in cities, I agree that contemporary Southern writing displays an impressive array of new and exciting frames of mind. Literature responds to changes in society, and Hobson is convinced that the economic success of the South will require a new voice, and less reliance on the models of the past.

Is it true that the preoccupation with the old themes and concerns is grinding to a halt, and that we should now listen for a new voice? Or have some old Southern concerns survived economic growth and massive immigration? Southern culture's meaning is carried in representations of actuality. And the only way to answer the questions is to see what Southern writers do with this century's main concerns: the haunting heritage, the biracial identity, and individual anxiety.

I am convinced that although the South has changed, it has also sustained its distinct character, and cultural traits have remained recognizable. I believe that these chapters will demonstrate that while doing justice to the individual existential experience of living in the South, some writers have, with a basis in a traditional ethical and racial knowledge, been able to strengthen the impression of a collective Southern consciousness. They have often succeeded in marrying the best of a tradition with the exigencies of modern living. As I see it, there is a continuity rather than a discontinuity in the treatment of ethics, prejudice, and existence in Southern literature.

What happened to me that evening, when I was enjoying a quiet moment of pre-talk relaxation, leaning against the red-bricked wall at Wingate University's Auditorium, was dramatic enough. I was alone, and suddenly out of the dark night the figures of two women appeared. As they were headed in my direction with determination and conviction and with coats and scarves streaming out, it became obvious that they were bearing down on me. And when they were closing in and I could see their big round eyes trained on me, I heard one of them crying: "It's him! It *is* him! I told you so. It had to be *him*." And as we were face to face, the other woman joined in: "You're right. It is *him*." My mind reeled swiftly through past transgressions, searching the agitated women's faces for clues. What sins were catching up with me? – It turned out that I was indeed the one they had in mind. We had met before, almost twenty years before.

In November of 1977 when we were all at the inaugural symposium, honoring Eudora Welty, at the new Center for the Study of Southern Culture, the kind North Carolina women had given me a ride from Ole Miss to Oxford. When they had heard that a Dane was to speak on Southern literature at Wingate University, one of them had argued that it had to be me. – It was me, I owned up immediately, and in 1977 it probably had to be me. But nowadays it could have been a number of Danish or other European scholars. Today a favorite part of university curricula all over Europe is the study of the stoic, biracial, and existential South.

---

[1] Carl N. Degler, *Place over Time: The Continuity of Southern Distinctiveness*, Baton Rouge, Louisiana State University Press, 1977.

[2] Lewis P. Simpson, *The Dispossessed Garden: Pastoral and History in Southern Literature*, Mercer University Lamar Memorial Lectures No. 16, Athens, Ga., University of Georgia Press, 1975, p. 71.

[3] Lewis P. Simpson, *The Dispossessed Garden*, 99-100.

[4] Jefferson Humphries, "Introduction," *Southern Literature and Literary Theory*, Athens, Ga., University of Georgia Press, 1990, pp. xv-xvi.

[5] Louis D. Rubin, Jr. as general editor, and Lewis P. Simpson, Blyden Jackson, Rayburn Moore, and Thomas Daniel Young as section editors.

[6] Michael Kreyling, "A Southern Dissensus?" *The Southern Literary Journal*, 19/2 (Spring, 1987) p. 102.

[7] Michael Kreyling, "The Extra: Southern Literature: Consensus and Dissensus," *American Literature*, 60/1 (March 1988) 83-95. A longer and more elaborate attack on the line of thought behind the *History of Southern Literature*.

[8] In an interview with me from 1993, unpublished.

[9] Fred Hobson, *The Southern Writer in the Postmodern World*, Athens, Ga., University of Georgia Press, 1991. And "Surveyors and Boundaries: Southern Literature and Southern Literary Scholarship after Mid-Century." *Southern Review* 27/4 (October 1991) 739-55.

Acknowledgements

I gratefully acknowledge that some of the essays in this book first appeared elsewhere, usually in a shorter version and under a different title.

"The Man at the Gate: Allen Tate and the Confederate Dead" was first published as "The Man at the Gate: Allen Tate's Ode," eds. L. O. Sauerberg et al., *The Practice of Literary Criticism*, Odense University Press, 1983, pp. 171-80.

"Katherine Anne Porter and the Old South" has its origin in "Katherine Anne Porter and the South: A Corrective," *The Mississippi Quarterly*, 34/4 (Fall 1981) 435-44.

"Madison Jones's Last Southern Agrarians" first appeared as "The Last Agrarian: Madison Jones's Achievement," *The Southern Review*, 22/3 (Summer 1986) 478-88.

An early version of "The Woman by the Side of the Road: Flannery O'Connor's Social Stoicism" was published as "The Side of the Road: Flannery O'Connor's Social Sensibility," *Realist of Distances: Flannery O'Connor Revisited*, eds. Karl-Heinz Westarp & Jan Nordby Gretlund, Aarhus University Press, 1987, pp. 197-207.

"Mint-juleping with Marcus Aurelius: Walker Percy's Stoicism" was first published as "On the Porch with Marcus Aurelius: Walker Percy's Stoicism," *Walker Percy: Novelist and Philosopher*, eds. Jan Nordby Gretlund & Karl-Heinz Westarp, Jackson, University Press of Mississippi, 1991, pp. 74-83.

"The Man in the Tree: Katherine Anne Porter's Lynching Story" first appeared as ""The Man in the Tree": Katherine Anne Porter's Unfinished Lynching Story," *The Southern Quarterly*, 31/3 (Spring 1993) 7-16.

"Americans in a Run-Away Buggy: Ralph Ellison's "And Hickman Arrives"" has its origin in "Protest and Affirmation in Ralph Ellison's "And Hickman Arrives"," *Delta* (France) 18 (April 1984) 15-23.

"Eudora Welty's Reaction to the Killing of Medgar Evers" has its origin in "A Neighborhood Voice: Eudora Welty's Sense of Place," *Where? Place in Recent North American Fictions*, ed. Karl-Heinz Westarp, Aarhus University Press, 1991, pp. 99-107.

"Southern Silence?: A. R. Ammons, James Dickey, and Donald Justice" was first published as "Southern Silence?" *Semantics of Silences in Linguistics and Literature*, eds. Gudrun Grabher & Ulrike Jessner, Heidelberg, Universitätverlag C. Winter, 1996, pp. 329-37.

"Eudora Welty's Existentialist Statement" first appeared as "Old Mount Salus Blues," in my *Eudora Welty's Aesthetics of Place*, Odense University Press & University of Delaware Press, 1994, pp. 286-314.

"Josephine Humphreys's New Southerner" appeared as "Citified Carolina: Josephine Humphrey's Fiction," *Southern Landscapes*, eds. Tony Badger et al., Tübingen, Stauffenburg Verlag, 1996, pp. 254-65.

The Stoic South

CHAPTER ONE

The Man at the Gate:
Allen Tate and the Confederate Dead

When I first came to the English Department at Odense University as an assistant professor in 1979, I was asked to contribute to a volume of essays that demonstrated the practice of literary criticism, which at the time meant New Critical analyses. I had just been ACLS Research Fellow at the Institute for Southern Studies at the University of South Carolina, 1977-78, and it was natural for me to contribute two essays on Southern literature. One was on Eudora Welty's "Death of a Traveling Salesman," and the other was on Allen Tate's "Ode to the Confederate Dead." The essays first appeared in The Practice of Literary Criticism, *ed. L.O. Sauerberg et al., Odense University Press, in 1983. Allen Tate's thoughts on the Stoic past have always meant something to me, it is still a good place to start, and this chapter is a revised version of my essay on his best known poem.*

The Man at the Gate

Allen Tate began the "Ode to the Confederate Dead" in 1925, and the poem was first published in 1927. Since then it has been revised several times, and a so-called "final version" was published in 1937 in Tate's *Selected Poems*. Nevertheless the "Ode" was revised slightly for its inclusion in *Poems: 1922-1947*.[1] From its first version the poem has had the rigid formality that is characteristic of T. S. Eliot's poetry. This is not surprising, for among the Fugitive Poets at Vanderbilt University, it was Allen Tate who first came to know Eliot's work and adhered most strictly to his example. Tate's "Ode" is an intellectual poem in the tradition of Eliot's "The Waste Land."

The "Ode to the Confederate Dead" was originally called "an elegy," which seems appropriate as the poem is set in a cemetery and contains a meditation upon the Confederate soldiers who were killed during the Civil War. The poem qualifies for the word "ode" in its present title in that it is serious in subject and dignified in style. Yet the title is partly ironic as the Greek ode was to be sung and danced on a public occasion. Tate's "Ode" is not spoken at a public celebration; on the contrary, the poem exists in the thoughts of a man who stands alone at the gate of a Confederate cemetery. Through his mind the poem reflects Tate's sense of history and his idea of the present meaning of the past. In 1938, Allen Tate wrote his own commentary on the "Ode" in an essay called "Narcissus as Narcissus."[2] It is an attempt in the tradition of Edgar Allan Poe at explaining the creation of a poem. Allen Tate died in Nashville, Tennessee in 1979. The "Ode" became his most famous poem.

The personal nature of the poem is apparent in the image of the anonymous man at the gate of the cemetery. He is excited by the sight of the graves, and he wants to claim for himself the vigor of the tradition of the buried soldiers. He considers how proudly the soldiers died, and how completely forgotten they are today. A wall separates the observer from the cemetery. It seems to represent the barrier he senses between himself and his tradition. He is unable to understand fully what the heroes stood for, and why they chose to die. All he is able to do at the moment is to watch the leaves pile up between the graves and contemplate death as a natural phenomenon. He tries to see the cemetery as a part of a historical and existential whole, but fails. He makes an effort to be honest to himself about his emotions and has to admit that for him there is no explanation for the unselfish bravery of the buried soldiers.

The poem is not so much about the tradition of heroism and self-sacrifice, as it is about the failure of the man at the gate in his effort to re-experience that tradition. The true subject is what the observer makes of what he sees, and the vision he tries to summon from his surroundings. Against his own situation, he evaluates his failure to live up to the example of his legendary ancestors. He realizes that *he* would not be able to act out of conviction. But it is not just a question of being judged by the standards of the past and found wanting. The real failure is that he is not even able to understand *their* conviction. He is unable to imagine an active faith beyond anything he can find in his own self. And it is natural for him to try to reduce the past to his own standards.

The refrain enumerates the details of the physical reality that the observer can actually see in the cemetery. But nature disturbs his vision of the past, as it occurs in 25-26. The "wind leaves refrain was added to the poem in 1930, nearly five years after the first draft was written," according to Tate's essay. The purpose was to make the commentary more explicit, and "to time" the poem better. The tone of the poem is set by the fall atmosphere of the refrain. If we see the wind-driven leaves as determined lives, we see that in his mortality man is like a leaf. But are there not qualities in a human life that separate it from the mere mortality of leaves? Were these dead men not *unlike* leaves in their heroism? This is the thought that the man at the gate would like to examine, but mostly he is "Seeing, seeing only the leaves" (42). The word "only" is important, for all he seems able *to know* is that the leaves are blown about among the tombstones. And the wind is as indifferent to human lives, as nature is in the poetry of earlier American poets like Emily Dickinson and Stephen Crane.

The blindly driven leaves serve as a comment on the meaning or lack of meaning of the scene. The last time the refrain is used (74-75), it is developed in the two following lines. The leaves are personified to the extent that they "whisper," and the summoned vision is almost present when his train of thought breaks down for the second time (83). The idea of personifying the leaves has its origin in Homer's *Iliad*. In a letter to Allen Tate of March 11, 1962, Donald Davidson, who was one of the Fugitive Poets, accepted the refrain of the "Ode" as a reference to Homer.[3] The passage in question is spoken by Glaucus, the Lycian commander, and in William Cowper's translation it reads:

> Why asks brave Diomede of my descent?
> For, as the leaves, such is the race of man.
> The wind shakes down the leaves, the budding grove
> Soon teems with others, and in spring they grow.
> So pass mankind. One generation meets
> Its destined period, and a new succeeds. (Book VI, 174-79.)

From the start of the strophe of Tate's poem, the first part of the classical ode, it is made clear that the Confederate dead in the cemetery are removed from the present, not only in time, but also by their anonymity (2). The soldiers are beyond historical identification for the passer-by; and the present generation has as little recollection of them as the wind (3). Below their strictly ordered tombstones the dead can rest "with impunity," for here they are no longer "blown around" and safe from further attacks and humiliation. The stones may surrender the individual names to the elements, but nature cannot be criticized or punished. The graves appear to be neglected. The piling up of leaves in between the graves seems to be the only ceremony performed to commemorate the dead (5). The dead leaves, which are driven by the wind in a casual manner, enforce the idea of decay. And the leaves are driven, as were the soldiers, by divine design (7-8). The wind serves to intimate what the many tombstones confirm: man is mortal, and only death is an eternal presence. These first nine lines imply a question: does anybody today care why the Confederate dead died, or is it only their being dead that is remembered?

The second stanza of the "Ode" offers us the consolation that the dead have entered the cycle of nature, now that their bodies fertilize the ground. And in this sense the bodies are ironically "inexhaustible" (11-13). The eternity that they should have ascended to is symbolically present in the cemetery as "uncomfortable angels." The stone angels are celebrators of the dead that have failed to withstand the passing of time. One angel catches the unnamed persona's attention with the "brute curiosity" of its stare. The fragment of crumbling sculpture seems to indicate the erosion of the tradition that put it there, but the angel so hypnotizes the man at the gate that he feels like a "blind crab" (20-24). He feels transformed to stone and plunged to a lower world, where he only has the "sea-space" of the crab. Modern man with his walled ego may have a certain mobility, but since his emotions and intellect have turned to stone, he is unable to use his animal energy with any sense of purpose. He must move blindly in the space allotted him.[4]

The third stanza begins with the refrain that makes it clear that the persona is unable to conjure forth a perfect vision of the dead heroes. He is "dazed," but only by the wind and the leaves. In this stanza he makes a second attempt at gaining access to the past by creating a vision of it in his mind. Although he comes much closer to succeeding than in his first try, he fails again. The key to the renewed failure lies already in the word "know" (27). It is obviously not easy to experience a total illusion or to completely suspend your disbelief, as Coleridge put it, if "you know" that it is *only* an illusion. The knowing ruins the vision. The expression "you know" is used to introduce three of the lines in the stanza.

The lines "You know who have waited by the wall" and "Here by the sagging gate, stopped by the wall" recall a photo by Matthew Brady, the Civil War photographer, of dead soldiers lying by a stone wall.[5] The stone wall in question may be the wall which played a major role in both battles of Fredericksburg. The wall was situated by the sunken road at the base of Marye's Heights, where there was a cemetery. Matthew Brady's photo shows General Barksdale's dead Mississippians, who were defeated in five attacks at the wall on May 3,

1863. They sacrificed themselves so Robert E. Lee could win at nearby Chancellorsville. But the man at the gate is also waiting by the wall. In an unexpected expression, we have been informed that modern man has only the "twilight certainty" of the crab, – now we are told why. He has been incapable of achieving the "restitutions of the blood" that are brought about by emotions and convictions. The word "immitigable" seems out of place with "pines," but by using the epithet the persona reveals his own need for steadfastness. The word "frieze" in the same line (30) prepares us for the following lines on Zeno and Parmenides.

Parmenides of Elea (c.540-470 B.C.) and Zeno, his favorite disciple, were Greek philosophers who doubted the reality of the phenomenal world. They thought that reality is entirely different from what we can experience through our senses. The mentioning of the philosophers, with their warning against the "way of seeming" of the world and their belief in the existence of only a changeless reality, is Allen Tate's way of warning modern man not to get lost in the illusions of apparent change. The philosophic scepticism makes belief in a heroic code possible. For if you can disregard the random sensual impression of the present moment, it is perhaps possible to act on the basis of convictions, as the soldiers and philosophers did in the past. The word "muted" (33) may refer to the heroic end of Zeno, who in his struggle against a tyrant was captured, but bit off his tongue in order not to talk; a heroic act that could well have been appreciated by the Confederate dead.

The "cold pool" of line 32 is not necessarily just a reference to the scepticism of Eleatic philosophy, it may also refer to the man at the gate who should experience, "the rage," but who is left with his doubts only. He has been waiting for the vision of the Confederate dead to bring an "angry resolution," and for a moment he hopes that it will give him a desire to live his life more fully (35), but it is implied that it will not. The word "shrift" in the next line reveals the almost religious nature of his worship of the dead soldiers. He praises their passionate commitment and their somewhat arrogant ability to believe fully in the justice of their circumstance and to act accordingly. But the man at the gate knows this only as a matter of historical record. The arrogance seen from his point of view was their conviction that their deaths would mean something. He throws in an ironic phrase to try to undo his already imperfect vision: the soldiers were "hurried beyond decision" (40). If the heroes did not *choose* to be heroic, but just escaped the decision-making in the "thick-and-fast" of battle, then he may perhaps regard their "arrogant circumstance" as a limited virtue.

In a letter to Donald Davidson, Allen Tate called lines 42-50 "the germ" of the poem.[6] In this section the persona resorts to echoes of the past through a silent enumeration of battlefields. In a famous line he advises us to turn our eyes to "the immoderate past." The past is "immoderate" in its demonstration of an excess of chivalry and courage.[7] The infantry is "inscrutable" because the observer is unable to understand their motivation. But they did not "last," for the South ran out of men and material. The battles named Shiloh, Antietam, Malvern Hill, and Bull Run were some of the bloodiest of the war. The South lost many of its veterans on these battlefields: so many in fact that the Confederacy could not claim a decisive victory during the remaining war period. On all four battlefields the fighting had to cease when the sun set; and a clear victory could not be claimed by either side. This is why the veterans had reason to "curse the setting sun." But the man at the gate sees the setting sun as a characterizing image for his own time and age. His is the end of the day when men could act. – The stonewall of line 47 is, of course, an echo of lines 27 and 41. But the word also invokes Thomas J. "Stonewall" Jackson, a famous Confederate general. He was shot accidentally by his own men *before* the battle of Gettysburg, and therefore he was not in "the sunken fields of hemp," where his presence might have made the difference.[8] Stonewall Jackson was another inscrutable "demon" who did not last.

The end of the strophe contains an emotional description of the failure of the "vision" produced by the enumeration of battlefields. In agreement with the classical tradition of the Greeks, the poet will not at the end of the strophe advance his ode any further in the direction it has been moving. In his essay on the poem Tate explains that 55-58 are the only lines he has written where he first considered the movement and then "cast about for the symbols." And they became very private symbols: crazy hemlocks, a mummy, and a toothless hound bitch. This is, of course, a section of the poem where the essay by Tate is most helpful, but even with the poet's explanatory remarks the lines remain a challenge. The general idea seems to be that as the man at the gate is losing his vision only sounds stay with him.

It is as if the shout he imagines, which is probably a shout of charging soldiers, startles him into awareness of his surroundings. He is terrified by the tree-tops that tossed by the wind appear crazed and ragged in their outline against the sky. The natural details are used to describe the turmoil in his mind; whereas images of the dead or dying dominate his thoughts about himself. He feels that he is not only dead, but a mummy, or a preserved dead, and as such a relic of the past and obsolete tradition. This is illustrated with a hound bitch: once, it took part in formal hunting, but now it is toothless and dying. There are no rituals any more for the dog or for the man at the gate. Just as there are no heroes. With this thought Tate changes the rhythm from the stately formal to the spasmodic irregular and finally breaks off after only half a line. Tate mentions that Milton's "Lycidas" was his model for the irregular rhyming.[9]

The beginning of the antistrophe is in lines 59-73. The stanza starts a movement in another direction. From being a private discussion within the mind of the man at the gate, the poem now becomes his address to us. The stanza begins to re-establish a formal rhythm by finishing the half line that ended the strophe. We are informed that the blood of the dead will serve to make the sea saltier, so even the comforting idea of bodies fertilizing the ground is withheld (60-61). The stanza illustrates our modern way of mourning the dead heroes. "Ribboned" dignitaries cannot mourn sincerely, Tate says, but they can achieve a "grim felicity" in their execution of formal grief. Everyone is dressed up for the "commemorial woe," but we have not only lost the ability to act, we have also lost any sense of purpose.

We do not have convictions that we would lay down our lives for. "What shall we say of the bones, unclean" (65)? We do not know what to do with the "insane" acres of buried soldiers. Is it that the past has too much control over the present, when we can imagine the shocking details and still not know what to do with them? The arresting line about "The ragged arms, the ragged heads and eyes" (67) is not only in the poem for its shock value, it substantiates the preceding line (which was contributed by Robert Penn Warren).[10] When the persona begins to talk of "gray lean spiders" (69), he no longer seems to be addressing an imaginary audience. As a memory of the dead Confederates in their grey uniforms, he sees only a few death symbols, such as the spiders, the owl, and the willows. Only nature reflects the natural valor of the dead. And Tate illustrates his emotions with the peculiar sound of the screech-owl. For a moment the sound recalls a "murmur of their chivalry," which the formal rituals had been unable to bring forth. The expression the "tangle of willows" may be meant to invoke the fighting in the Wilderness south of Chancellorsville. But for the man at the gate it is not invoked, for he cannot return to his half-vision of the charging infantry.

The ending of the antistrophe is in lines 74-83. Modern man is not even able to express himself as lyrically as the screech-owl, says Tate, we cannot sing but only "say." Our time is "In the improbable mist of nightfall" (77), as he puts it with an unusual negative. Time has borne down upon us and has limited our sensibilities.[11] Estranged from the past, modern man can exist from day to day only. Past and present become indistinguishable, and both the remembrance and the natural surroundings are now obscure to the man at the gate. There is nothing but night, whatever the distractions. As the antistrophe comes to its end, the symbolism again becomes private, but the petrifying speculation and the leaping jaguar elucidate the theme. The "mute speculation" seems to be the intellectualism that blinds man, so that he will ultimately jump for his own image, just as the jaguar leaps for its own reflection in the pool. The individualism that results from the scepticism will lead to narcissistic self-destruction. The egocentric soul becomes suicidally narcissistic, and therefore Tate called his essay on the poem "Narcissus as Narcissus." Compared to the formal rhythm of lines 59-73, all of this is presented in a distracted rhythm, and it finally stops on the weak ending of the word "victim."

If line 84 is lowered, which it is in some editions, the classical structure of the "Ode" would be evident, for the line begins the epode of the poem. The movements in both directions cease, and we are left with some questions.

What shall we say in the face of decay? What are we supposed to do when we realize that our values are only so much narcissism? Shall we sit down and write poems about our sad existences? "Shall we, … , set up the grave/ In the house?" (86-87). Notice, however, that these questions are not answered in the poem. The idea of "knowledge/ Carried to the heart" (84-85) indicates that in our hearts we *do* know what motivated the dead heroes. And the knowledge implies that the answer to the questions of the first four lines of the epode is clearly negative. The lines may even suggest a liberation from the spiritual tyranny of the past. The man at the gate may have only a limited capacity for action, but after all his chance of a significant battle is also limited. The observer is fully dislocated: he is not ready to worship death or a dead tradition, nor is he at home in his own time. Yet, he seems resigned when he decides to leave the cemetery, "the shut gate and the decomposing wall." The decision to leave may be a positive act in itself. The past seems inaccessible and less than useful, and he is leaving because he has a life to live, whatever his present situation.

As the persona is leaving, he sees a snake in a mulberry bush. It is green, quick, and "rioting" with its tongue. The snake and the shut gate bring to mind another place that man was shut out from, at the beginning of time. The exploring snake may be seen as a symbol of life in time. And the concept of time is the only absolute the man found at the gate. Whatever else "Ode to the Confederate Dead" may be read as saying, this is certain: man is inextricably in time. Beyond that, we can be sure of nothing except our estrangement from the past and our mortality. In his essay Tate calls the closing image of the snake "the ancient symbol of time"; but as Radcliffe Squires has pointed out, Tate "might have remembered that when Aeneas prays at his father's grave, a serpent wriggles up from the earth. That serpent was the spirit of his lineage, the spirit of the past, present, and future of the house."[12] The passage in question is from Virgil's *The Aeneid*, Book V, where Aeneas hails his father's ashes. In John Dryden's translation they read:

> Scarce had he finish'd, when, with speckled pride,
> A serpent from the tomb began to glide;
> ....
> With harmless play amidst the bowls he pass'd,
> And with his lolling tongue assay'd the taste:
> Thus fed with holy food, the wondrous guest
> Within the hollow tomb retir'd to rest.
> The pious prince, surpris'd at what he view'd,
> The fun'ral honors with more zeal renew'd,
> Doubtful if this place's genius were,
> Or guardian of his father's sepulcher.

Grand-style heroism is an obvious theme in the "Ode to the Confederate Dead." The poem celebrates the past as a storehouse of heroic and stoic values. The use of the legend of Confederate valor is dramatic rather than decorative. We are not meant to see the Civil War battles as idyllic moments, there was nothing idyllic about them. The war was characterized by disintegration and dislocation, and in this respect the times were not unlike our own. But the antebellum South had a framework of accepted codes that made life tolerable even under adverse circumstances. Is it possible for the modern Southerner to draw any strength from his tradition by defining, reviving and re-possessing the past? The memory of the legendary soldiers seems to promise that the heritage can be reclaimed, and that there is a potential nobility also in modern man. The continued pursuit of integrity that the "Ode" exemplifies is proof of the lasting influence of the past in the present. But the man at the gate finds it impossible to understand the short "happy" lives of the Confederate soldiers. His attempt to celebrate the past disintegrates into a reflection of the decline of his own time. The awareness of the past gives him a perspective on the present, and the memories become the backdrop for a commentary on the state of man. In this respect Robert Lowell's "Ode to the Union Dead" (1959) may be read as a "companion piece." Neither poem is ultimately about the Civil War, but both draw on the past in the analysis of the situation of modern man.

Solipsism is an important theme in the poem. By solipsism is meant the egocentricity of being locked in the sensibility of one's own ego. The man at the gate may have inherited some passions and loyalties, but he is first and foremost a modern intellectual, who suffers from an emotional poverty. He has the malaise described in much twentieth century literature, in that he feels cut off from the objective world of nature and society. According to the version of the past that he has created, the Confederate soldiers did not confuse subjective appearances with reality, and they were able to believe fully in the objectives they fought for. This is what the man at the gate envies. In his attempt at relating his problems to those of other people, he finds no absolute values to believe in. His solipsism arises from his failure to find worthy commitments. And his thoughts and feelings do not lead to action.

But even though we have lost the ability to act in accordance with convictions, we can still recall the time when people did. It is a part of us, as our history and tradition. Although the memory is often rejected and ignored, the tradition implies that it is rewarding for us to struggle with our limitations. One of these is scepticism. And if the man at the gate believes he creates the world in perceiving it, it is no wonder that he finds it difficult to relate to the past. Death can have no explanation beyond the physical cessation of consciousness, human experience cannot have any validity outside the individual consciousness, and the past can exist in the present only as a submerged and distant reality. So for the solipsistic sceptic tradition offers no bulwark against *Angst* and despair. He is forced to realize that he leads a life of isolation, and that this is the origin of his ineffectualness.

Allen Tate struggles with our limitations in the poem. To what extent do we have a free will, and to what extent are our lives determined? We live in the hope that we can act freely, but we have strong intuitions that everything has already been decided. Our heroic potential on one hand and our obvious limitations on the other do not offer an enviable starting position for an inquiry into the meaning of life. But the "Ode" records Allen Tate's attempt to wrest some meaning out of his life and the lives of those who died long ago. In his meditation on the relationship between the subjective and objective worlds of the poem, he points out that the overstressing of the purely intellectual is the cause of the rift between our thinking and our emotions. For the dead soldiers the rift did not exist, or perhaps it was just bridged for a moment when they were "hurried beyond decision" and stoically followed their orders. Donald Davidson was no doubt right when he wrote to Tate that the poem "is not for the Confederate dead but for your own dead emotion." But as S. T. Coleridge wrote his famous "Ode to Dejection" complaining that he could not write poetry any more, Tate wrote his best poem explaining that he felt no emotion any more. He does not celebrate the Army of Northern Virginia, but he does manage to celebrate his supposed inability to celebrate. Some may see the poem and the poet's use of philosophy as an excuse to avoid any possibility of taking action. But the very writing of the poem is an active attempt to bridge the gap between our emotions and our intellect. Allen Tate may not be able to achieve a fusion of sensibility and intellect; like the dead soldiers, he fails, but not without revealing the importance and the dignity of trying.

1. Lawrence Kingsley, "The Texts of Allen Tate's "Ode to the Confederate Dead"," *The Papers of the Bibliographical Society of America*, vol. 71, no. 1 (1977), 171-89.

2. *Essays of Four Decades* (Chicago, The Swallow Press, 1968), pp. 593-607.

3. *The Literary Correspondence of Donald Davidson and Allen Tate*, eds. John Tyree Fain & Thomas Daniel Young (University of Georgia Press, 1974), pp. 383-84.

4. There are echoes in Allen Tate's "Ode" of T. S. Eliot's "The Waste Land," "Gerontion," and "Four Quartets."

5. Keith Ellis, *The American Civil War*, The Putnam Pictorial Sources Series (New York, G. P. Putnam's Sons, 1971), p. 80, photo 179.

6. April 12, 1928. *The Literary Correspondence*, p. 212.

7. Hart Crane described what he considered the theme of the "Ode" in a letter to Allen Tate as "a theme of chivalry, a tradition of excess. " *Essays of Four Decades*, p. 599.

8. See Louis D. Rubin, *The Wary Fugitives* (Louisiana State University Press, 1978), p. 108.

9. Allen Tate elucidates his use of rhymes, particularly in ll. 10-24, in "Narcissus as Narcissus," *Essays of Four Decades*, p. 603.

10. John L. Stewart, *The Burden of Time: The Fugitives and Agrarians*, (Princeton University Press, 1965), p. 386.

11. "Allen Tate and John Peale Bishop: An Exchange of Letters, 1931," eds. Thomas Daniel Young and John Hindle, *The Southern Review* 16 (Autumn 1980), 898.

12. *Allen Tate: A Literary Biography* (New York, Pegasus, 1971), p. 82.

CHAPTER TWO

Katherine Anne Porter and the Old South

During my ACLS Fellowship in South Carolina, 1977-78, I received my first invitation to speak at an American University. Lewis A. Lawson invited me to speak at the University of Maryland at College Park. It became the beginning of our friendship. I savored the chance to do some research in the Katherine Anne Porter Room at the university. I also tried to get to meet the ailing Miss Porter, who lived nearby. But her health was so poor after several strokes that Paul Porter, the writer's nephew, politely asked me not to insist on meeting Miss Porter. My talk was on Katherine Anne Porter, Eudora Welty, and Flannery O'Connor. My comments on Katherine Anne Porter and her life in the South were the origins of this chapter. An early version was first published in The Mississippi Quarterly *in the fall of 1981 as "Katherine Anne Porter and the South: A Corrective."*

Katherine Anne Porter
and the Old South

> *It is my conviction that when events*
> *are forgotten, buried in the cellar of*
> *the page – they are no longer even history.*
> Katherine Anne Porter

Katherine Anne Porter was liberal with information about her family history. She took pride in it and claimed that she was the great-great-great granddaughter of Nathaniel Boone, who was Daniel's nephew, on her father's mother's side.[1] On several occasions K. A. Porter enumerated the distinguished Porters among her ancestors. She traced the family back to the Virginia of 1648. But from a literary point of view, it would have been more interesting if she had told us of her early years in greater detail, for her Southern childhood was a decisive influence on her fiction.

It is not unusual for authors to try to cover their trail when it comes to the actual biographical background. Porter did more than just cover her trail, she consciously built up several myths about her family and her youth in Texas. The surprise is that as she was cultivating these myths, she was also gathering every scrap of evidence that she knew would eventually explode the myths. And with her usual courage she gave the facts to her hand-picked biographer when she thought the time was ripe for such a gesture. She picked Joan Givner, a British-born writer who lives in Canada, who wrote the fine biography *Katherine Anne Porter: A Life* (1982). Porter's motivations are easily understood: when you have spent a life, or ninety years, repeating that facts should be rendered honestly in fiction, it does not make much sense to leave behind a biography consisting of imaginative lies. The biography should at least have a chance to live up to the quality of the fiction.

Unfortunately, Porter told us very little about her first thirty years. Therefore, all accounts of that part of her life differ considerably even as regards basic data. There is incorrect information in the *Paris Review* interview of 1963, and also in the *Bibliographical Guide to the Study of Southern Literature*, although these are among the most reliable sources. The many facts enumerated in Givner's Porter biography, and the more reliable biographical information, have proved valuable in correcting some of the common misreadings of her fiction. The publication of Enrique Hank Lopez's inaccurate and unreliable *Conversations with Katherine Anne Porter* (1981) proves in itself that a biographical corrective is necessary. Besides Givner's biography the best sources of biographical information about Porter are the letters and manuscripts at the University of Maryland. And in the Katherine Anne Porter Room in the McKeldin Library at the university, there are some books from the author's private collection. Her copy of George Hendrick's a *Katherine Anne Porter* (1965) is full of extensive marginal comments. The widely read book is simply full of factual mistakes; and the reader of K. A. Porter's marginalia sees that the corrections are meant to be read. Besides Givner, the autograph comments in Hendrick's book are the main sources of my information.

K. A. Porter *was* born in Indian Creek, Brown County, Texas. Note that this is about a hundred miles due west of Waco, and therefore close to the geographic center of the state. This is often overlooked when we try to estimate the importance of the Old South in the country of her childhood. The old order, to the extent it did exist in Brown County, was an import, which does not, however, mean that it did not survive in the true spirit of the antebellum South. As for her date of birth, K. A. Porter was not herself without blame for some confusion, as she informed interviewers and others that she was born in 1894. But in spite of other suggestions, it can be established with certainty that she was born on May 15 in 1890. The mother, Mary Alice Jones Porter, died at Indian Creek in 1892 after giving birth to her fifth child. "She died of childbirth complicated with pneumonia."[2] When she died, she had been married to Harrison Boone Porter since 1882. They had five children and Katherine Anne was their fourth, not the third or fifth child as critics sometimes have it. The sisters and brothers were Ann Gay, Mary Alice, John and Paul – names that are familiar to readers of K. A. Porter's fiction. The writer's full name is Katherine Anne Maria Veronica Callista Russell Porter, as the writer wrote in the margin of George Hendrick's book (p. 18). As a child she was simply called Callie Russell.

K. A. Porter was herself somewhat uncertain as regards some details of the early life of her family. On her request, her father sent her some information in 1935, and of his wife's death he wrote: "Baby was born in January and your mother died in March. – Your mother is buried at Lamar Churchyard near our old home ... she was only 33 years old."[3] The death of Mrs. Porter meant that Harrison Boone Porter decided to move from Indian Creek in order to live with his mother in Kyle, Hays County, near Austin. The move took place shortly after Mrs. Porter's death; on November 27, 1892, Harrison Boone Porter wrote to Miss Cora Posey, his former neighbor in Indian Creek, to thank her for her help during his wife's illness. The letter was probably sent from Kyle.[4] And it was in this little village that K. A. Porter lived during the most formative period of her childhood. Critics disagree about the time of the arrival in Kyle, and there is also, surprisingly enough, some disagreement in their evaluation of the importance for the writer's development of the nine years with the grandmother in Kyle.

In a letter to Louise Gossett, the critic, K. A. Porter described the town: "Kyle was a little town of about five hundred people. Grandmother had a house there, and her farm was about five miles away between Kyle and Buda."[5] She always remembered Kyle vividly. Here she grew up in the care of her paternal grandmother Catherine Anne Porter, born Skaggs. "Catherine" was also the original spelling of the writer's name. But, as she put it in a letter: "I was named for my grandmother and of course, you know how, at a certain age – the young want to change things, have something of their own, so I changed the spelling, which I now regret. But it's a little late for changes."[6] As should be obvious to any reader of her fiction, life in the grandmother's house would prove an inexhaustable source of material for the writer.

The grandmother had lived in Kentucky in her youth; and she had brought some former slaves with her to Texas as servants. She was known as Aunt Kat "affectionately over the whole region between San Marcos and Austin."[7] For nine years Katherine Anne lived in Kyle. The Porters' town house, though altered, may still be seen there, whereas nothing is left of the country house, which was situated near Kyle. But people in the town still know the original site of the farm. The Porters from Indian Creek and Kyle were Methodists, not Catholics, as it is often claimed. This is obvious in K. A. Porter's "Notes on the Texas I Remember," which she published in the *Atlantic Monthly*, in 1975. It was only as an adult, on April 5, 1910, that she adopted her husband's religion, Roman Catholicism.[8]

To my surprise I find that Givner regards the nine years from 1892 to 1901 in the grandmother's house in Kyle as "one of the most unhappy periods" of Porter's life. The facts do not bear out Givner on this point, and surely Porter would have disagreed violently with the conclusion. The life in Kyle was "pinched" and perhaps somewhat "unharmonious," but all sources indicate that it was far from "disorderly," as Givner maintains.[9] There is no reason to call the period the "nine terrible years." It is at best a very materialistic evaluation which ignores the spiritual values the young Porter learned in her grandmother's house. If we judge by her correspondence and stories, the nine years in Kyle seem to have been among the happiest in her life. Givner writes of "the absence of strong parental models." But that is an underestimation of Aunt Cat. The death of a mother is a great loss for any child, especially if the child is only twenty-two months old. And it was a tragedy for the Porter children, but there is no evidence that it "ruined" their childhood. The love of the strong-willed grandmother did not allow a ruined childhood.

The importance K. A. Porter herself attached to this part of her childhood can hardly be overestimated. From the grandmother she inherited some Old South values, which stayed with her for the rest of her life. When the grand old lady died in 1901 an important formative period in K. A. Porter's life was over. In one of her essays, she was later to write that she had little interest in biography after the tenth year, for "childhood is the fiery furnace in which we are melted down to essentials and that essential shaped for good."[10] She seems to have been right about her own case, at least. The memory of life in her grandmother's house from age two to age eleven served K. A. Porter well in her career. – After his mother's death, Harrison Boone Porter and his children moved to San Antonio. This was in 1902, *not* in 1903 or 1904, as it has often been claimed.[11] It is doubtful that Porter would have recognized her father in Givner's description of him as a weak, shiftless character.[12]

Under the influence of the Miranda stories, I assume, several critics have maintained that K. A. Porter's early schooling took place in a convent school in New Orleans. In all fairness, it must be said that there are references in her correspondence which indicate that she was taught by Jesuits at one time, and that she *was* in New Orleans as a girl.[13] But when and for how long she was there, or if she went to school there, have not been established. It may well be that the so-called convent schooling belongs to the life of Ione Funchess, the writer's uncle's wife, called Tante Ione, who made a significant impression on the young Katherine Anne. For years she pretended that parts of Ione's life were her own. Fortunately, we do know a little about her early schooling in San Antonio, where she attended Thomas School, a nonsectarian boarding school. In an unpublished letter to Louise Gossett, December 6, 1965, Porter wrote:

> I haven't seen San Antonio for many years, and, when I lived there, it was mostly a little, shabby Spanish town with plaster houses and red-tiled roofs and narrow, muddy little streets, and downtown young girls could not walk alone because there were at least three saloons to every block. Just the same, I liked the place. We did not live in town, but out near West End Lake [now Woodlawn Lake] in a pretty, little 1880-style house, which had belonged to a very fashionable young woman named Smithie Reily. It was rather rundown when my grandmother bought it, but I remember the gilded moldings and the imitation raised Spanish-leather wallpaper in the dining room. I have forgotten how long we lived there. Time has a way of folding up on you.
>
> I went at least one year to a school for girls on the other side of the lake. It was really on the upper end of the lake and was called the Thomas School, which is now extinct. All I remember about that school is that the art teacher taught me to draw an inch. An accomplishment I practiced for many years. The French teacher tried to make me pronounce "le coeur" as "lay coor," but I knew better, having learned a little French in New Orleans. I remember going to parties and little dances at the nearby Peacock Military School very pleasantly. I wonder if that school is extinct too. Kyle was a little town of about five hundred people. Grandmother had a house there, and her farm was about five miles away between Kyle and Buda.[14]

In 1906, when she was sixteen years old, K. A. Porter decided to leave school. And in the same year she married John Henry Koontz, a clerk on the Southern Pacific Railway.[15] The marriage lasted for nine years, not just for three years, as it is often claimed (see Porter marginalia in Hendrick, p. 19). After she left school, it seems she taught classes in music and dramatic reading in Victoria, Texas. But as K. A. Porter chose not to talk about her life between 1906 and 1914, very little is known about these years. But it was important for her development that she remained in Texas until February 1914, when she left alone for Chicago. – She tried to get into the movies, and, among other things, worked for a newspaper for one week. But she was not ready to leave her home state yet, and she returned to Texas in September of the same year – possibly because she thought she had contracted tuberculosis. She spent eighteen months, *not* just six weeks as it is often claimed, in a sanatorium; but during a part of that period, she ran "an outdoor school in Dallas for tubercular children."[16] In 1917 K. A. Porter was in Fort Worth, where she wrote for *The Critic*. She covered social and theatrical events; and she acted in the Fort Worth Little Theater. – In 1918 she went to Denver, where she worked for *The Rocky Mountain News* from September 1918 to August 1919. During this period she was critically ill with the dangerous 1918 influenza. There is a letter from Harrison Boone Porter, dated October 23, 1918, to his daughter Gay, Katherine Anne's elder sister, in which he expresses his fear for Katherine Anne's life. After Denver, she moved to Greenwich Village, where she lived until she went to Mexico in December 1920.

In her *Truth and Vision in Katherine Anne Porter's Fiction* (1985) Darlene Harbour Unrue attaches much importance to Porter's Mexican experience. She does not, however, address the question of how long Porter was actually in Mexico. But the facts are that if we allow for childhood visits across the border and a couple of brief touristy visits, Porter went to Mexico twice. The first time she went to live in Mexico City was late November 1920, when she was thirty years old. She stayed less than a year and was in Fort Worth by September 1921. The second and last time she went to Mexico to live was in the middle of October 1929, but she had left again by the beginning of December the same year. She returned to Mexico City at the end of April, 1930, and stayed for a year and a half in her Mixcoac home. Porter left Mexico for good when she sailed from Vera Cruz for Bremerhaven on 22 August, 1931. She had spent a total of two years and a few months in Mexico, and was thoroughly disillusioned with the country by the time she left. These facts do not mean that Mexico is not important for Porter's early career as a writer, or that her time there should be ignored. But the Mexican experience must be seen in the perspective of her long creative life. Porter's early years, the first twenty-eight years of her life in the South, are important for her best fiction and merit more attention. It is significant that her first published poem and the first poem in Darlene Unrue's excellent edition of *Katherine Anne Porter's Poetry* (1996) is her

"Texas: By the Gulf of Mexico" (1912). It speaks of her preference over "the frozen North" for the warm climate of Texas with "sunkissed fruits and flowers" and "fluttering jessamine trees."[17]

K. A. Porter did not, then, leave the South for good until 1918, when she was twenty-eight years old. This is much later in her life than it has been supposed by most critics. Although she traveled all over the world for the next eighteen years, she always remained a Southerner. Under the influence of foreign sights, it was her Southern inheritance that came into focus. The most important of the early stories reflect the experiences of her twenty-eight years in Texas. She did not return *to live* in the South until 1937. Her father stayed in Texas until he died in 1941, at the age of eighty four.[18] K. A. Porter's reasons for leaving the South were sound: "I didn't want to be regarded as a freak. That was how they regarded a woman who tried to write. I had to make a rebellion. .... It was a confining society in those days."[19] As recently as March 1975, Porter told us that she left the South to return only once in fifty-five years.[20] We should not, however, take the statement literally because she lived in New Orleans again (?) from October 1937. In April of 1938 she married Albert Erskine, Jr., and lived with him in Baton Rouge, Louisiana, until June 1940. They were divorced June 19, 1942. After WW II, K. A. Porter made only brief visits to the South. Some of the important visits were with Eudora Welty, in March 1952,[21] and with the O'Connors at Andalusia, in March 1958 and again in October 1960.[22] Flannery O'Connor described the visits in great detail in her letters. And Eudora Welty told me about Porter's 1952 visit with a genuine joy of recollection:

> We drove round the Coast, then pretty unspoiled; it bears no resemblance to what is there today after hurricane Camille. Katherine Anne loves that part of the world, we were getting near – you know she is from Texas near Louisiana, so driving into Southwest Mississippi and Louisiana, we were nearing her bailiwick, and I think she felt that. And she lived in Baton Rouge a long time, where I first met her. All of that country means something to her.[23]

And it is a fact that K. A. Porter was as emotionally involved with the South as William Faulkner. In his second essay on Porter, Robert Penn Warren pointed out some of the similarities between the oeuvres of the two Southerners:

> There is a peculiar similarity, among all the dissimilarities, between Porter and Faulkner. They both turned to the past for a significant part of their material, but turned to an informed and moralized, not romanticized, past; and both in the end tell a story of the passing of the Old Order and the birth of a New Order. Both regarded the present as a product of the past, to be understood in that perspective, and both, though repudiating the romance of the past, saw in it certain human values now in

jeopardy, most of all in jeopardy the sense of the responsible individual, and at the same time man's loss of his sense of community and sense of basic relation to nature. To return to our beginning, both lived through the twenties unreverent before, even inimical to, the shiboleths of the age.[24]

Porter's love for her South is reflected in her writing. A well-known instance of this is her essay on the sources of her "Noon Wine." But an even better is, of course, her comments on Faulkner's writings. She admired his work, especially *The Sound and the Fury, Absalom, Absalom!,* and "The Bear," all of which she taught in classes in several universities. She also taught "Spotted Horses," "Raid," "A Rose for Emily," and "That Evening Sun." Some of her lecture notes on Faulkner are in the Porter Collection in the McKeldin Library. In her notes she called Faulkner the "old green man of the woods." The explanation for that phrase may perhaps be found in an interesting part of an interview for "Camera Three," WCBS, New York, that Porter gave October 14, 1956 (an interview that has been overlooked by Porter critics). The interesting part of the interview in question is where it becomes obvious that Porter to a large extent identified with the rural South portrayed in Faulkner's work. She seemed to see the land as their common ground of human reality and possibility. Porter said:

> Faulkner is rooted as a tree; almost as natural, almost as organic. He is a natural force. And of course, he has – he does get the strength of the man that stands on his native earth and knows who he is and where he is and what he's doing ... the love of the land, but it's that land; it's not just any. You know, if he was from another place, it may not have been.
>
> The South – a great deal of the South has a great hold, some kind of terrific emotional hold. I understand it perfectly, and I can't explain it, but the Southerners are very emotional about the South, and it means the land, it means the way of the land and the things that grow on it, don't you know, and also the lives that have been lived there. We are attached to it. (ms. 18-19)

Another illustration of K. A. Porter's love for the South is her essay "Audubon's Happy Land" about her trip to St. Francisville, Louisiana, together with Mrs. Cleanth Brooks, in 1939. In a private letter she wrote about the trip: "Suddenly after all these years I went back and saw it in one day, and it gave me an extraordinary sense of peace and happiness."[25]

John M. Bradbury has claimed that the Porters, for all their ties with the "aristocratic" heritages of Kentucky and Louisiana, had begun to shake off the traditional sanctities of code and agrarian tradition.[26] I have found no evidence of this. On the contrary, K. A. Porter was brought up in accordance with the best of Southern codes. The results of her early training were a lack of sentimentality, an emphasis on decorum, a moral stamina, and an emotional stability, all of which helped her greatly as a fiction writer. It is not surprising that she remembered the family life in Kyle with pleasure, "I look back on it now and think how perfectly wonderful, what a tremendously beautiful life it was. Everything in it had meaning."[27] No Southern writer has been in a better position to use her own background to advantage. And in the best of her fiction, she did manage to create a dialogue between the past and the new order of the present. It is a dialogue of a universal significance.

Some critical comments demonstrate how fatal it can be to overlook K. A. Porter's emotional involvement with her native area. She created a myth from her family history, but she did not mistake the myth for reality. And she did not idealize or sentimentalize the past, yet she made it clear that there is no escape from it. The characters in her fiction see the past for what it is, so they may organize their lives in terms of the actual. And the past provides the standard by which they finally judge, and by which they are judged by the readers. Without knowledge of K. A. Porter's Southern background, it is easy to misjudge the perspective on the past in her fiction. It is only too easy to overestimate or underestimate the biographical elements.

The Miranda figure seeks self-definition through her past and present. She rebels against the Old Order; but she is at once a part of the Old Order and apart from it, in the way K. A. Porter herself was. It would be a mistake, therefore, to see the Miranda stories as ending in "isolation and desolation," as claimed by George Hendrick. In a marginal comment, K. A. Porter has pointed out that she meant the stories to end "in an exhilaration of having faced one's destiny – [Miranda] wasn't frightened, wasn't sad, only resolved. A very positive state of being" (in Hendrick, p. 75). As a consequence of the "isolation and desolation" interpretation of the stories, Cousin Eve's negative view of the past has been accepted as speaking more of the truth. "In what way?" asks K. A. Porter in another marginal comment, "is a venomous view any more true than a romantic one? Is hatred more *true* than love?"(in Hendrick, p. 74). Only a complete disregard for her love for the South makes the narrow negative interpretation possible.

A sound knowledge of K. A. Porter's biography could have prevented critics from obvious blunders. One critic has argued that she named one of her characters after James Joyce's Gabriel in his long short story "The Dead." In a comment Porter makes it clear that she "called him Gabriel, because that was his name, my Uncle Gabriel Gay." And when the same critic also traces the name "Eliza" to an origin in Joyce's fiction, K. A. Porter gets impatient: "Listen to me for once .... She was my grandmother's sister and she was named *Eliza*! I saw no reason to change it" (in Hendrick, p. 73 & p. 65). She often refers to fig trees in her fiction, not because of the obvious possibility of creating a symbol, but because "we really had fine fig trees, a fruit that was my delight and now a pleasant memory" (in Hendrick, p. 64). And when a critic claimed that the ending of her short story "Rope" refers to Walt Whitman's "Out of the Cradle Endlessly Rocking," she responded, "I never read more than four poems of Whitman – I detest him – always did – I have heard whippoorwills all my life!" Critics have also seen it as symbolic that Miranda is taken to see Miss Honey, Gabriel's second wife, in a hotel in *Elysian Fields*. But as Porter comments, "They *were* living in a slumming hotel in Elysian Fields in New Orleans" (in Hendrick, p. 74).

It is commonly held among critics that the closer K. A. Porter worked to the world of her youth, the more successful she was. When "The Fig Tree," a long lost story, was published in 1960, both critics and readers were pleased. But she chose not to restrict herself to the Texas material. Her work does not, however, have to be *about* the South to reflect and embody the Southern experience. Could *Ship of Fools* have been written by anybody but a Southerner? As Louis D. Rubin, Jr., has put it: "The way that Miss Porter looks at human beings, the things she thinks are important about them, the values by which she judges their conduct, are quite 'Southern,' even though none of the major characters are Southern" in the novel.[28] The novel became the object of many negative comments. The adverse criticism came from readers who could not accept that Porter saw life as devoid of heroes and all mankind as flawed. It is a troubling and dark truth about our moral and spiritual impotence, which it is difficult to accept fully. But Porter knew from experience that people could be agreeable one minute and most disagreeable the next. In her novel she refused to genuflect and did not even add a comforting hint that there could be some universal order. For as she saw it, there is none.

Porter's only faith was in her art and in her duty to tell the truth as she saw it. She saw lust, cruelty, contempt, egotism, and hate. And she had the courage to say so. Her passengers cling to false hopes and ideals while they withhold the love and compassion needed to break their isolation. Some critics looked in vain for a dramatic center in the lives of Porter's characters, but she did not see such a center in the lives of people about her. The tragedy is in man's struggle toward the illusion of something better. The existence of a safe harbor, which was denied already in an early working title for the novel ("No Safe Harbor"), remained an illusion in her fiction. She looked courageously at life and had the artistic integrity to write a novel that offers no real hope. The fact does not make a book popular, but we should try to read it without flinching. The novel offers a terrifying vision of mankind that Marcus Aurelius, Thomas Jefferson, in his final years, and Robert E. Lee would have recognized instantly. Lashing out at Porter in order to get rid of the unpleasant vision does no good. It cannot all be Disney. The novel ends by focusing on a young German's hopes for the future. When he sees Bremen from the Vera, he greets the city as if it "were a human being, a good and dear trusted friend who had come a long way to welcome him." It is the 17th of September, 1931, and his hopes can only be false.

In *Ship of Fools*, as in all her fiction, Porter faced the present and offered her commentary on it. The comments would have been different if her background had been different. Once she wrote, "Of the three dimensions of time, only the past is 'real' in the absolute sense that it has occurred, the future is only a concept, and the present is that fateful split second in which all action takes place."[29] And what statement could be more "Southern"? – To Porter the Southern past was real and *not* a myth, for a part of Southern history is her own history. In one of her marginal comments in Hendrick's book on her, Porter wrote: "The South is no myth to Southerners who live through its history" (p. 75), which is an ambiguous statement that also invokes the Southerner who only lives through history. In view of her mental attachment to Texas, it is perhaps surprising that she never went back to live there. In fact she once planned to return, but nothing finally came of it. In the summer of 1959, she considered a permanent change of address to Austin, Texas, about which she wrote Dr. William J. Handy:

> It is time my peripatetic career should end itself and why not in a place where I can grow cape jessamine and camellias and black figs and pomegranates and mangoes *outside*? Another earthly paradise, though naturally full of mosquitoes, red ants, and chiggers. I think it was the chiggers that ran me off the first time.[30]

As it turned out, Austin could not offer Porter the recognition and celebration she demanded, so she ended her career in Maryland, but her early life in the South was always on her mind.

---

[1] See an autograph letter to Miss Ford of September 2, 1970, among the K. A. Porter manuscripts at the Special Collections Division, McKeldin Library, University of Maryland

[2] Porter marginalia in George Hendrick, *Katherine Anne Porter* (New York: Twayne, 1965), pp. 17-18. Some references to this book will appear in the text marked "Hendrick."

[3] Harrison Boone Porter to Katherine Anne from Mission, Texas, February 13, 1935. See also K. A. Porter to Glenway Westcott, February 6, 1942.

[4] Mr. Porter's correspondence proves that he was in Kyle, Texas, by June 1893; but he was probably already there when he wrote Cora Posey on Nov. 27, 1892.

[5] K. A. Porter letter to Louise Gossett, December 6, 1965. Quoted with Louise Gossett's permission.

[6] The letter to Miss Ford, September 2, 1970. See note 1 above.

[7] See K. A. Porter's letter to Brother William Nance, S. M., from Venice, Italy, no date.

[8] Joan Givner, *Katherine Anne Porter: A Life*, 1982, p. 100.

9 Joan Givner, *Katherine Anne Porter: A Life*, 1982, p. 45.

10 "Reflections on Willa Cather," *The Collected Essays and Occasional Writings*, Delta Books, 1973, p. 31.

11 See K. A. Porter marginalia in Hendrick, p. 18.

12 See Porter's letter to her sister Gay, from Salem, Massachusetts, March 5, 1928, which brings us closer to the people who brought her up. K. A. Porter Collection, McKeldin Library, University of Maryland.

13 Three K. A. Porter letters to Glenway Wescott dated New Orleans, October 11, 1937; December 5, 1936; and March 27, 1940.

14 Quoted with Louise Gossett's permission.

15 K. A. Porter: "At sixteen I ran away from New Orleans and got married." In "The *Paris Review* Interview," reprinted in *Katherine Anne Porter: A Critical Symposium*, eds. Lodwick Hartley & George Core (Athens, University of Georgia Press, 1969), p. 8.

16 See Joan Givner, "Katherine Anne Porter," *Southern Writers: A Biographical Dictionary* eds. Robert Bain et al. (Baton Rouge: Louisiana State University Press, 1979), pp. 360-62.

17 *Katherine Anne Porter's Poetry*, ed. Darlene Harbour Unrue, Columbia, University of South Carolina Press, 1996, p. 65.

18 K. A. Porter's marginal note in her copy of Flannery O'Connor's *A Good Man Is Hard to Find*, 1955, p. 155. The volume is in the K. A. Porter Room in the McKeldin Library.

19 An interview with Archer Winsten, "The Portrait of an Artist," *New York Post*, May 6, 1937, p. 17.

20 "Notes on the Texas I Remember," *The Atlantic*, March 1975, p. 104.

21 There is a K. A. Porter postcard to Monroe Wheeler, dated Pass Christian, Mississippi, March 9, 1952, in the McKeldin Library.

22 *The Habit of Being*, ed. Sally Fitzgerald (New York: Farrar, Straus, Giroux, 1979), pp. 275-77, 279-80, 414, 416.

23 "An Interview with Eudora Welty," *Conversations with Eudora Welty*, ed. Peggy W. Prenshaw, (Jackson, University of Mississippi, 1984), p. 219.

24 Robert Penn Warren, "Introduction," *Katherine Anne Porter: A Collection of Critical Essays*, Englewood Cliffs, N. J., Prentice-Hall, Inc., 1979, p. 8.

25 K. A. Porter to Glenway Wescott, March 23, 1939, pp. 2-3.

26 *Renaissance in the South* (Chapel Hill, University of North Carolina Press, 1963), p. 70.

27 "The *Paris Review* Interview," *Katherine Anne Porter: A Critical Symposium*, p. 7.

[28] *The Curious Death of the Novel: Essays in American Literature* (Baton Rouge, Louisiana State University Press, 1967), pp. 138-39.

[29] *Collected Essays*, p. 449

[30] The letter is dated Washington, D.C., June 30, 1959. The letter is at the Humanities Research Center, the University of Texas at Austin.

CHAPTER THREE

Madison Jones's Last Southern Agrarians

In May of 1978 I was in Alabama at Auburn University to speak on the role of education in Denmark. It was a success, embarrassingly my talk drew a larger crowd than René Wellek did. He was speaking there the same evening, fortunately not at the same time. Madison Jones was the local writer-in-residence, and I met him when he was signing his new novel Passage through Gehenna *in the university bookstore. I reviewed the novel for* South Carolina Review *in the fall of the next year. Later we did an interview which appeared in* Contemporary Authors *in 1983. Ever since our first meeting I have written about Madison Jones, and I still believe that his fine fiction will eventually receive the recognition it deserves. In 1985 I published an essay on Walker Percy, Barry Hannah, and Madison Jones in* Revue Francaise d'Etudes Americaines, *which together with my essay on Madison Jones in* The Southern Review *in the fall of 1986 are the early versions of this chapter.*

Madison Jones's
Last Southern Agrarians

Madison Jones has spent most of his life in the South and most of his fiction is set there. When Jones was thirteen, his father bought a farm twenty-five miles north of Nashville, and the boy spent every summer there until he was grown. At eighteen he worked on the farm and remained there for almost two years before enrolling at Vanderbilt University. There he studied under Agrarian poet and critic Donald Davidson, whose lectures have had a lasting influence on him. It was also at Vanderbilt that his first fiction was published; he broke into print in 1948 with a story called "The Red Bird" in the *Gad-Fly*. After graduating from Vanderbilt University with a B.A. in 1949, Jones returned to the farm in Cheatham County, where for nearly a year he considered becoming a farmer. When he writes about "setting, topping or suckering" plants in the tobacco patch, it is based on his personal experience of tobacco growing, and the many passages about horses in his novels are based on his experiences as a trainer of Tennessee walking horses.

Returning to school, this time to the University of Florida in Gainesville, Jones found another major influence in Andrew Lytle, Agrarian novelist and critic. Under his guidance, Jones specialized in creative writing and received his M. A. there in 1951, staying in Florida until 1953 to do further graduate work. During the early fifties Jones's stories in *Perspective* and the *Sewanee Review* began to win him notice. While serving his apprenticeship, he maintained himself by teaching first at Miami University, Ohio, in 1953-54, and then in 1955-56 at the University of Tennessee, Knoxville. Between these teaching assignments in 1954, he received a *Sewanee Review* Fellowship and spent a year in Florida writing most of his first novel. After 1956 he taught at Auburn and has now retired.

Madison Jones's literary heritage has been the Agrarian movement. He has absorbed fully and somewhat pessimistically the concerns of the earlier Agrarian group, the Fugitives, which included (in addition to Davidson and Lytle) Allen Tate, John Crowe Ransom, and Robert Penn Warren. In the younger generation of writers, he is the best preserver of their traditional ideals. He depends largely on established conflicts between the native and the alien, the old and the new, tradition and "progress," and he is a neo-Agrarian in practice as well as theory. On a piece of land twenty miles north of his home at Auburn,

Alabama, Jones keeps a herd of Hereford cattle. At times he writes there in a rock-and-log cabin that he built with his sons.

The split life of farming and teaching is reflected in his fiction. His seven books are not attempts at creating a Tennessee Yoknapatawpha, but they do constitute an extensive chronicle of the South. A homogeneity of theme makes them cohere as a body of fiction. While Jones is concerned about the encroachment of the New South on old values, he is even more concerned with the concepts of guilt and innocence. His protagonists come to grief because they follow the optimistic philosophies of idealists such as Jean Jacques Rousseau or Thomas Jefferson. Jones believes that evil has an absolute existence and that man needs God's grace to be delivered from evil. On the general nature of his fiction he has said, "On a more obvious level, my fiction is concerned with the drama of collision between past and present, with emphasis upon the destructive elements involved. More deeply, it deals with the failure, or refusal, of individuals to recognize and submit themselves to inevitable limits of the human condition." Jones's world is emphatically a moral one. Since his early childhood the greatest literary influence on him has been the Bible; he was brought up in a fundamentalist area and retains strong memories of faith-healing meetings and tent revivals. But he has found himself unable to believe with "the absoluteness of the Christian."

In Jones's first novel, *The Innocent (1957),* Duncan Welsh returns to his father's farm in rural Tennessee after seven years in the North. Profoundly dissatisfied with the materialistc nature of life in the North, where he has had an unsuccessful newspaper career and an equally unsuccessful marriage, he settles on his inherited land, trying to rediscover the uncomplicated life he remembers from his childhood. But the forces of "progress" have also reached his native area, and they confront Duncan from the moment he returns. In a wrestling match at a fair, he sees a farm boy killed by Tiger Sloan, a professional wrestler. The incident, in which the boy dies because Sloan employs a new style of wrestling, prefigures Duncan's defeat in his battle against the encroachment of specialization and mechanization on the old ways. Nature is rapidly retreating in the Tennessee of the novel; and with the "renewing" occasioned by industry, there is little space for independent men.

Change has come to the South, and Duncan cannot stop it. He tries to uphold ideals that the past had held untouchable, so he will not be perverted into casting off his own nature. He devotes himself to the restoration of the large but worn-out farm, and above all, he works to save from extinction the once famous Mountain Slasher breed of Tennessee walking horse. It is a breed of horse that has been replaced by the more elegant Allen breed, which is preferred by the *nouveaux riches* of the area. His attempt to preserve the Mountain Slasher bloodline is also an attempt to preserve his own past. All his values are summed up in the colt Chief, which gives him hope. But the colt grows to be a stallion that belongs not in the Agrarian past, but in the virgin wilderness.

The horse is uncontrollable and is shot by Dickie Jordan, who is of a family of Allen horse breeders. Duncan's mono-maniacal work with horses has isolated him from the community. When he allies himself with Aaron McCool, a depraved moonshiner, Duncan knows that he has lost his fight against the New South. After an initial endeavor to maintain his integrity in a disintegrating world, he is reduced to seeking primitive vengeance by murdering Dickie Jordan. Duncan's doom is inevitable because like his horse he seems to belong to "a vanishing bloodline": both he and McCool are shot by the representatives of law and order. Jones's first novel is deeply pessimistic, for the old ways are surely irrecoverable.

The Innocent is a disturbing novel even today, almost thirty years after its publication. It is still good reading because it is an expression of good craftsmanship. Few first novels are as well written and soundly constructed. The evocation of woods and fields, and horses and men, is perfect. The novel is full of powerful visual images, convincing characters, and sudden dramatic scenes. While Jones was criticized for cluttering his novel with scenes and characters and for attempting to do too much, these are minor flaws in a moving affirmation of Agrarian values. *The Innocent* is a first novel which made it plain to most readers that a major talent was on the scene. In a review of the novel Robert Penn Warren wrote: "Madison Jones has written an intensely interesting story, and one that clearly declares his talent."

In his second novel, *Forest of the Night* (1960), Jones goes back to the early 1800s, following a young man into the Tennessee wilderness and down the Natchez Trace. Jonathan Cannon, who represents American innocence in its encounter with the wilderness, regards his mission to establish a school in order to bring "light" into the forest of the frontier. The novel rejects the New Eden myth, and it also rejects the notion of man's innate moral nature. Ignorant of the ways of wild animals, Indians, outlaws, and pioneers, Jonathan discovers that his idealized virgin forest, during the progress of "civilization," has become a forest of the night, where most of the pioneers are fugitives from the law. In the climate of hopelessness he succumbs to his desire for a girl who lives in the forest. He does not know that she has been the lover of the notorious Harpe brothers, outlaws who operate along the Natchez Trace. Because Jonathan bears an uncanny resemblance to the younger Harpe brother, he is finally pursued by the people he has set out to educate.

As in his first novel, Jones describes the shock of an idealist who is faced with the reality of innate human depravity. There is no room for innocent visionaries in this world, and there is little comfort in the fact that the pioneers endure on a primitive level. Unlike his first novel, *Forest of the Night* received little critical attention. It seems to have been too pessimistic and too direct in its portrayal of mankind's degradation to become popular. Yet, as John M. Bradbury said of the novel in *Renaissance in the South*, "Jones's linguistic power and ability to evoke the concrete image of living reality raises his allegory far above the common run of historically based fiction." It would be a challenge to try to find a more underrated and more completely forgotten novel than *Forest of the Night*. Yet there is not a more revealing exposé in American literature of the truly unromantic nature of pioneer life. It is perhaps Jones's best novel, but it will never be popular.

Jones's third novel, *A Buried Land* (1963), is set in the valley of the Tennessee River at the time when the Tennessee Valley Authority flooded the lowlands of Tennessee and northern Alabama. The destruction by the water of a whole community plays a central role in the novel. Jones rages against the betrayers of the past who allowed the flooding of the green valleys; he sees it as the last outrage against ancient modesty. The novel protests the loss of identity and memory through the inundation. The main character is the callous Percy Youngblood, who works for the TVA even though his family will lose their ancestral farm to the waters. As in his first two novels, Jones is concerned with the integrity of individuals and communities in the face of change. The Youngblood family breaks up when industry comes to Tennessee. But this does not worry Percy, who concentrates on his seduction of Cora Kincaid. She is a young woman who has been abandoned by Percy's friend Jesse Hood. The girl becomes pregnant by Percy and then dies at the hands of a Nashville abortionist. Jesse and Percy bury her secretly in the old cemetery, which is soon to be flooded. The end of the ballad-type plot is that Percy Youngblood leaves, makes a career for himself as a lawyer, and returns to the area thinking that his past is buried.

Fowler Kincaid is the dead girl's brother and easily the most interesting character in the novel. Like Aaron McCool in the first novel, Fowler believes in freedom without obligations, and he will defend that right with savage brutality and a primitive wisdom "as cold as snake's," if necessary. It seems that every novel by Jones has at least one character who displays the naked visceral hatred of any authority. Fowler tries to discover what happened to his sister. Because of a drought, the water level of the new lake is receding and the valley lies like a huge black pit. Percy is haunted by his own conscience, and Jesse, his accomplice, is too shiftless and unreliable to be trusted. Percy attempts to escape the moral responsibility for his past. He turns against his family and his friend in order to hide the truth about Cora. But when Jesse is murdered by Fowler Kincaid, Percy panics, kills Fowler, breaks down, and confesses to his mother. He realizes that the destruction of his ancestral home parallels his own spiritual bankruptcy and that he cannot live with the moral ambiguity in his life.

After she had finished reading *A Buried Land*, Flannery O'Connor told Jones that, although she liked all of his books, this one impressed her the most. She told him, moreover, that she had read the story carefully, wishing she could write with such conciseness and force. In *A Buried Land* Jones is so furious with the outsiders who destroy his native area and the local people who would not even help with the removal of the remains of their ancestors that Percy Youngblood's existential rebellion against "the impossible lack of proportion in things" tends to be overlooked by the reader.

In the mid-sixties Jones wrote a book of picaresque comedy, *Tales of Dixie*, which borders on farce. With the exception of two sections, "Home Is Where the Heart Is" and "A Modern Case," the book has not been published.[1] One of the unpublished episodes deals with a young novelist who has been hired by a northern newspaper to report on civil rights demonstrations in Mississippi. It is primarily a satire on northern ideas of what was happening in the South at the time. The published fragments show what Jones can do in a humorous vein and they look forward to the comedy of the first chapters of *To The Winds (1996)*.

An Exile (1967) has been Jones's greatest popular success to date. John Frankenheimer made it into a film called *I Walk the Line*, starring Gregory Peck and Tuesday Weld. Columbia Pictures decided to use the title of the country song which lends atmosphere to the film. Mèrimèe's *Carmen* was the source for Jones's short novel, and the plot possesses a classical simplicity. Sheriff Hank Tawes is torn between loyalty to his office and his passion for a bootlegger's daughter. He ought to arrest bootleggers, but he is looking for a way to change his life, and he believes for a short time that he has found it in Flint McCain's bootlegger camp. Although he is unhappily married and bored with his life, there seems to be little reason why Sheriff Tawes should strip himself of all the virtues he has defended for years. Yet, this "good" man abandons duty and honor to cover for the liquor traffic.

Sheriff Tawes is a believable person; he displays the frailties of mankind, and there is tragedy in his fate. His motives are not sexual fulfillment, but he sees the girl as a chance to escape from a world which has lost all sense of moral values. Tawes is modern man who, faced with evil, decides to seek the peace which follows self-destruction. As in earlier Jones novels, the protagonist is caught in a web spun partly by his own actions, but he is primarily the victim of his human heritage. Tawes's marriage breaks up, one of his men is killed, and he disintegrates. The bootleggers are brought to justice, but the restitution costs Sheriff Tawes his life. He has been tempted with a spiritual and physical peace he has never experienced a before, and he succumbs.

An Exile is a novel with a clear moral message of a neo-Agrarian nature. The characters are so fully realized that the message is not read as didactic, but as an organic part of a well-structured and low-keyed story. The psychological portrait of human weakness is convincing and deserves its success. The problems of the physical passion and moral disintegration of an aging man are rendered honestly and with great skill. *An Exile* is an exciting novel on the ambiguities of life. Jones is supposed to have declared that he himself should have acted the part of Sheriff Tawes in the film. This is said to have been upon seeing his friend James Dickey act the part of Sheriff Bullard in the film version of

Deliverance. As it was, the part of Sheriff Tawes was played by Gregory Peck, and Madison Jones remains relatively unknown. He has always shunned publicity efforts, and his novels have not received the attention they merit.

Jones considers his fifth novel, *A Cry of Absence* (1971), his best book. It is set in a small Southern town during the most bitter period of the civil rights struggle, and it is an attempt at providing an objective statement on the South and its main problem in the sixties. In his review of the novel, Monroe K. Spears calls the action "austere, powerful, and inexorable as any in Greek drama, and as evocative of both pity and, terror." It depicts the old conflict between family affection and duty to the law. The dilemma is that for one kind of right to be achieved, much of value must be destroyed. Ames Glenn and his mother Hester are at the center of the plot: the body of a black civil rights agitator is found in Cameron Springs, and Ames discovers that his brother Cam is one of the killers. When their mother learns of the murder, she is quick to blame the killing on "white trash." She has always romanticized the past and idealized her family. She has never wanted to recognize the truth about Cameron Springs and her heritage.

The Glenns are one of the old families in the town, and there is a good deal of tension between them and newcomers. Among the newcomers are the Delmores, a family of industrialists, who intend to make the town over. They do not see anything worth preserving. In the name of "equality" they want to break all links to the past of Cameron Springs, even "the tenuous threads of common memory." Little by little, Ames manages to make his mother see that Cam, the high school baseball star, is one of the killers. When she is finally aware of Cam's guilt, she encourages him to commit suicide. It shocks her to discover that her own son believed she would consider murder to be within "moral" bounds in the present situation. In the final part of the novel, Hester Glenn accepts her responsibility for her son's action. She realizes that it was her uncritical identification with the past that Cam had totally misinterpreted, and she takes her own life.

The triumph of the novel is that Jones manages to make the reader understand why Hester reacts as she does. The details of her childhood and married life in the house of her great-grandfather are convincing. She would be the one to circulate a petition for restoration of the Confederate monument of the town. Her fatal flaw is that she has been blind to the moral ills of the past and therefore can only be partially aware of ills in her own time. She does not realize that blind racism, here personified by Hollis Handley, is also a part of the tradition she passed on to Cam. Hollis Handley seems closely related to Aaron McCool, Fowler Kincaid, and Flint McCain of the earlier novels; and it is with Pike Handley, a representative of these sinister poor whites, that Cam Glenn commits the murder. Ames Glenn does what he has to do, although it leads to the deaths of his mother and his brother. His loyalties are, of course, divided, but he does not repudiate his heritage. He accepts full knowledge of the Southern past, and therefore he can avoid contributing to the evil of his own time. Ames stays in Cameron Springs and decides to keep his mother's house, for "who could say – since a spirit that had lived once could live again – that much more than this was not recoverable." *A Cry of Absence* was well received by the critics, but never achieved the popularity of *An Exile*.

The discovery of the existence of evil by an "innocent" young man is also the theme of *Passage through Gehenna* (1978). But in this novel Jones writes with a greater compassion, and with the savage ironic humor usually associated with Flannery O'Connor. *A Buried Land* and *A Cry of Absence* were topical novels. *Passage* is, however, a timeless allegory; of the earlier novels it is akin to *Forest of the Night*. The novel is set in the small river town of Hallsboro, Tennessee. Although Jones creates an Old-Testament world, these rural Tennessee characters smoke as much pot and hash as their cosmopolitan neighbors. The scene is set for a clash between modern ways and traditional values. The novel focuses on the testing of Jud Rivers. He is brought up in the Church of Christ, one of the fundamentalist churches in the Tennessee hills. The stern religion of Jud's childhood emphasized rectitude at the expense of love. The novel traces his struggle to liberate himself from his early training in order to be capable of loving. But Jud must also come to terms with evil in the form of Lily Nunn, a modern witch doing the devil's work. She hopes to prove to Jud that all Christians of Hallsboro are hypocrites. Ultimately, Lily's efforts cost the lives of Salter, a fundamentalist preacher, and Hannah Rice, who is in love with Jud.

The uneasy relationship between fundamentalism and sexuality leads to a good deal of comedy. Jud tries to stare down his libido, in vain. His first sexual encounter with Goldie from the local café has all the eye-opening impact of reality on the dreamer's mind. He discovers that his impulses run counter to the morality he has been taught, and he seeks refuge in the world of the flesh. Yet, through the self-sacrifice of Hannah, who commits suicide, Jud makes it through his Gehenna. Like other Jones protagonists, Jud is caught in a trap only partly of his own making. But unlike the situations in earlier novels, the hero is here offered a chance to recognize his condition before it is too late. Repentant, he is allowed to tell his story as a memory. And Jud Rivers is finally at least capable of love. It is no secret that Jones had difficulties in getting *Passage through Gehenna* published. And without the advantage of advertising, the novel received little attention.

Season of the Strangler (1982) depicts both continuity and change in the South. It is a short story cycle with the effect of a novel, in the manner of Sherwood Anderson's *Winesburg, Ohio,* William Faulkner's *Go Down, Moses,* and Eudora Welty's *The Golden Apples*. There are twelve interrelated stories, all related to the central matter of a local strangler. Together they make up the tale of the long hot summer of 1969 in the fictive town of Okaloosa, Alabama. The book is a portrait of the community during a period of great drama and anxiety.

In spite of the title, the stranglings are relatively unimportant. They take place off-stage and may be read as symbolic incidents that frame the everyday life in town. The emphasis is on the individual, his relations with family and community. The central motif of the strangler links the twelve portraits of black and white, old and young, men and women. Jones makes it clear that in a sense we strangle ourselves.

The stories detail individual roads to spiritual bankruptcy. Mr. Cecil Peck, in "Break," is the owner of the local shoe store and a henpecked husband. When an employee quits, Mr. Peck is informed that he is "a feist-voice, bully-boy, playing with ladies' feet." He admits the truth of this to himself, but one day as he is holding a woman's foot, he has a vision: "And it was a sort of vision starting with her foot." The incident changes his life. Like another Francis Macomber, he rebels against his domestic role and his short yappy wife. At first he satisfies himself by frightening his wife into believing that he might be the strangler. This is a sadistic enjoyment of the ability to terrify that he shares with others in the town. Finally he liberates himself by moving out of his home: "He did not so much as send home for his clothes. Instead he bought new clothes, of a kind with a sort of subdued flashiness about them that made him look a little seedy." The fate of Mr. Cecil Peck is rendered with an irony worthy of Sherwood Anderson, but Jones's compassion for the shoe-store owner is unmistakable.

"Familiar Spirit," the last story in the book, is about young people and the Civil War (the "waugh"), and the difficulty of preserving a commitment to history. The skirmishes that Douglas Bragg witnesses are between his mother and grandfather over integration. In a fine comic scene, Douglas sends his half-dressed, bugle-blowing grandfather into a meeting of the local "Interracial Dialogue Group." When the effort kills the old man, his old black friend turns up for the funeral. This is Jones's only Civil War fiction before *Nashville 1864: The Dying of the Light* (1997). This is surprising as he grew up with a grandfather who loved to tell him about the War Between the States. (The grandfather was born in 1856, remembered details from his childhood, and had become a Civil War scholar.) "Familiar Spirit" ends as Douglas tries to invoke the scene of the Okaloosa Creek skirmish and fails: "There was something missing, something needed to focus things the way a memory did."

Often the characters in *The Season of the Strangler* fail to recognize the rules of the community and consequently must pay the price. The book can be read as a study of fear. There are the old men who realize they are not wanted in their families; young men who do not fit in, or do not live up to their parents' expectations; sexually frustrated housewives who attempt to live double lives; and panicky middle-aged men and women who realize they have wasted most of their lives. When the summer is over the murders stop and Okaloosa is dropped from the headlines; but the self-inflicted psychological stranglings continue. No evidence that might have led to the strangler's identity ever appears. "It was almost as if a spirit, having finished its evil season in the town, had gone back in just the same way it had come to whatever place it belonged."

Fortunately, it is too early to sum up Madison Jones's career. But certain merits are conspicuous. Jones is a consummate stylist. He writes with the order and economy of great art. Whether he uses rural dialogue, country preaching, or the filthy whisper of the local whore, the language is convincingly unaffected and authentic. He is an experienced storyteller in the best Southern tradition and does not let us off until the story has been told. A great tension is maintained also between climactic scenes, for Jones always works hard at reducing "the elocution." He always moves on to new aspects at exactly the right moment, and the transitions are unrivaled in smoothness. The economy is praiseworthy and every detail is essential in relation to the novel as a whole. But the austerity of the form does not diminish the richness of the texture. Every detail is fully dramatized, and entire scenes are brought to life with just a few specifics. As an expert craftsman, Jones avoids coincidences, but accepts the unavoidable. People kill, have abortions, and commit suicides also in Jones's fiction, but the events are not merely shock effects. The reader accepts the violence as organic and unavoidable. Jones has a natural sense of fiction; in the words of Robert Penn Warren: "he has a strong, natural power of narrative; he can tell a story."

There is a noticeable development in Jones's narrative technique over the years. In *Season of the Strangler* tension is still one of his primary considerations, yet he is now willing to risk the "loose moment" in several stories. And they gain from the willingness to leave the reader time for the individual imagination to cooperate through a moment's relief. There is also a noteworthy development in Jones's attitude toward his fellow man from the pessimism of *The Innocent*, through a growing optimism in *Passage Through Gehenna*, to the nuanced, complex, and compassionate vision of *Season of the Strangler*. Jones's work-in-progress concerns the age-old conflict between the new and the old, in this case about a small town and its academic community. It incorporates drug dealing, corrupt car salesmen, exploited students, and a heroic grandmother. It promises to be in the lighter vein of some of the amusing stories in the short story cycle.

Madison Jones has a dark view of the human condition, but he also has self-knowledge, humility, and real compassion for his characters. In his fiction they are often caught by irresistible forces and hurled to an inescapable doom. But even when their world is changed beyond recognition against their will, his characters retain their pride, courage, and dignity. Jones demonstrates that it is almost impossible for an individual to exist apart from a social framework, but also that every individual is ultimately responsible for his own actions.

Jones is true to his own time and his South. The Southern concerns of place, community, and history figure prominently in his fiction. He shares the traditional regret at the loss of inherited values in the South, and in this respect he is, perhaps, the last Agrarian. But his fictional world goes beyond this. He has created a moral world which transcends its region and reflects the universal.

---

[1] The two published sections are: "Home Is Where the Heart Is," *The Arlington Quarterly*, 1 (Spring 1968), 12-69; and "A Modern Case," *Delta Review* 6 (July-August, 1969), 42-52, 72-75.

CHAPTER FOUR

The Woman by the Side of the Road: Flannery O'Connor's Social Stoicism

Flannery O'Connor's fiction was one of my early interests. I have spent much time in Milledgeville, Georgia, and had the good fortune to interview Mrs. Regina Cline O'Connor. In the Flannery O'Connor Collection at Georgia College I found the unpublished story "An Exile in the East," and "The Shiftlet Fragment" by O'Connor and had them published in 1978 and 1981, respectively. In 1984 Karl-Heinz Westarp, O'Connor scholar and my friend from our student days at Aarhus University, Denmark, suggested that to commemorate her death twenty years before, we should host the first international Flannery O'Connor symposium abroad at Sandbjerg in Jutland. In 1987 we published the essays from that symposium as Realist of Distances: Flannery O'Connor Revisited. *My own contribution was a reply to Sally Fitzgerald, the Flannery O'Connor friend and biographer, who participated in the symposium. I expressed my disagreement with the attempts on the part of religious O'Connor critics to minimize the social awareness in her fiction. The chapter has its origin in my paper at the 1984 symposium.*

The Woman by the Side of the Road

St. Cyril of Jerusalem, in instructing catechumens, wrote: "The dragon sits by the side of the road, watching those who pass. Beware lest he devour you. We go to the Father of Souls, but it is necessary to pass by the dragon." No matter what form the dragon may take, it is of this mysterious passage past him, or into his jaws, that stories of any depth will always be concerned to tell .... (Mystery & Manners, p. 35)[1]

When Flannery O'Connor first published "The Displaced Person," the first sentence read: "Mrs. Shortley stood on a small prominence to the left of the pump house."[2] In the final version of the story the pump house was dropped, and understandably so. Yet, the pump house and all the rest that make up "the side of the road" are not without interest. The side of the road is likely to be forgotten once the dragon appears, and so is the pump house when the peacock is in sight. This is perhaps the way it should be, but for the critic the side of the road is interesting in itself.

For a writer whose social concern is not supposed to have been notably pronounced, O'Connor displays a remarkable social sensibility.[3] She takes into account the social problems of her day and comments in much of her fiction on the social order of her native society. Several stories reflect the racial situation in much of the South during the 50s and 60s. Even if her concern is not to improve the material situation of poor whites and blacks, her fiction reveals her sympathies. Her characters, who often live in the country and mostly in Georgia, become concrete illustrations of social behavior through unsentimental characterizations. It was no accident that she majored in sociology, though many critics do not like to hear this.[4] From the beginning of her career she had a highly developed social sensibility, and it served her well in her writing. She took great pains in her lectures to show that good fiction demands a sound knowledge of people in time and place. It is a question whether it is possible to understand her work fully if we see it as sermonizing. Not to consider the social experience that she presents, is to simplify and underestimate both her and her fiction. The purpose in stressing her social sensibility is to call attention to a neglected side of her genius. The purpose is not to try to obscure her Catholic faith, which manifests itself in all her work. For her the social realism is her access to the mystery of life. She believed that if the novelist "doesn't make these natural things believable in themselves, he can't make them believable in any of their spiritual extensions" (*MM*, p.176). The social and the

Christian concerns do not exclude each other; on the contrary it is her Christian faith that makes O'Connor, who obviously loves her neighbor, observe and describe social problems and conflicts.

Flannery O'Connor's writing career can be seen as a development from an early stereotyping tendency to the allegorizing skill of her final years. This career structure has often been recognized by critics, but it has been less readily accepted that she also had a creative middle period when she wrote fiction of obvious social concern. The characters in her fiction of this period are not just economic and social exemplars, though they are obviously also that. The middle period may be said to begin during the fall of 1949 with "A Stroke of Good Fortune," and it seems largely to end with "The Artificial Nigger" in the spring of 1955. The social concern was not sudden or new in 1949, it is obvious already in O'Connor's first stories. In "The Crop," from before February 1946, Miss Willerton encounters intruding reality in the shape of a poor white couple that she passes downtown, and she gives up her idea of writing "arty" fiction about poor white sharecroppers, at least for the moment. "The Barber" from the following year is a comment on the racial issues of the time and the frustration experienced by Southern liberals. By June 1955, when "Good Country People" was published, O'Connor's social concern had become less obvious, while the religious symbolism tended to be increasingly heavy-handed.

It should perhaps be pointed out that it is impossible to overlook the social sensibility in several of her stories from after 1955. In "A View of the Woods" (1957) she records the rape of the land in the creation of a site for the new fishing club. Finally, the site is deserted except for the presence of Mr. Fortune and "one huge yellow monster which sat to the side, as stationary as he was, gorging itself on clay" (*CS*, p.356). With "Everything That Rises Must Converge" (1961) she has given us one of the best fictional accounts of the breakdown in the late 50s of the old order of the South. In the story Julian is forced to realize that you cannot take off your Southern heritage as easily as you take off a tie. The social stratification of Southern society and the end of it are also the subject of Mrs. Turpin's vision in "Revelation," the last story O'Connor saw in print. Mrs. Turpin had not expected "whole companies of white-trash" and "bands of black niggers" to precede her own tribe of middle-class respectability in the vast horde of souls "rumbling toward heaven" (*CS*, p. 508). The most astringent social comment from her final period is probably the glimpse of starvation in "Parker's Back," the last story she completed. Sarah Ruth has skin that is "thin and drawn as tight as the skin on an onion" (*CS*, p. 510); and when she is offered an apple, she takes it quickly, "as if the basket might disappear if she didn't make haste. Hungry people made Parker nervous. He had always had plenty to eat himself. He grew very uncomfortable" (*CS*, p. 515). As most of us would feel uncomfortable at the thought of hunger in our own backyard.

In 1953 the social concern was often central to O'Connor's fiction. Several of the short stories from that year had their origin in newspaper articles.[5] The inspiration for her most famous story "A Good Man Is Hard to Find" was a newspaper headline that read: "'The Misfit' Robs Office, Escapes With $150." O'Connor's story is about a criminal called The Misfit and also about why he is a misfit. A second story from 1953 "A Late Encounter with the Enemy" is about our Hollywood version of the past, and what it does to our concept of everyday life. It originated in a newspaper headline that reads: "Confederate Vet to See Wife Get Degree at GSCW." A third story from 1953 is "The Life You Save May Be Your Own," whose main character called Mr. Shiftlet is clearly a have-not, who is out to have something. "The Shiftlet Fragment" shows how he became so materialistic.[6]

Several fragments among O'Connor's manuscripts at Georgia College tell us about Mr. Shiftlet. Some of the best known are the alternative endings of "The Life You Save May Be Your Own." In one of these Lucynell Crater out-foxes Mr. Shiftlet, he does not get her car, and he is forced to leave town with his bride by train. And in another fragment Mr. Shiftlet returns frustrated to his family in the city, only to smash the TV set that his wife bought in his absence. These fragments are of scholarly interest, and they are obviously alternative versions of parts of the published story. The interesting circumstances about manuscript Dunn 156a (Driggers 153a), which I have called "The Shiftlet Fragment," are that it is marked "II" and paginated "17-25", is chapter two and as such an attempted continuation of the story.

The relentless humor in O'Connor's stories is often that of the social satirist. It is true, of course, that the critic has to be careful not to exaggerate the importance of social criticism in her fiction. But he should also take care not to overlook it completely. She herself felt that "the larger social context" should not be excluded from her fiction (*MM* p. 198), and it is in her account of what modern society does to us that she demonstrates her powers as a satirist. In "The Life You Save" she plunges us into the life of "good country people," and we do not have to read far to understand that the social situation of these people is *not* enviable. Lucynell Crater, Sr., does not go about without teeth because she enjoys being toothless; and she would probably not refuse help to her retarded daughter, if it were offered. But it is not.

Although the social portrait was never an end in itself, O'Connor was always concerned about giving as realistic a picture as possible. In a manuscript passage, later crossed out, Mr. Shiftlet takes Lucynell Crater, daughter, for a ride in the car that he has repaired. In the passage, the girl is not a deaf-mute but a hunchback:

> The girl sat as if she were leaning forward and the top of her hat nearly touched the top of the car. After a while she began to have a pain in her back from the bumping, but she didn't say anything about it. Mr. Shiftlet was telling about himself and all the things he had done in his life. He

gave her the ages of all his female kin, "Did you know I come over the radio oncet?" he asked. He had played gitar with Uncle Roy's Redcreek Wranglers. He asked her if she knew Shorty Allen? She didn't but she asked him if he knew Mr. B. J. Waters that ran the A&P grocery store in town; he had spoken to her once. "Shorty played gitarr too," Mr. Shiftlet explained. He considered in his mind stopping somewhere and buying the hunchback a hotdog but he decided not to; he didn't want to get her to expecting one every evening. (Dunn 156e, p. 8)

Is there a clue to the character of Mr. Shiftlet in this passage? He is obviously self-centered, sentimental, and materialistic. He can mouth pieties and practice cruelty at the same time. He is "a poor disabled friendless drifting man," as he is described in "The Life .... " But how did Shiftlet come to be this way? He probably did not become a poor jack-of-all-trades by choice. In "The Life ..." his egoism, which is the basis of his incompleteness, is never explained. It is as if O'Connor did not wish for us "to understand" Mr. Shiftlet; we are not to pass judgment on him.

The comedy emerges as a revelation of his stunted spiritual life. When stated without a trace of sentimental identification, Shiftlet's egoism, which is the basis of his incompleteness, becomes grotesquely amusing. The readers may recognize their own absurd selves. And there are no extenuating circumstances, and there is nothing relative about the shock of recognition. We gather that Shiftlet is enslaved by material objects. His booty consists of a retarded girl, seventeen dollars and fifty cents, and a car that has not run in fifteen years. Moreover, one of the fragments shows us that Mr. Shiftlet originally had his eye on a radio: ""I couldn't live nowhere like this where there isn't even a radio. I sho couldn't stay here for long without a radio." The old woman didn't like music, even bad music. "If you had you a sweet wife," she said, "you wouldn't be thinking about no radio." "Ain't nothing a substitute for a radio," Mr. Shiftlet said sullenly, and they sat there for a while at this impasse, not saying anything" (Dunn 156e, p. 10.). Many readers prefer it when O'Connor's prophetic vision called for "large and startling figures," as in the mocking demonstration of Shiftlet's greed, that even the blind must see.

But the main object of Mr. Shiftlet's worship in "The Life ..." is the automobile that he is able to resurrect. He had always wanted a car, but he had not been able to afford one. He needs a car to move as he chooses, just as Hazel Motes did in *Wise Blood*. For a psychological explanation of the obsession we have "The Shiftlet Fragment," in which Shiftlet reasons about the social role of a car owner. If he drives, he is no longer forced to see his surroundings clearly; thus he is able to concentrate on "larger matters." For this reason Mr. Shiftlet desires to see only a blur around him. He is certain "that there had to be a unifying power and that it could only be speed." His life is an attempt to find out just what does please him. His selfishness and material greed cannot be overlooked, but "The Shiftlet Fragment" informs us that he has been conditioned by his environment, which makes the evil in him appear less absolute than in "The Life ... ,"[7] which may well be the reason she chose not to publish it. O'Connor had no use for compromises.

"The Shiftlet Fragment" makes him more psychologically interesting; his hypocrisy, duplicity and frauds are enlightened by our knowledge of his self-deception. Just who is the man who tours the countryside discoursing on the identity of man? "The Shiftlet Fragment" shows that there is no real mystery about him; he has the background and the personality of Everyman. Mr. Shiftlet is in all of us in part: he runs away from problems, he is self-centered, he pays lip-service to ordinary morals, he is sentimental about his childhood and the memory of his mother, and he really does not adhere to any absolute standards. Mr. Shiftlet is provincial, superstitious, ignorant, and basically unheroic. At one time O'Connor was truly worried that Ronald Reagan would be chosen to act the part of Mr. Shiftlet in the TV version of "The Life You Save May Be Your Own." (As it turned out Gene Kelly acted the part of Mr. Shiftlet, and the ending of the film was changed to a happy ending.) It is interesting that the earliest title of "The Life... ," which was "Personal Interest," at one point was changed by O'Connor to "The World Is Almost Rotten."[8] It appears that O'Connor originally intended to make Mr. Shiftlet the central figure of a novel. She attempted to develop the figure by taking him back to his tenth year. Her letters tell us that she was revising "The Life..." and writing what became the first chapter of her second novel at the same time. However, one day during the fall of 1952 O'Connor decided to drop Mr. Shiftlet in favor of Francis Marion Tarwater.

The social criticism is obvious in the harsh contrast between poor and rich in "The River" (also from 1953), in which the city is seen as "a cluster of warts on the side of the mountain" (*CS*, p. 165). The city vs. country opposition is also essential in "A Circle in the Fire" from the following year, in which the boy named Powell clearly feels displaced in Atlanta. One of the boys tells Mrs. Cope that Powell's mother "works at a factory and leaves him to mind the rest of them only he don't mind them much" and that "one time he locked his little brother in a box and set it on fire" (*CS*, p. 184). Just how bad it is in Atlanta's urban wasteland is obvious in "The Artificial Nigger" from 1955. For Mr. Head and Nelson it seems to be a fate worse than death to be lost in the labyrinth of the city. The social sensibility and the true concern are unmistakable in all the stories from the period. O'Connor follows her own precepts for the novelist and descends "to the concrete where fiction operates" (*MM*, p. 92) and draws "large and startling figures" (*MM*, p. 34) of "what-is." There is no excuse for a novelist who fails to notice the situation of his immediate surroundings, as far as she is concerned: "The novelist is required to open his eyes on the world around him and look. If what he sees is not highly edifying, he is still required to look" (*MM*, p. 177).

The novels follow the pattern of the short stories. The social concern is more pronounced in *Wise Blood* (1952) than in *The Violent Bear It Away*, from her final years. In the first novel we have no doubts about Leora Watts' function in Taulkinham. She is one of the ugly and sad products of the city, like shallow lives and loneliness. Enoch Emory's background is sad, Hazel Motes' background is sad and so is their social situation. And the same is true of everybody they meet in Taulkinham. The city is just as frightening and sad in her novels as in her stories, and her writing of life in the metropolis is full of concern. In her second novel the Tarwaters live almost completely cut off from the community and their relatives. Social concerns are remote from the Tarwaters' universe and from the novel in general. The novel is full of obvious Christian symbolism and the social concern expressed is insignificant in comparison. The side of the road is simply not described in most of *The Violent Bear It Away*.

In "An Exile in the East" it is also through the world of matter that spirit gleams. In retrospect it can be accepted, as Mr. Robert Giroux has suggested, that the story is "an intermediate version" of "Judgement Day."[9] But in 1954 Flannery O'Connor considered it a finished story, one which she was ready to include in the collection *A Good Man Is Hard to Find*, and it is significantly different from both "The Geranium" and "Judgement Day." Therefore "An Exile in the East" has a claim not just as a manuscript version of a familiar story, but as a story in its own right (ms.: Driggers 207, pp. 1-16). It belongs to O'Connor's middle period. It was written between "The Displaced Person" and "The Artificial Nigger," at a time in her life when she was physically as well as she would be, and when she was at her peak as a writer. Her growth as a short story writer manifests itself in her continued use and development of certain thematic elements. In "The Geranium," "An Exile in the East," and "Judgement Day," similar short stories from three decades, O'Connor emphasizes different aspects of the same concerns. She often uses the same elements in the three stories, but she employs them with a different effect in each story. The similar passages clarify O'Connor's shifting emphasis on the thematic elements common to the three stories.

The "Exile" passages often avoid the sentimentality of "The Geranium" and virtually all the melodrama of "Judgement Day." "Exile" manages to show something profound about life in the South and in the North, without some of the heavy literary symbolism of the first story and without some of the manifest theology of O'Connor's last story. Above all, "An Exile in the East" treats the racial theme in greater depth than her other stories. In the "Exile" story it is clear *why* Old Tanner believes in the possibility of a friendship with a black man, and the emphasis is consistently on the Coleman-Tanner friendship. The two men in the tin and crate shack are dependent on each other. For forty years they have stayed together, voluntarily. Tanner knows that he has been "on a nigger's hands" for a long time, but he has not thought of it that way until his daughter points it out. In his mind Coleman and he share the burdens of their everyday existence equally. He has had Coleman on his hands for many years earlier in their lives, and he still provides his share by giving Coleman shelter. The element of sharing the burdens is toned down in "Judgement Day," where Coleman is *paroled to* Tanner, and where the shack belongs to both of them. In "Judgement Day" the dialogue between the friends does not ring true. The men have been together for thirty years (in that story), and this influences what they say and what they do not say to each other. It is only in "An Exile in the East" that the two men talk and behave consistently in accordance with their common knowledge of their life in a small Georgia town.

In April of 1959 when O'Connor had refused to meet with James Baldwin in Georgia, she wrote in a letter to Maryat Lee that it would be nice to meet Baldwin in New York. She added: "I observe the traditions of the society I feed on – it's only fair."[10] O'Connor makes several comments on farm laborers and blacks in her correspondence with Fanny and Brainard Cheney that would place her in the company of so many limited characters in her own fiction, if we did not have her fiction to prove her sincere compassion for the poor and the displaced. O'Connor told the Cheneys several incidents involving the black tenants of Andalusia, in which they appear as amusing children. And her 1962 (August 9) account of an attempt to integrate a Milledgeville drugstore by means of "outside ajittaters from Atlanta" is in a satirical vein, yet with a serious note at the end: "But that night the klan met right across the road from us .... Our colored man has been gone from here ever since. I hate to see it all get started."[11] O'Connor's true concern for each black individual on Andalusia is above suspicion of racism. When Shot, one of the black tenants, is sucked into a hay baler up to his elbows and injures both arms, O'Connor's letters are full of concern, for more than a year she keeps returning to the subject. But the great political changes of the 50s and 60s remain unimportant in her letters. Like so many white Southerners of the time, O'Connor was worried about the African Americans she knew well, not about the racial situation. In this attitude she is not unlike Old Tanner of "An Exile in the East."

The "Exile" story, unlike the "Judgement Day" text, explains why Coleman hangs about at the sawmill. He wants to be accosted by a white man, and he is willing to wait a week, "because he has never been accosted before, only ignored." In "An Exile in the East" Coleman is a human being with human motivations. He is in perfect accordance with O'Connor's definition of a black man in the South: "The uneducated Southern Negro is not the clown he's made out to be. He's a man of very elaborate manners and great formality, which he uses superbly for his own protection and to insure his own privacy" (*MM*, p. 234). When Tanner faces Coleman in "Exile," he does so with authority and intelligence. We can understand that Coleman is awed by the white man. In "Judgement Day" Coleman has been reduced to a clown, and it does not take much to impress him. Note that in "Exile" Tanner reaches his immediate goal, Coleman is going to go to work for the mill, and he is going to get the other black workers back to work.

Flannery O'Connor was not exclusively a religious allegorist. In "An Exile in the East" the social context is necessary, believable, and vividly described. The Georgia setting and characters are rendered with an eye for detail that makes them more than a backdrop for abstract themes. The story shows two old men caught in a conflict between rural and urban ideas. The two men seem equally expendable in the North and in the South. O'Connor's religious concern is implicit, resting in the theological foundation which informs the story, and it is illuminated by her religious knowledge. The story reminds us that O'Connor could be sociological as well as theological, and that she could accomplish both at once. There is no conflict between the sociological and Christian themes. On the contrary, it is O'Connor's Christian mind that makes her turn to the racial conflict at a time when a crisis in racial relations is developing.

It would also be fairly easy to demonstrate the presence of O'Connor's social sensibility in stories such as "Everything That Rises Must Converge" and in "The Artificial Nigger." But "The Displaced Person" (1954), also from her middle period, will be considered here, as it is a typical O'Connor story in several ways: the setting is rural Georgia, the theme is clearly Catholic, and it deals with a universal problem. In the story she is right at the crossroads where time and place meet eternity (Cp. *MM*, p. 59). The religious concern in the story is obvious as always and so is the social criticism. Not to see the latter is to underestimate O'Connor. She portrays reality as it manifests itself in the concrete sensual lives of everybody on the farm. It is important that a sense of place is established in order for the tale of spiritual displacement to work. To avoid over-emphasis on the abstract and the risk of impoverishing the imagination and the capacity for prophetic insight, the farm and its social hierarchy must first be made concrete. (Cp. *MM*, p. 203). This is done through the observation of the farm and inhabitants by Mrs. Shortley and later by Mrs. McIntyre. The final version of the story is twice as long as the first version, which stopped already at Mrs. Shortley's death. The story as it now stands consists of two confrontations, first between Mrs. Shortley and the displaced person, and then between him and Mrs. McIntyre, the owner of the farm. And throughout the story there is Father Flynn, who drops in. Both women experience failure and death, but O'Connor does not permit these events to become sentimental. She does not want our sentiments to obscure the absurdity of the lives she describes, so she makes sure that we cannot identify wholly with her characters. She hopes, of course, that we will recognize the absurdity as a part of our own lives. Mrs. Shortley dies at the moment of her final vision, whereas Mrs. McIntyre lingers on after her revelation. At the end of the story all the survivors are thoroughly displaced both spiritually and socially.

On July 21 in 1949 the *Union Recorder*, the local Milledgeville paper, carried the story: "Displaced Family Arrives On Farm From Poland" on the front page. And a week later the same paper featured a photo of the displaced family also on the front page.[12] The newspaper was probably a source of inspiration for O'Connor. The main difference between the newspaper article and O'Connor's plot is the death of the displaced person in the fictional account; the Poles mentioned in the newspaper left the area unharmed. From O'Connor's letters we can see that a displaced Polish family was also at Andalusia, the O'Connor farm. On March 3, 1957, she wrote Mrs. Rumsey Haynes: "Our [Polish displaced][13] family has got a better job and they are moving next week and so my mother is busy getting in another family. This is always a trying time because you never know what you are getting until you get them. This will provide her [Mrs. O'Connor] with an additional headache and me with an additional story probably" (*HB*, p. 205).

The social milieu and characters of "The Displaced Person" are close to the milieu on Andalusia and the people there; this is confirmed by a letter to a friend known as "A." On May 19, 1956, O'Connor wrote: "The two colored people in "The Displaced Person" are on this place now. The old man is 84 but vertical or more or less so. He doesn't see too good and the other day he fertilized some of my mother's bulbs with worm medicine for the calves. I can only see them from the outside. I wouldn't have the courage of Miss Shirley Ann Grau to go inside their heads" (*HB*, p. 159). In spite of the disclaimer in the last sentence, it is her intimate knowledge of the local people and their ways that make O'Connor's stories such excellent material for the social observer and the film maker. She is a master of convincing dialogue, sensitive as she is to the speech of her native area. And she is aware of its importance for her fiction: "A distinctive idiom," she maintains in one of her talks, "is a powerful instrument for keeping fiction social. When one Southern character speaks, regardless of his station in life, an echo of all Southern life is heard. This helps to keep Southern fiction from being a fiction of purely private experience" (*MM*, p. 199). In her fiction she demonstrates that she can render the speech of any Southern character regardless of station in life. Here is a conversation between a poor white, Mrs. Shortley, and a black man, old Astor, upon the arrival of the displaced family on the farm:

> The old man, Astor raised himself. "We been watching," he said as if this would be news to her. "Who they now?" "They come from over the water," Mrs. Shortley said with a wave of her arm. "They're what is called Displaced Persons." "Displaced Persons," he said. "Well now. I declare. What do that mean?" "It means they ain't where they were born at and there's nowhere for them to go – like if you was run out of here and wouldn't nobody have you." "It seem like they here, though," the old man said in a reflective voice. "If they here, they somewhere." "Sho is," the other agreed. "They here." The illogic of Negro-thinking always irked Mrs. Shortley. "They ain't where they belong to be at," she said. (*CS*, p. 199)

O'Connor demonstrates a remarkable ability in creating dramatic scenes out of the concrete details of life on a Georgia farm. Her characters not only sound right, they also look right. It cannot be doubted that the characters who are actors in the great tragi-comedy of man, are also Georgia people.

Mrs. Shortley dominates the first half of the story. She seems to be indifferent to the beauty of nature and blind to its spiritual value. She ignores the peacock and calls it "Nothing but a peachicken," (*CS*, p. 198) and she ignores "the white afternoon sun" (*CS*, p. 194). But when the Poles try to become members of the social system, she takes up religion and dwells much on vengeance and destruction. But she still ignores the clouds that look like rows and rows of "white fish" (*CS*, p. 210) and perhaps suggest Christian mercy. O'Connor's social concern in the story becomes obvious if we consider Mrs. Shortley as a representative of her class. She represents the malnutrition and marginal economic existence of the poor white South. Anni Maude, one of Mrs. Shortley's daughters, "had never got her growth," and Sarah Mae, the other daughter, "had a cast in her eye" (*CS*, p. 197). These are medical problems that nothing seems to have been done about, although the girls are fifteen and seventeen years old.

Mrs. Shortley herself is in bad health. Her distorted visions are made plausible by her ignorance and her bad physical condition. When she drives home the cows, she climbs a hill and probably suffers a minor heart attack. She knows she has heart trouble, but receives no medical treatment. She does prophesy the manner of her own death, whereas her Sunday afternoon revelation originates, it seems, in war newsreels, her distrust of foreigners, and her highly selective Bible reading. The entangled limbs of the Shortleys during her last moments recall the tangle of bodies in the newsreels. In this way Mrs. Shortley is united with the dead concentration camp victims through her own death (*CS*, pp. 213-14).

In the second part of the story Mrs. McIntyre takes over from Mrs. Shortley as "the giant wife of the countryside" (*CS*, p. 194). As her language reveals Mrs. McIntyre is of another class. Her ultimate concern is and has always been the finances of the farm. And it is through Mrs. McIntyre's materialism that O'Connor voices her most direct social criticism in the story. Mrs. McIntyre's worst worry is her tenants. Over the years she has had the Ringfields, Collins, Jarrells, Perkins, Pinkins, Herrins, and now the Shortleys. It is obvious that Mrs. McIntyre thinks of them as so much cattle, as human beings she considers her tenants completely "worthless." She behaves and sounds like Mrs. Hopewell in "Good Country People," who "had averaged one tenant family a year" (*CS*, p. 273). Mrs. McIntyre feels that she has been fooling with "sorry people" for years. And she cannot understand why the people she hires always leave her. But it is no wonder, for while she works tirelessly for material success, she thinks of the hired help as just means to her end.

To be a tenant on the McIntyre farm is not an enviable life. When the Guizacs arrive, they receive "things that Mrs. McIntyre couldn't use any more herself" (*CS*, p. 196). They are allowed to move into a tenant's shack, and they are told that "they should be grateful for anything they could get" (*CS*, p. 196). For their labor the four Poles will receive seventy dollars a month. Mrs. McIntyre's self-seeking callousness towards the Guizacs illustrates the cruelty of the system. Tenants are only valued in proportion to the money they earn for the farmers. Mrs. McIntyre claims that "people are selfish," (*CS*, p. 216) but she herself wages a regular war on mankind: "She had survived a succession of tenant farmers and dairymen that the old man himself would have found hard to outdo, and she had been able to meet the constant drain of a tribe of moody unpredictable Negroes, and she had even managed to hold her own against the incidental bloodsuckers, the cattle dealers and lumber men and the buyers and sellers of anything...." (*CS*, p. 218). In short every human being she gets into contact with is a menace to her, or at least superfluous in her eyes: "All of you are extra. Each and every one of you are extra!" she screams at her black and white help (*CS*, p. 232). She feels that she alone is essential, for the farm is "her place."

The criticism leveled at Mrs. McIntyre's pride, egotism, and materialism constitutes O'Connor's violent denunciation of the whole social system that breeds these characteristics. At times she suspects her own insufficiency. She then seeks her tabernacle, which is a room with a safe surrounded by old ledgers and bank-books. It is the room where her first husband had conducted his business. It is here, facing the safe that she tries to understand why "there was nobody poorer in the world than she was" (*CS*, p. 221). She never suspects her own shortcomings or those of the social order. Father Flynn understands her nature very well, and he uses the introduction of the displaced family on the farm to try to save Mrs. McIntyre from her own materialism and her all-devouring self-interest. She becomes a benefactress, even if her motive is greed. The old priest is well aware of this and lets out "a great ugly bellow" when Mrs. McIntyre asks him "if he thought she was made of money" (*CS*, p. 230).

When Mr. Guizac threatens to upset the social and the racial balance on the farm by working too much and by planning to let Sulk marry a Polish girl, Mrs. McIntyre's reaction reveals no uncertainty: "Mr. Guizac! You would bring this poor innocent child over here and try to marry her to a half-witted thieving black stinking nigger! What kind of a monster are you!" (*CS*, p. 222). Clearly, it is Mrs. McIntyre who is the monster. She feels no obligation to other human beings, but she does feel that "*her* moral obligation" is to "her own people" (*CS*, p. 228). "He's upset the balance around here," she says about Mr. Guizac. And for her this is more important than some girl's suffering in distant Europe. It is significant that it is Astor, the old black man on the farm, who helps remind her of the traditional order on the place. Their relationship reflects the social order which is the gauge for everything they do. – Astor's presence is a flaw in the story in one respect. It is hard to believe that he would not have put a quick end to Sulk's plans, it is impossible to imagine that Astor did not know, and given the time and place it is difficult to imagine that Sulk would ever get the notion to marry a white girl, even when encouraged by Mr. Guizac. O'Connor sees the weakness and indicates that Sulk is half-witted.

It is only at the murder of Mr. Guizac that Mrs. McIntyre begins to suspect that she may not be in full control even on her place. She watches the figures bending over Mr. Guizac's body. Among them is Father Flynn (who has gotten there unbelievably fast); he is administering the last rites to the Pole when Mrs. McIntyre wakes up after she had lost consciousness. She now experiences the sense of displacement that supposedly also characterized Mrs. Shortley's last moments. Though it all takes place on her own farm, Mrs. McIntyre feels that she is "in some foreign country" (*CS*, p. 235). The irony is, of course, that the class conscious Mrs. McIntyre would never have expected to share an experience with one of her "sorry" tenants. Her punishment is that she is not allowed to die right away as Mrs. Shortley did. All of her life Mrs. McIntyre has hated discussions about religion, they embarrassed her, and now she has to accept the weekly visits of Father Flynn, who comes to explain the doctrines of the Church. Ironically, the proud, practical and materialistic Mrs. McIntyre is condemned to suffer religious instruction she has not asked for.

The difficulties between the displaced person and the two women represent a confrontation of value systems. One system derives from the social stratification of Southern society, the other is the product of a frightening European experience. Mr. Guizac's foreign social behavior brings the value systems into violent opposition. He poses a threat to a society that has always dealt with class, race, and sex in its own ways. The Pole's willingness to work hard and his ability to improve his financial position together with his willingness to accept blacks as equals are potentially lethal to the established social order. It is when Mrs. McIntyre realizes this that she complains: "He's extra and he's upset the balance around here" (*CS*, p. 231).

The daily life on the farm depends on everyone's tacit acceptance of the social stratification. Everybody on the farm knows that Astor and Sulk steal, but in doing so they confirm the stereotype image of blacks, so nobody thinks much of it. Mrs. McIntyre knows that Mr. Shortley smokes in the milking barn, but that is what can be expected of poor white help, so she only hints at it. Both the blacks and the poor whites run stills on Mrs. McIntyre's property. It seems that everybody knows it, but it does not constitute a transgression against the accepted behavior patterns for blacks and poor whites, so nobody even considers interfering. This is the system that the Guizacs threaten to disrupt by their mere presence. Mr. Guizac is finally sacrificed, because the accepted social order is considered more important than any moral consideration could possibly be. It could be argued that the Polish immigrant must die because he undermines social patterns whose existence he does not even know about. "The balance" that is upset is finally not so much based on divine justice as on social convention. What threatens is the dissolution of all social distinctions through the planned marriage between a young black man and a blond Polish girl. Surely the social satire is too obvious to be overlooked.

The social context is always clear in "The Displaced Person," as O'Connor feels it should be in all fiction: "The larger social context is simply left out of much current fiction, but it cannot be left out by the Southern writer," she said in one of her talks (*MM*, p. 198). It is, after all, the portrait of the class-divided society that makes the story about the displaced person so convincing. This is always the case O'Connor maintains in her advice on writing: "You can't cut characters off from their society and say much about them as individuals. You can't say anything meaningful about the mystery of a personality unless you put that personality in a believable and significant social context" (*MM*, p. 104). The social situation of the Shortleys is only too plain when they load their boxes and "old battered suitcases from under the bed," two iron beds with the mattresses rolled up between some rocking chairs, and "a crate of chickens" on top of their old car (*CS*, p. 212). They prepare to leave the farm in their "overfreighted leaking ark" before they are asked to leave. The only ones worse off than the Shortleys are the blacks; and they will be next to go, according to Mrs. Shortley, now that nobody has mules any more (*CS*, p. 205). The only comfort for the blacks is that their social position is too low for anybody to dispute with them for it. It is her "moral obligation" to the social order that makes it impossible for Mrs. McIntyre to prevent the killing of Mr. Guizac. She becomes the accomplice of the poor whites and blacks in "collusion forever" (*CS*, p. 234). She is bound by her particular past and by the institutions and traditions that the past has left to her, and, ironically, she is bound to the very people she rejects.

Flannery O'Connor's social and moral ideas invoke the milieu of her region and the society of which she was a product. In this sense large social issues were always the stuff of her work.[14] A true appreciation of O'Connor as a fiction writer must also take into account her rendition of her time and place and the people there. Her style in "The Displaced Person" is that of the social satirist. In her story of what the social order and the accepted system can do to us, she demonstrates her social awareness. There is no reason to exaggerate the importance of her social sensibility, but it should not be ignored. Whenever she tells us about the lives of good or bad country people, we learn that their situation is often less than enviable. She obviously enjoys showing that we are human and made of dust, but it is also obvious in her fiction that Flannery O'Connor had great love for the people who try to pass the dragon by "the side of the road."

1. Flannery O'Connor, *Mystery and Manners*, New York, Farrar, Straus and Giroux, 1969.

2. *Sewanee Review*, 62/4 (Autumn 1954) 634.

3. See Sally Fitzgerald, "Introduction," *Three by Flannery O'Connor,*" New Jersey, 1985, p. xxiv. Fitzgerald claims that O'Connor did not treat "a current social issue" in her fiction until "Everything That Rises Must Converge."

4. See e.g., Sally Fitzgerald, p. viii: "... she had majored – for the last time ever – in Sociology."

5. Harvey Klevar, "Image and Imagination: Flannery O'Connor's Front Page Fiction," *Journal of Modern Literature* 4/1 (September 1974) 121-32.

6. "The Shiftlet Fragment,"*The Flannery O'Connor Bulletin*, 10 (1981) 78-86.

7. See the letter to John Hawkes of December 26, 1959.*The Habit of Being: Letters of Flannery O'Connor*, ed. Sally Fitzgerald, New York, Farrar, Straus and Giroux, 1979, p. 367.

8. See the letter to Elizabeth McKee, October 15, 1952, *The Habit of Being*, p. 44.

9. "Introduction," *Flannery O'Connor: The Complete Stories*, New York, Farrar, Straus and Giroux, 1965, p. xvi. And "An Exile in the East," *The South Carolina Review*, 11/1 (November, 1978), 12-21.

10. *The Habit of Being*, p. 329.

11. *The Correspondence of Flannery O'Connor and the Brainard Cheneys*, ed. C. Ralph Stephens, Jackson, University Press of Mississippi, 1986, p. 154, p. 155.

12. Harvey Klevar, pp.126-27.

13. The brackets contain the actual wording of the letter on deposit with Georgia College, Milledgeville, Ga.

14. See Sally Fitzgerald, "Introduction," *Three by Flannery O'Connor*, p. xxv: "Large social issues as such were never the stuff of Flannery O'Connor's work."

CHAPTER FIVE

Mint-juleping with Marcus Aurelius: Walker Percy's Stoicism

At the MLA meeting in Houston in December, 1980, I participated in a workshop on Walker Percy's achievement with a talk on the reception of his fiction in Scandinavia. By April 1982 my focus had shifted, and I talked on "Walker Percy and the South" at the University of South Carolina. When I had been awarded an ACLS Fellowhip to Vanderbilt University, 1984-85, to study Southern literature, I gave talks on Walker Percy and the Stoic tradition at North Carolina State and Wake Forest universities. The topic was still on my mind in 1989 when I suggested to Karl-Heinz Westarp that we should host an international symposium on Walker Percy's "faith, fiction, and philosophy" at Sandbjeg in Jutland, which we did in August. Some of the papers from the symposium were published by University Press of Mississippi in 1991 as Walker Percy: Novelist and Philosopher. *My contribution to the symposium was on Percy's stoicism and it was an early version of this chapter.*

Mint-juleping with Marcus Aurelius

Walker Percy's Stoicism is one circumstance of his mental makeup that needs critical attention. In his existential search Percy has not separated his imagination from the Southern community. He was born of a region that endows him with character and purpose, and he seems to know that he can only deny its parenthood to his own hurt. He confronts the world from his region, he tries to comprehend its past, he considers the values and limitations of his heritage, and in his search he also takes into consideration the continued presence in the South of the Stoic tradition. So far, Walker Percy's critics have only talked of his Stoicism in general terms. The use of the word is often biased, and it is treated as if it were simply a synonym for all non-Christian ideas, but it should not be dismissed so lightly. We need a critical discussion of what is meant by Stoicism in connection with Walker Percy's fiction.[1]

The theology of the Christian church owes much to the ethical doctrines of Stoicism. Emperor Marcus Aurelius Antoninus advised the readers of his *Meditations* to keep their temper with the foolish and ungrateful and "even care for them" (8.8) because "men exist for each other" (8.59). In view of the reputation of Roman Stoics, it is perhaps surprising for some Christians that Marcus Aurelius considered the idea of "man's brotherhood with his kind" inherent in the constitution of every human being (12.26); but the existence of a brotherhood of man is one of the ideas that Christian theology shares with Stoicism. Epictetus, whose handbook *The Enchiridion* was the moral guide for generations of Southerners, anticipated Marcus Aurelius by pointing out that a brother's injustice can be borne when we keep in mind that he is our brother (43). In this way brotherly love was accepted as a principle by Roman Stoics, if not as an emotion. The emperor's meditations on the lantern of eternal "truth, wisdom and justice" (12.15) became a guide for distinguished Southerners such as William Byrd II, Thomas Jefferson, and Robert E. Lee.[2] Stoicism offered them a gospel of endurance rather than hope, enabled them to reconcile social dependency with personal independence, allowed the idea that God is not separate from the world, and confirmed their suspicion that what is happening now will happen over and over, whatever our passions. Stoicism did for them the most that religion can do for any man, to paraphrase Henry James on Epictetus: it enabled them to live hopefully in a miserable world.[3]

There are, of course, essential differences between Christian belief and Stoicism. Whether God exists or not, the moral issues remain unaffected for the Stoic. Marcus Aurelius wanted to adopt "strict principles for the regulation of impulse" (8.1) simply for "the happiness of real integrity and dignity" (10.9). And for Epictetus the goal was the preservation of his own honor and fidelity and self-respect (24). The Stoics did not offer the promise of an afterlife. The emperor wrote, "One thing only is of precious worth: to live out one's days in truthfulness and fair dealing" (6.47). In this way the Stoic philosopher looks to himself for all help or harm (48) (compare the egoism of Aunt Emily in *The Moviegoer*). And he does good in order to be virtuous, that is, in order to be able to live with himself. It is a small but truly decisive step from the Stoic maxims to the ethical precepts of the Gospel.

During Walker Percy's childhood his foster father was an explainer of the region to outsiders. William Alexander Percy felt a strong commitment to the preservation of the human values of the Southern community, but he rejected its fundamentalist religion. The dominant evangelical protestantism emphasizes the individual's own role in saving his soul. Each individual is supposed to maintain his personal relation with God and is expected to work out his salvation without the help of any man-made institution. William Alexander Percy would have thought it natural that ultimately all responsibility is individual. What made him a skeptic about the dominant faith of his native region was its intense emotionalism in defense of revealed knowledge and mystery. Southern fundamentalism holds that temporal ends are not ultimate ends and that there is knowledge to which all "facts"are either subordinate or irrelevant. Most Southerners live in a world peculiarly balanced between such Christian otherworldliness and the Greco-Roman ethics of individual responsibility, but in William Alexander Percy's home there were only the philosophers of antiquity.

It was to the Roman Stoics that he turned when faced with the task of educating his cousin's sons, LeRoy, Walker, and Phinizy. Throughout his autobiography, *Lanterns on the Levee*, it is obvious that William Alexander Percy admired the Stoic sense of duty *(kathékon)*, which is the duty to do the most rational thing possible under the circumstances. And he considered the virtues of reason, courage, justice, and self-discipline ends in themselves. In writing on the education of the boys, he revealed his gloomy view of his time: "Should I ... teach deceit, dishonor, ruthlessness, bestial force to the children in order that they survive? Better that they perish. It is sophistry to speak of two sets of virtues, there is but one: virtue is an end in itself.... Honor and honesty, compassion and truth are good even if they kill you, for they alone give life its dignity and worth."[4] He was here writing of "the unassailable kingdom" of Marcus Aurelius, which is simply a moral state where absolute virtue reigns supreme. It is "unassailable" as it remains with us whatever happens. It was not to Christian humility but to the "remaining fastness" that he hoped to guide his adopted sons. As their first books the "young Enzios" received the gospels and the *Meditations* of Marcus Aurelius. In his choice their educator had drawn the lines for an intellectual conflict between Christianity and Stoicism that in Walker Percy's fiction remained unresolved.

William Alexander Percy rejected truths that are considered fundamental by most Christians. He wrote, "We trouble our hearts with foolish doubts and unwise questionings – the fear of death, the hope of survival, forgiveness, heaven, hell. Rewards and punishments hereafter? What bribes we ask for our perfunctory righteousness! ... There should be no question of reward: to function is the task assigned" (*LOL*, 320-21). He found that the prodigal son could have stayed in a more sanitary place than the hog-wallow, that he did not deserve a party but a whipping, and that the hardworking son, who did not go and get himself "hog-smelly," was quite right in being upset about the party for his brother (*LOL*, 28). It was a natural reaction for a man who believed in character, talent, and performance. He realized that the instruction offered his wards by the churches was not what he wanted for them; their teachings seemed but a burden. In his poem "Enzio's Kingdom" he wrote:

> When I have made my tablet of the laws
> To guide the flight of my young Enzios,
> 'Thou shalt not' shall be missing from its rubric.
> Perhaps two words will make its decalogue:
> 'Courage: Unselfishness.' These two suffice.[5]

He knew that the standards he offered had already been defeated; and he knew that if they were to accept his standards, they would appear as boys left over from the age of chivalry. But, as he asked himself, "What could I teach them other than what I myself had learned?" He shared the concerns of the Southern aristocrat, who thought churches more palatable when they were behind rows of Greek columns. And he hoped people would return to the old standards, but he was not optimistic about it.

William Alexander Percy's concern with ethical standards became Walker Percy's concern. In his novelized philosophy the tension is always between the inherited Stoicism and the adopted Catholic faith. For Uncle Will the main torment in life was what seems to be "eternal isolation" (*LOL*, 321). Loneliness was seen by him as the saddest fact of our existence; and Seneca, Epictetus, and Marcus Aurelius do not suggest ways to overcome the problem. The existential concern is also a part of Walker Percy's heritage. And the inadequacy of Stoic philosophy and evangelical Protestantism in the face of isolation and loneliness gave rise to his search for other values. But William Alexander Percy's Stoic ideas remain essential for an understanding of Walker Percy's fiction.

From the start the novelist defined his fiction in relation to his uncle's ideas, as if he were having a crucial argument with him. In 1973 *Lanterns on the Levee* appeared in a new edition with an introduction by Walker Percy. There he states, "Even when I did not follow him, it was usually in *relation* to him, whether with him or against him, that I defined myself and my own direction" (*LOL*, xi). The statement should not necessarily be in the past tense, for Walker

Percy was still defining himself and his characters in relation to what Uncle Will taught him. Several passages in his early work attest to William Alexander Percy's presence in his mind. In the early 1930s the influence made itself felt in the poems and reviews he wrote while he attended Greenville High School. In *The Pica*, the high school paper, the young Walker Percy published an interesting poem, "If I Were King." One of the more notable lines asserts, "No sloth I'd be if I were King."[6]

Under the influence of the social issues of the 1950s, Walker Percy became increasingly aware of the gap between his uncle's Stoicism and his own thinking. He had an intuition of man's radical dependence which did not justify his uncle's stress on individualism. Walker Percy's 1956 essay "Stoicism in the South" reflects the conflict in his mind. He maintains that through the centuries the South has managed to have the stoa beside the church, "one for living in, the other for dying in."[7] The Old South, Percy claims, always had a stronger Greek flavor than it ever had a Christian. He argues that the South is still on the porch with Marcus Aurelius and suggests that it is time to leave the stoa behind:

> The Southern gentleman did live in a Christian edifice, but he lived there in the strange fashion ... of a man who will neither go inside nor put it entirely behind him but stands forever grumbling on the porch. From this vantage point he caught sight of Pericles and Hector and the Emperor, and recognized them as his heart's elect. Where was to be found their like? In Abraham? In Paul? He thought not. When he named a city Corinth, he did not mean Paul's community. How like him to go into Chancellorsville or the Argonne with Epictetus in his pocket; how unlike him to have had the Psalms.[8]

In his essays from the 1950s and 1960s, Percy again and again referred to the Stoicism in the Southern mind. In "The Failure and the Hope" (1965) Percy repeated his praise for the old Stoic tradition, but he allowed that it possessed "fatal weaknesses" (primarily that it was based on personal relationships and did not possess resources for renewal) and that it could not offer a viable alternative to racism. He recalled "the gentle tradition" with "affection and admiration" but found that its code had little relevance in the social and political order of the day. And again he implored the old-style, quasi-Christian gentleman of the South to get off the porch and into the church. Percy's polemical essays from this period no doubt amount to a rejection of Stoicism, but it is a peculiarly loving rejection. In January 1985, I asked him about his view of Southern Stoicism. He replied: "Stoicism is the main Southern ethos, which is not ordinarily recognized.... Everybody took Greek and Latin. And they called their cities Corinth, Ithaca, and Demopolis. All well-educated Southern gentlemen knew their Cicero and their Horace, their Virgil, and their Seneca, as well as their Marcus Aurelius.... People don't usually know how strong the Greco-Roman Stoic tradition was among the educated classes."[9]

The reassessing of ethical heritage that Percy has accomplished is characteristic of the present mode of Southern fiction. The existential search is not the only search; Percy is also struggling to comprehend the nature of memory and history. This possibly with the idea that it will ultimately prove to be one search, whether we seek answers in the past or in our present existence. *The Moviegoer* is an engaged analysis of man's situation in the twentieth century. Brainard Cheney reviewed the first Percy novel in the *Sewanee Review*, and his piece was praised by Percy.[10] Cheney claimed that Binx and Kate are left at the end of the novel in "Christian swaddling clothes" and that the moviegoer discovers "a candle-lit footpath" to faith. Whereas it is clear that at the end of the novel "grace has somehow *rubbed of*" on Binx, it is difficult to find an overt acceptance of faith. Binx is Percy's John Falstaff, a man of the little way, a man who finally turns out to be determined by the heritage of his Aunt Emily, who is a true Stoic and who thinks that the world makes perfect sense without God.

Binx may not understand or accept Aunt Emily's Stoic values, but as he matures, he acts in accordance with them. The facts of the ending of *The Moviegoer* are that we leave Binx at the ethical stage of existence, fighting physical and mental illnesses. In the final scenes Binx does behave like a responsible citizen, and everything he does, Marcus Aurelius would have applauded. But he is still dislocated, still caught between the Stoicism of his father's family and the Catholicism of his mother's family, and he is still exiled from both traditions. Like Percy himself, Binx is forever trying to combine individual ethical responsibility with faith in revealed knowledge. It may only be a short way from belief in the revealed knowledge of fundamentalism to the mysteries of the Catholic faith, but as Percy's fiction reveals, the journey from the sanctity of the inner self of Stoicism to the sanctity of the "we" of the Catholic community is arduous.

Williston Bibb Barrett of *The Last Gentleman* loves to hear his father's stories of their ancestors. He admires his father, who gave speeches on topics such as *noblesse oblige* and the importance of character, which are also important subjects in *Lanterns on the Levee*. Will Barrett reads Douglas Freeman's *R. E. Lee;* and in his mind he is constantly correcting Confederate foul-ups before they happen. At Princeton he blows up a small Union monument because it offends him (*LG*, 267). And when he is accused of being absentminded, Will admits that he was "thinking of the summer of 1864." He occasionally finds that the Southern stoic in him surfaces when he is most in need of it. At one point, when he is being ignored but needs the quick help of a nurse, Will finds the voice of his ancestors:

> 'Nurse,' he said sternly, four feet away. He actually raised a forefinger. She answered the telephone. All at once time fell in.... He seemed to be listening. 'You hear me, goddamn it,' thundered a voice terrible and strange. It was for the two of them to listen as the voice went on,' – or else I'm go-

ing to kick yo' ass down there.' An oddly Southern voice, then not his surely. Yet her glossy eyes were on *him* (*LG*, 394).

The voice may not be Will's, but it is surely a part of his voice. The Southern stoa may have been "discredited as a viable way of life in the twentieth century," as Ellen Douglas phrases it,[11] but in the critical situation where Will Barrett is faced with his duty toward another, the force of the stoic thought exerted upon him reveals itself. But Will is also a representative modern man; he is insecure and concerned with what the world is coming to, and he is lonely. The battle formations of the lingering Stoicism that is Will's heritage and the Christianity that he hopes will help him are clearly visible.

When we meet Will Barrett again in *The Second Coming*, he is uncured of his malaise, and he is still preoccupied with the past. He distinguishes between two versions of the old Stoicism – one, represented by a Greener and *Ivanhoe*, which he inherited from his grandfather; the other, which is from his father, is represented by a Luger and *Lord Jim*. They both had enemies; the grandfather, like Ivanhoe, hated his enemies. Like Jim, Ed Barrett, Will's father, felt guilty and had only one hated enemy: himself. He hated his death-in-life existence so much that he decided to kill himself and planned to kill Will, too. Years later Will imagines that he hears his father urging him to kill himself: "Go like a man, for Christ's sake, a Roman, here's your sword" (*SC*, 337). Will tries to get away from the "secret love of death" by doing the exact opposite of his father. Because his father did not, he tries to believe in the Christian God, but does not succeed.

His father's brand of Stoicism is summed up for Will by Ewell McBee, who heard Ed Barrett tell "a preacher" how to define "a soul": "A soul is a man like you and me and Ewell here. You want to know what a man is? I'll tell you. A man is born between an asshole and a peehole. He eats, sleeps, shits, fucks, works, gets old and dies. And that's all he does. That's what a man is" (*SC*, 176). This is not Stoicism according to Epictetus or Marcus Aurelius. The primitive summing up of our existence is realistic enough, but it ignores the noble principles and codes that Ed Barrett also believed in. But in his irritation with the "savior of souls" he reveals his defiant despair. To the *Los Angeles Times* Percy explained that in the novel Will "actually sees a possibility of achieving love, work that he likes, a sense of identity, ... freedom to choose for himself, and he demands the presence of God on top of that."[12] And Percy thinks it is clear that he gets it. That Will's achievement is topped by the bonus of the presence of God is about as clear as Binx Bolling's footpath to faith at the end of Percy's first novel. Throughout *The Second Coming* the reader has been waiting for Will to act in order to set things right, and he finally does. In a Stoic effort to make life tolerable for the people about him, he decides to put to work all the old, bored, maimed, and generally miserable people in a project of building log cabins. Will finally accepts that he has to create his own answers and sets about ordering life for himself and others. What Will actually does would have been praised by the emperor.

Lancelot, in Percy's novel named for the knight, is a moralist concerned with the lapse of decorum and values, and he is disgusted with the cynicism and corruption of the present. He finds it difficult to live with dignity in a pornographic age. His story is an unpleasant statement of man's moral, psychic, and spiritual impotence. Behind Lancelot's perpetual jeremiad we can hear the voice of William Alexander Percy, and it is echoed by Walker Percy in a *Paris Review* interview, where he explains that his anger is caused by "the widespread and ongoing devaluation of human life in the western world." Lancelot's disgust with the modern world makes him plan a new society based on Stoic precepts, and this time Percy lines up his battle formations so that they are impossible to overlook. In an interview with me Percy explained:

> Instead of dealing overtly with Christianity I deal with the old Roman ethic: what's wrong with him taking revenge in the way he did? Would Aunt Emily object to that? What he is doing is carrying Aunt Emily's ethic to its logical conclusion. If he has been cuckolded by somebody, a Hollywood producer, then what Lancelot does is *kill* him. That's what Ulysses did, and we look on Ulysses as one of the great heroes of Western culture. Ulysses and Telemachus kill everybody! Lancelot only kills three people.... And we applaud Ulysses. (*Conversations*, p. 209)

Percy brings it down to an either/or. The choice is between Lancelot and Percival, his Christian counterpart. The choice is also between the tradition of the stoa and that of the church, which may well be the reason why the book never became popular in the South. Percy tries to force his reader off the porch and into the church, but he has a hard time ridding himself of the Stoic stand in *Lancelot*. And it is no wonder, for he realizes the values that will be sacrificed if Lancelot's ideas are rejected. It is painful for a Southerner to bracket Robert E. Lee with Adolf Hitler and Idi Amin because they all ordered killings, but a good Christian does not kill under any circumstances.

Lancelot represents the madness of our Judeo-Christian Western culture, but is he more insane than he has to be in order to survive in the society in which he lives? He makes some frightening statements about life in the Western world, but it is much too convenient to write him off as a madman. Linda Hobson's interpretation, for example, is simplified so that the reading of the entire novel becomes a nice equation with a predictable result: "Lance's rantings ... of madness and indifference are stilled by the priest's affirmative "Yes" at the close of *Lancelot*."[13] The fine ambiguity of the fiction is here lost in the interpretation. If Lancelot were indeed mad and therefore *not* responsible for his life, the moral questions raised through his actions would be uninteresting. If the novel were a pat moral tale, what would Father John and Lancelot talk about "beyond the pages of the novel"? If Lancelot were mad, his opinions would not have caused Father John's rediscovery of his faith, for he would probably not have attempted a dialogue with a mad person. Like Hamlet,

Lancelot is "but mad north-north-west; when the wind is southerly [he knows] a hawk from a handsaw."

Lancelot chooses the Stoic tradition as an instrument to tackle the problems of the modern world, and his reasoning cannot be written off as madness just because it is a secular revolution that he plans. "No, Lancelot is not beyond the reach of Percival and accordingly Lancelot is not beyond hope," as Percy has stated.[14] But Lancelot Andrewes Lamar is so deeply rooted in the Stoicism of the Old South that it would be impossible for him to start a new order from scratch – the Stoic past will be too much with him. It is because of his heritage that he feels the necessity to plan a new life in Virginia. If he had lived in the twentieth century, the emperor would probably accept the need for a new order and perhaps even sanction Lancelot's plans.

The alluring tale of how Lancelot in the tradition of Western culture defended his family heritage by revengeful murders has awaited Percy's further rejection. But in *The Second Coming* Will Barrett combined Stoic and Christian thinking in an effort to help the elderly. In *The Thanatos Syndrome* it becomes clear that Percy now polarizes abstract scientism and Christianity as extreme opposites. Percy said, "My purpose is ... to challenge science, as it is presently practiced by some scientists, in the name of science."[15] The idea is already clearly present in *Lost in the Cosmos*, where Dr. Aristarchus Jones plans to leave the genetically defective children behind on the dying planet Earth, as these children do not fit into his plans for a new society on another planet. The new society is to be based on reason and science; it will be a society "freed from the superstitions and repressions of religion" (*LC*, 246). Colonel John Pelham, C. S. A., known as "the Gallant Pelham," artillery officer under General J. E. B. Stuart, personifies old Stoic values in *Lost in the Cosmos: The Last Self-Help Book* ... (1983). On a Donahue show he lectures the audience on a gentleman's obligations. With Epictetus he believes that man achieves freedom through self-discipline; and even though he respects religious convictions, he believes that right behavior has little to do with religion (*LC*, 53). Because he reminds them of a character from *Gone with the Wind*, Colonel Pelham is well received by the *Donahue* audience.

In *Love in the Ruins* Percy gives us a frightening portrait of the demise of Western culture. As always in Percy's fiction, hope lies in putting into practice the Christian ethic, which in the novel is personified by the rather stoic Father Smith. The priest tells Tom More that he should think about doing his job, be a better doctor, and worry about people and the state of his unhappy country, and he advises him to stop daydreaming (*LR*, 399). When we meet Tom More again in *The Thanatos Syndrome*, he has just been released from Fort Pelham, after two years at the minimum security facility. Significantly, he was detained for trafficking in drugs. It was a minor offense that nevertheless anticipated Van Dorn and Comeaux's use of science in their Gnostic attempts to improve on man. The time in Fort Pelham has restored Tom More's humanity, if not his faith (*TS*, 81). He returns to become an ally for Father Smith's Christian forces against an enemy that worships human intelligence. The social engineering that Tom More faces has its roots in Gnostic dreams of purifying the race. It is akin to, albeit much worse than, the self-help or how-to-live books so suspect to Percy because they imply that truth is revealed in our material world, and that we have the ability to improve on our world. All of which would make God an unnecessary extra. It is ironic that Thomas More in his first appearance, in the novel *Love in the Ruins*, hoped by his invention called the lapsometer to be able to rid man of his despair and *Angst*, in other words to do so by purely scientific means. And for the achievement he expected to receive a Nobel Prize.

In *Lost in the Cosmos* and in his last novel Percy warned us specifically that Gnosticism is at work in our everyday lives. He warned us that acceptance of Gnosticism ultimately will lead to the use of gas chambers; by which social engineers, sentimentalists, and technocrats will try to improve on man by removing undesirable specimens. The true nature of the enemy is revealed in "Father Smith's Confession." What Tom More should do to stop the scientists from experimenting on the people of Feliciana is implied in Father Smith's account of what he did not do or understand in Germany in the 1930s. This is why Father Smith talks of "the Louisiana Weimar psychiatrists" (*TS*, 252). Helped by the stoical Vergil Bon and Uncle Hugh Bob, Tom More does stop the "Blue Boy" heavy sodium experiment. By forcing Comeaux to transfer them to Father Smith's hospice, Tom More saves the infants who are considered undesirable specimens and therefore candidates for a swift "mercy killing." All in all, it is not a bad achievement for a man living in the Age of Not Knowing What to Do. Marcus Aurelius would have been pleased with Tom More.

My argument with Linda Hobson and other Percy critics is with their evaluation of the Stoicism in Percy's thought and fiction. His Stoicism is treated as if it were Gnosticism or simply a synonym for all non-Christian ideas in the world. Hobson's definition, for example, of ethical Stoicism is much too general and biased: "Make a separate peace, uphold good manners oneself, or die on one's own sword like a defeated Roman general, runs the thinking."[16] Whose thinking "runs" like that? It is not the thinking of Epictetus in his discourses, or of Marcus Aurelius in his meditations, or of William Alexander Percy in his poetry and biography. Is Hobson thinking of the many Stoics in Percy's writings? Emily Bolling Cutrer, Ed Barrett, Sutter Vaught, Ellen Oglethorpe, Lancelot Andrewes Lamar, and Colonel John Pelham, just to mention some of the Percy characters of the Greco-Roman persuasion. Others such as the important Father Boomer and Father Smith show essential Stoic virtues: reason, a sense of duty, courage, justice, freedom, compassion, dignity, and self-discipline. Surely the Stoicism of these characters should not be dismissed too easily. The Percy hero needs "to define a way to live without borrowing from Southern Stoicism," Hobson argues, but is that at all possible for them?

It is not Walker Percy's theological insight that makes him an important artist but his accomplishment in the art of fiction. Percy wants to testify to the consequences of God's becoming incarnate, and he has chosen to do so not through theology but in his fiction and through a discussion with his heritage. It is obviously impossible for the Roman Catholic Percy to rid himself of the Old South Stoic Percy or to extricate one from the other; instead, he can use his heritage to define his faith. Stoicism and Christianity are not necessarily antithetical, although it took Percy some time (and his critics somewhat longer) to realize this. What Percy showed us about his ethical Stoic heritage is *not* that something is wrong with it but that Stoicism is not enough.[17] My argument is that Percy saw Stoicism as a formidable ally in the struggle against the devaluation of human life in the western world, but found Stoic thought painfully lacking in the celebration of human life, mystery, hope, and communion with others. He did not reject his inherited Stoicism, but warned of its limits: for the Christian it is not enough to do the right thing for the preservation of "the unassailable kingdom," he also has to face the alienation from himself and from God.

1. All references to Walker Percy's fiction are to the first editions.

2. Lewis A. Lawson, "*The Moviegoer* and the Stoic Heritage," in *The Stoic Strain in American Literature: Essays in Honour of Marston LaFrance*, ed. Duane J. MacMillan (Toronto: University of Toronto Press, 1979), pp. 180-82.

3. *Literary Criticism: Essays on Literature, American Writers, English Writers*, eds. Leon Edel and Mark Wilson (New York: Library of America, 1984), p. 12.

4. William Alexander Percy, *Lanterns on the Levee: Recollections of a Planter's Son* (Baton Rouge: Louisiana State University Press, 1984), p. 313 (hereafter cited as *LOL*). This edition has an introduction by Walker Percy.

5. William Alexander Percy, *"Enzio's Kingdom" and Other Poems* (New Haven: Yale University Press, 1924), p. 112.

6. Walker Percy, "If I Were King," *The Pica*, 22 February, 1933, p. 8.

7. Walker Percy, "Stoicism in the South," *Commonweal*, 6 July 1956, p. 344.

8. Walker Percy, "Stoicism in the South," p. 343.

9. Walker Percy, "Difficult Times," *More Conversations with Walker Percy*, eds. Lewis A. Lawson & Victor A. Kramer, Jackson, University Press of Mississippi, 1993, pp. 105-106.

10. Brainard Cheney, "To Restore a Fragmented Image," *Sewanee Review* 69 (Autumn 1961): 691-700. Walker Percy's letter to Brainard Cheney, dated 30 Oct. 1962, is in the archives at the Alexander Heard Library, Vanderbilt University.

11. Ellen Douglas, *Walker Percy's "The Last Gentleman": Introduction and Commentary*, Religious Dimensions in Literature, no. 11 (New York: Seabury Press, 1969), p. 8.

12. Marc Kirkeby, "Percy: He Can See Clearly Now," *Los Angeles Times Calendar*, 3 August, 1980, p. 52.

13. Linda Whitney Hobson, *Understanding Walker Percy*, Columbia, S.C., University of South Carolina Press, 1988, p. 107.

14. Zoltan Abadi-Nagy, "The Art of Fiction XCVII: Walker Percy," *Paris Review* 103 (Summer 1987): 69.

15. Walker Percy, "The Fateful Rift: The San Andreas Fault in the Modern Mind," Eighteenth Jefferson Lecture in the Humanities, 3 May 1989, transcript from the National Endowment for the Humanities, p. 2.

16. Linda W. Hobson, *Understanding Walker Percy*, 1988, p. 14.

17. See my second interview with Walker Percy, "Difficult Times," *More Conversations with Walker Percy;* p. 106.

The Bi-Racial South

CHAPTER SIX

The Man in the Tree:
Katherine Anne Porter's Lynching Story

I had come upon Katherine Anne Porter's unfinished lynching story in the collection of her papers in the McKeldin Library at the University of Maryland during my first visit there in April 1978. But it was in May 1991, when I was a Fulbright Fellow at the University of Southern Mississippi, that I could present my ideas on the unpublished story at the centennial celebration of Katherine Anne Porter at the University of Maryland. A version of this chapter was published by The Southern Quarterly *in the spring of 1993.*

The Man in the Tree

Katherine Anne Porter always considered it a favorite gambit of writers in the Northeast to imply that Southerners suffer from a burden of guilt about slavery. She thought it a smug and pious Yankee notion that Southerners in this way are deservedly still being punished for the sins of their ancestors. She knew, of course, that guilt is a tremendous motive in literature, and she often stated that one famous Southern writer had created his fiction out of his obsession on the subject. Among her manuscripts in McKeldin Library two pages are titled "About Southern guilty conscience about slavery," which Porter also called "Copied Notes: Piece about the Negro." Throughout the last half of the 1950s she was gathering notes for an essay on the racial issue. The mentioned note begins by Porter evaluating the question of guilt in the light of her own family history:

> I think my grandparents suffered from it [guilt] – or it may have been simply that they themselves were tired of their slavery to slaves, and the terrible hopelessness of their situation, for as early as 1820, according to some family wills I have found in old courthouses in southern towns [in] Virginia, Tennessee, North and South Carolina, Kentucky – they were freeing their slaves by will and providing for them as well as they were able: an acre and a cabin for life, or a few dollars a year to be paid out of the estate; or maybe just that they should be fed, sheltered, and clothed for life; sometimes the heir was burdened to ruin with these bequests. Other more practical and worldly wise among them quite simply set them free with the clothes on their backs and a dollar in pocket; turned them out, because there was nothing else to do: there was nothing left to give them, but their freedom, and a sad, melancholy sort of freedom it must have been; a cruelty, in short; for they had nowhere to go, no work, and no charity from their Abolitionist friends who, having once got them emancipated, didn't care what became of them just so they stayed in the south and became an intolerable burden to their former masters; just so they didn't go wandering off to the north and making trouble there.

The traditional partisan Southern incantation leads up to Porter's total rejection in the same note of the idea of inherited guilt: "Let me confess for myself that I do not feel one trace of guilt because my grandparents and all my known ancestors were slaveholders." But the rejection of the guilt complex does not mean Porter was unable to identify with the African Americans. She understood their situation very well. She was still preparing an essay on the topic in the late 1950s, possibly for *The Reporter*, and in another note to herself called "More or less a starting point," and with the title: "Negro Question" added in holograph, Porter tried to make us realize just exactly how "strange and painful" black American history is:

> So that we may really understand it, put yourself in the place of any of them, even those three generations removed from slavery: suppose you were captured along with other white people, [(added in holograph:) and not only that, but sold by your own rulers, your own people] taken to Africa, in chains – put under the whip, treated like a wild but trainable animal, taught a strange dialect, a strange religion, made to eat unfamiliar food, to suffer a climate against the grain of your being, to be in short, a stranger in a strange land, in captivity that seemed hopeless: well, how would you feel and what would you like to do about it? (ms p. 2)

As we see, the rejection of the notion of guilt as regards slavery did not prevent Porter from identifying with black Americans and regretting their painful history. The identification and sympathy did not lead Porter to support rapid integration. Like William Faulkner and Robert Penn Warren in the late 1950s, Porter wanted integration to come slowly, if at all. She considered the Supreme Court's decision about desegration both "rash and abrupt." Deep in her soul she was convinced that total integration would prove a disaster for black Americans. After a long absence from the South Porter visited Texas, Mississippi, and Louisiana, probably in 1952, and returned with an optimistic view of the racial situation. In a note with the heading "By Katherine Anne Porter" she describes the change she saw in the South. It was mostly that black people were better dressed and fed, drove their own cars, and had their own "moving picture theatres." She acknowledged that it was "not the Millennium, by a long shot," but it was obvious to her that "it was all going in the right direction." Porter was pleased to see that in her South the black race was still "intact and pure": "I thought, God bless them both – meaning both black and white; and I blessed them for maintaining, each within his own race, his own human dignity and self-respect. For we know well and bitterly that black and white blood in this country or any other do not mix often in the marriage bed. I am one of those who believe that they are both better for not mixing at all." Nobody has to feel particularly shocked by the separate-but-equal statement by an about sixty-five year old woman, who was raised in the South at the beginning of the century. Many other Southerners said and believed the same sort of thing at the end of the 1950s. What is important is that in spite of her anti-desegregation attitude Porter was never a racist. Fortunately there is a manuscript that proves this beyond a shadow of a doubt.

Katherine Anne Porter's manuscript[1] "The Man in the Tree" focuses on the racism of her native region at the turn of the century.[2] The notes for the story read like a contribution to later debates on integration, and I always felt that it was unfortunate that she chose not to finish it. Her strong opinions on racial issues, as expressed in the manuscript, deserve to be remembered. Porter seems to have worked on the story in 1933 and 1934, as Joan Givner reports,[3] but the state of the manuscript and the use of different typewriters show that she returned to it over the years. The manuscript is also valuable for what it shows about Porter's compassion at a time in her life when she did not yet take the preponderance of evil for granted.[4] These pages are a treat for lovers of the stories collected in *The Old Order* for what they add to our knowledge about white and black lives in mythologized Kyle, Texas. Porter enthusiasts will stir to the sound of names such as Gay, Maria, Miranda, Uncle Gabriel, Uncle Squire, and Old Nannie. And some of the writing in "The Man in the Tree" is excellent.

For the Porter critic the manuscript offers pleasures that a published story could not hope to equal. In the writing process the author addresses herself in her notes and creates an intimacy with the reader of the manuscript. As Porter never intended to publish her comments to herself, the manner of her metafiction is less formalized than Virginia Woolf's experiment in talking to herself and to her reader in her story called "An Unwritten Novel" (1921), but it is equally brilliant. Porter reminds herself of the existence of a character, advises herself of what to concentrate on, asks herself questions on whether she should use biographical material based on her father's relationship with black people and on her grandmother's "boast that no negro had ever been formally whipped on the place," and she uses "etc" as if she knew exactly what she would add to a conversation. Porter's advice to herself includes: "put in here" (a dramatic incident at a fruit stand), "let it be the woman instead" (who cheats a black boy), "let this be the real reason for the attack and the accusation," "with the crux maybe being in old Nany [sic] sending word she'd come and work out the ten dollars" (to pay for the boy's funeral), "the scene – rather slimy" (with Brigadier-General Angus Kirkendall), "describe the sweet dark country" (the Louisiana swamps), "change her name" (that of the black cook), "have the scene when they go to the jail," "express this better" (Gabriela's reaction to the lynching), and "for the lynching story." The most intimate moment is on a page marked "written in Paris," where Porter seems to be well aware that some day her manuscript would have a reader: "Just stopped to roll and light a new cigarette, and this smell of Scaferlati is astounding ... Like new mown clover mixed equally with very high class barn yard fertiliser, ... Hayfield and ill kept stables recur to me, country life and good weather. But think of *smoking* it!"

One title Porter considered for the material was "The Southern Story." It is an account of a lynching and its aftermath, and the focus is on pride and shame *within one household*. It is embarrassing for the white family the Gays, or Townsends, or Beauregards, that the lynched boy is the grandson of their respected black mammy, called Nannie Bunton (corrected by hand to Bunting), named for Maria Gay's grandfather; so, "the lynching had practically occurred in the family." Porter anticipates that "the crux" of the story will be Nannie's proud refusal to accept money and mourning clothes from "the white folks." Hasty, which is really Hastings, Bunton, "named for old Madam Hastings who owned his grandfather," is described as a decent, hard-working field Negro, who ran perpetual errands with "a wide never fading smile." Porter does not want any suspense about why Hastings was lynched:

> The fat woman with oily light brown hair, who ran the fruit and soda water stand etc, accused him. She ran screaming into the street in a thin pink silk nightgown, she screamed until she drew a crowd of men from all over, and standing there before them, tossing her wild head from one of her hands to the other as if it were a football, she accused the negro boy, Hasty Bunting, of an attempt on her virtue and life.

Later in the ms the woman is given the name Tarleton, possibly with a reference to Banastre Tarleton, who was a particularly cruel British officer in the South during the American Revolution. Porter's Tarleton lives on the edge of town, and as her husband works on the railroad, she is often alone. Porter calls her "a sluttish poor white woman." She is described twice as being mostly in a "prostrated" position; the fact is probably without any religious connotations.

What really happened between the woman and the boy is explained on a page and a half of the manuscript. The woman runs a fruit stand, Hasty bought an orange for a quarter, paid with a fifty-cent piece and did not receive any change. This is the reason for his "attack," which is not defined. On a later page Porter lets Maria observe the Tarleton woman in some detail, and Maria is close enough to overhear the argument about the quarter. On still another page Porter tries to understand the psychology of the woman that any white man can have for a dollar. The woman knew she could count on the mob to believe her, but "believe" is perhaps the wrong word. They simply needed a pretext to indulge in a need, as Porter explains, and the woman senses that the accusation would be believed because it is "consecrated by a tradition equally false." But Porter also writes about another element of the public mind that the Tarleton woman has forgotten in the heat of her anger. Afterwards, when the moral hangover is in effect, they will turn on her. She will be ostracized, for nobody in the community will go near a woman who has been "handled by a nigger." They will blame her for her having the power that made them lynch an innocent young man. So the Tarleton woman will become a victim of the racism she herself set in motion.

The incident at the fruit stand and Maria's final encounter with old Nannie are two dramatic scenes Porter returns to throughout the sixty-three unnumbered large pages of the manuscript.[5] But of even greater import is another visual scene that is also mentioned on what appears to be the first page: every morning Maria Gay sends her girl of four (or five) called Gabrielle (or Gabri-

The Man in the Tree

ela) to school accompanied by Loute (or Lute), a black girl of thirteen. Porter describes the daily scene: "They flew out of the gate the instant it was opened like two escaping birds, Lute flapping her flat black bare feet, her little bur of a head thrust forward between her shoulders as she ran, Gabrielle, in her pink organdy sun bonnet and thin dress, streaming out at the end of Lute's long dry black arm like an afterthought." Porter then imagines the fright of Loute who literally bumps into Hasty's body hanging from a tree in the center of the square. And it was such a "pleasant green square with the live oaks and magnolias and Spanish moss and the cape jessamine bushes and the bandstand." On another page, where the title "The Man in the Tree" is used, Porter describes the scene after the lynching: "He hangs there, dark among the dark branches, a reproach and a witness, not only against his murderers, but to the shame of those who believed they were his friends."

Beside the "blood guilt" of the lynching, Maria is also worried about Gabrielle's and Loute's reactions to what they saw. And as if this were not enough, Marty, a young black girl, brings a postcard of Hasty hanging from the tree; he is in his work-day overalls. The souvenir photos are already being sold in the square at a quarter each. Maria feels the grief, she feels a responsibility for what has happened to "the culled branch of the fambly," as Hasty used to say, but she feels helpless. On another page she says to herself: "It is something I know well and remember with shame as if I had done it." Severely she tells Marty always to pay the exact amount.

Another fragment is called "Courtney and Maria." Porter describes Maria's state of mind. She longs for peace and hates having to manage people. This includes managing her husband Courtney (or Richey) who is county attorney, i.e. prosecuting attorney, which is important in one contemplated variation of the plot. When Courtney tries to talk to her, Maria is so troubled that she turns her husband away with "forbidding coldness." The general situation also makes it a trying time for their marriage. (Caroline, the presiding cook, knows it and warns her child that Maria will have a fit "if theys a blow struck or a voice raised in this house today.") Their financial situation is such that they should sell the farm, but Maria cannot imagine her life "without its foundation in this piece of land." The place is the family tradition, her great-grandfather had brought up eleven children and supported sixteen blacks on the land.

Maria, who is described as "the flower of southern womanhood from her head to her foot," tries to talk about the lynching to old Brigadier-General Angus Kirkendall, a representative of the old ways. The only result is a rebuke: a Southern lady should not even mention such a topic. To make it worse, the general is obviously getting sexually excited by talking about the lynching to *her*, "a pure and high bred lady." Maria gets no help from "the filthy old buzzard," which is her outraged opinion of Angus Kirkendall. On a page with a title she was to use years later, "The Never-Ending Wrong," Porter speculates on the nature of lynching:

Any one reading the newspaper stories about it would have said it was an entirely stupid and ordinary lynching like any other; the stupid kind of cruel thing that must happen now and again when men, needing to remind themselves of their power, wanting terribly the smell of blood and the sight of pain more intimate and understandable to them than the kind they can cause by torturing animals, seize a human being, – and it is necessary this creature should be helpless and in the wrong about something or it would be dangerous, – and murder him. It is not ordinary murder, but has religion and morality on its side, by some fearful perversion of fact, and a special tang to it for the killers.

Another scene is focused on Gabrielle, who is described as being "sleek and grey-eyed and peach colored." She is seen in her relationship with Loute, the black girl who looks after her.[6] (Porter introduces a page on everyday black-white relations as comic relief here. Loute has worms and is unable to stay on a bed at night; she rolls all over the house in her sleep. Maria worms her and the girl calls her "Miss Kathin Ann.") In her fear of white people, Loute becomes hysterical, which has its effect on Gabrielle. On what is probably the day after the lynching, Gabrielle does not want to be washed and combed for "convent school" (later, "kindergarten"), she throws a tantrum and Anna (also, Caroline) slaps her. Porter notes that Gabrielle will not admit that she has been slapped by a Negro and wonders whether this an example of racism bred in the bone? Maria decides to take the terrified Loute to the next parish so she can stay on their rice farm, a family asset that is not doing well. Maria realizes that Loute, with the image in her mind of Hasty in the tree, now believes that white people are capable of any cruelty against her.

The tension in the community is reflected in a scene where two black women (Lillie and Mamie) talk about keeping their sons (whom Porter describes as "pot bellies of chronic undernourishment") clear out of town to keep them safe. They make sure Maria overhears their conversation. The tension is also brought out in a verse sung by Skid (possibly Hasty's younger brother) who is mowing a lawn:

> You gointa git sumthin you don' expeck
> It aint no money and it aint no check
> And you're going home all wropped up in
> A wooden kimona trimmed with tin.

When Loute absolutely refuses to stay with strange white people on the farm, the Gays take her back home. Porter makes it a point to show that Gabrielle and Loute are delighted to see one another again. Maria later hears them talking about the lynching. In one version the children saw "a knot of men collected around a big tree. There was a ladder and a black wagon standing by, and a big man in a black hat and a pistol at his belt, and they were scrambling around up in the tree and on the ground, and they were terribly quiet, like people in a moving picture."

The Man in the Tree

In another scene, Loute has not actually seen Hasty's body, but the child has. Porter brilliantly dramatizes Maria's worries when Gabrielle shocks her mother by pointing out the hanging tree:

> "Look, Mama, there's where they had the man in the tree this morning!" "I suppose they're getting ready to cut off some of those big branches," she said. "No Mama," said Gabrielle, "there was a man climbing in the tree, but there was another man there too; he was tied on." She put her hands up to her neck. [The last sentence was added in ink.]

In one fragment Porter imagines Hasty on the run, a mob is gathering and she introduces us to a black woman who hides Hasty in a cowshed. The black woman comes fully and wonderfully alive in just two short paragraphs. In the most moving fragment of the manuscript, Hasty gives her the infamous orange, and she persuades him to wait while she makes coffee for him.

> In the middle of the night I warmed up the coffee and took a cup out to him. He drunk it up, and I brung another. But he said he had to get on, he didn't feel safe there, and I begged him to jes try and drink one mo' cup cawfy. I kep tellin him, go on, drink that cawfy. You gonn want it this time tomorrow and I'm gonna wish you had it ... You gonna be sorry you didn't drink it while you had the chance, I kep tellin him. So he said, "I'll try to drink it latah on." So I lef the pot there, and when I went back in the mawnin, he was gone and the cawfy still standin there jes like I lef it.
>
> I know now he ought nevah to a stopped a tall ... he jes lost time hidin out in that barn. He jes los the time he needed to git across the swamp where the dawgs couldn't take up the trail. I knows that now. I oughta tole him to run, instid of tryin to make him drink cawfy. I knows it now. [Porter's ellipses throughout]

On the same page "All the Evidence?" is suggested as a possible title for the story. The word "evidence" seems to have brought the law to Porter's mind for another fragment of the text features Sheriff Carleton in a conversation with Richey (or Courtney) Gay, the prosecuting attorney. The sheriff, whom Porter brings to life through language and attitude, tells Gay how he and his posse tracked down Hasty just in time:

> Me and my possy was just one lope ahead of that mob all the way. They never had a chance't. Say, that nigger was glad to see us. I says "Come on out, Hasty, it's the sheriff," I says, "if you know what's good for you." And he sure did crawl right outa the brush with his eyes big as saucers, and says, small like, "here I am, Mister Carlton." So we've got him all jailed up and he's sure one relieved looking nigger. He'd be a mess of skin and bones by now if that crowd had got him.

On this page it is implied that Hasty is guilty and the accusation is murder rather than attempted rape. And on a stray half page titled "airless jail," there is a description of how Hasty, upon being arrested, "stopped feeling sick at his stomach for the first time since he had killed the woman." The sheriff and the attorney decide to transfer Hasty to Waco so there will not be a lynching in their town. This is the first indication of location in these notes; on another page of the manuscript the setting is Louisiana. Porter seems to have given up on the transfer to Waco. Instead she describes how Hasty is pursued with dogs, captured in a deep gulch, and brought back to town.

> Here they hanged him to a fine branch of the live oak in the center of the public square, near the band stand, and they left him hanging, as an example, no doubt, until about eleven o'clock the next morning. They did not shoot at the body, or mutilate it, nor had they beaten him extraordinarily; they simply hanged him, and left him there, in a strangely cold blooded and methodical way: and dispersed ... it almost appeared that they had got no real enjoyment of it.

At another point Porter experimented with a description of bullet holes in the body and dried blood on Hasty's feet. She lined this out, probably because the type of cruelty suggested would only obscure the point of the story.

Maria, the main character, interestingly named Miranda on the particular page, reveals her furious anger in a conversation with her sister, also named Gabrielle (here, Gabriela). She refuses to be a passive witness to the lack of justice in the town: "I – I – I'm going to leave ... get as far away as I – I can ... I w-won't stay in this filthy country ... I won't s-stay here and – and – and be murdered too!" Maria considers how white people are enslaved by their relationship with blacks; she feels that she herself is a victim and an "unwilling propagator of a state of affairs she did not believe in." Maria remembers that her grandparents did not believe in slavery, but is pointedly reminded that they had slaves just the same (her last name here is Beauregard). And the idea of mutual victimization of the races seems to be Porter's main theme. She advises herself to write of "the emotional aftermath of such a crime, about the poisoned feeling that comes after excess." Maria is genuinely scared, not of the blacks, but of the whites "who go mad periodically with blood lust."

As her lynching story demonstrates, Porter had no illusions about the nature of man. Her misanthropy so powerfully expressed in *Ship of Fools* had been a life-time in the making, and should have surprised nobody. Although she was not a Catholic, except on paper during her first marriage, Porter believed as firmly as her friend Flannery O'Connor in the existence of evil. In a letter to Andrew Lytle of 15 September, 1947, summed up her experience:

> We have always a preponderance of evil because Man loves it, he cannot live without it. Times change, but human nature does not ... the scales crash inevitably on the side of evil, because that is the line of least resistance. Did you ever hear of the world falling into the state of good? If Evil is the true God, it is because Man prefers it so. He has only to choose. And he does choose. But he will not accept the responsibility of his choice ... – oh why can he not? This to me is the riddle of the universe – face the truth of his own motives ....

Four pages in the manuscript are called "newspaper comment." They serve as comic relief. The newspaper editor could have been created by Mark Twain. These pages show a side of Porter's genius that she did not often allow into her fiction, for this is humor in the tradition of antebellum southern humorists. The plot is brought forward by the information that Courtney and a small group of men cut Hasty's body down, give it burial, and protest to the sheriff. The latter is the most serious provocation and starts a hilarious and sad newspaper row. Porter obviously enjoyed writing these pages and reminded herself to add more letters to "the most fearless editor" in the South. She uses these pages to illustrate the division in the white community, where the Angus Kirkendalls are decidedly the majority.

It is in the light of the type of Southern male that Porter wrote about in the manuscript that we should read her reaction to a Faulkner comment on women and race, as reported by Malcolm Cowley: "If the race problems were just left to the children, they'd be solved soon enough. It's the grown-ups and *especially the women who keep the prejudice alive.*"[7] [Porter's emphasis]. Porter's marginal comment to the statement is dated and to the point: "Liar – the old Adam still putting it all off on us ... curse the filthy cowardice of men in this question KAP 9 Jan, 1967." She thought Faulkner showed a general resentment against women that amounted almost to vengefulness and suggested that he was "paying off a grudge of some sort."[8]

As "The Man in the Tree" continues, Maria, who worries, knows she must go and see old Nannie Bunton, who took to her bed after the lynching. Maria had offered her some food, a black dress, and ten dollars to pay for the funeral. The old woman refuses the offer but later is ready to accept the money and the clothes on condition that she make it up in work. Maria is shocked by Nannie's sudden display of hatred for all whites, she has only seen her as mammy and granny over the years. Maria's feelings are hurt when Nannie's reaction to her offer is reported to her, and she dreads the meeting; she knows she will be held responsible for all actions by whites.

Maria cannot face Nannie alone and wants to bring Hector, a Great Dane, on the visit to Nannie's cabin. Hector is a kindred spirit, not quite the dog he seems to be. The point is that Maria has always refused to discipline any beast or child, and as a result has permanent problems with her servants, her children, the horses, and Hector. But the accepted violence in the families around her is so dominating that it frightens her. This is especially true of the black families where the children are beaten "unmercifully at all hours." Maria wonders "why southern people, even the best of them, beat their children so much." Porter sees the parallels between the private and the public violence and makes the point that the common everyday accepted violence will finally "justify" even lynching as an act of necessary discipline. Maria, therefore, enjoys the company of the undisciplined and timid dog, especially on this trip. – With the five pages dealing with the dog and violence, Porter may have realized that with these themes she was really working on a longer story, maybe even a novel. Perhaps it was the main reason she never finished it as a short story.

Maria finally faces old Nannie, who is on the bed with a Whig Rose quilt covering her. If she could, Nannie would have refused to see even Maria, but she is trying to get Hasty buried. She is finished accepting money from white people for "they turn on you, they say you stole it." Porter remarks to herself: "try to explain the burden on the soul of any decent person in this situation." Trying to invoke the past, Maria says, "Why Nanny, my Uncle Bill and your Charlie were foster brothers, don't you remember?" But Nannie wants to die, and when she does speak, it is to "some invisible presence in the corner nearest the fireplace." The reference is most likely to Maria's grandmother, which brings us once again close to the old order stories. Nannie sums up her life's experience with these words: the "cullud branch of the fambly always git de worst of it."

Six pages are titled "after scene with the old woman." The boy called Skid has been fired from his job, because he is related to Hasty. Maria and Courtney try to persuade him not to run away and tell him he can sleep in the garage. Courtney complains: "So help me there simply isn't enough to go round, another mouth'll ruin us ... Oh, damn that whore!" And he adds, "all this for a quarter!" The Gays decide to keep Skid and plan to persuade Mr. Runge, his employer, to take him back. The wrong never seems to end, and Maria and Courtney are still paying for the sins of their ancestors. Courtney thinks to himself: "It had been going on for five generations, and what was he going to hand on to his son? [A baby called Stuffins.] The same hellish insufferable endless load to carry." At times Maria regrets that they did not choose New Orleans, where they could have lived in the Vieux Carré, and Courtney could have worked in "Uncle Gabriel's law office." They mourn with Nannie and ponder the existence of the "buzzardly poor white trash" who had lynched her harmless grandson. "They both lay there quietly, not talking or moving any more, but filled with a dark confused sense of grief too great even for the present event, as if it was something half remembered, brought over from another life, a bequeathed memory of wrong done." They are shocked into awareness of the present by Skid's blood-curdling screams from the garage where he is convulsed by a nightmare, or as Porter puts it, "in a death struggle with an invisible enemy." That night Nannie dies in her sleep.

In what looks like the end of the manuscript Loute is seen leading Gabrielle across the bridge once again, Skid is working in the garage, Courtney goes off to the rice farm, and everything seems to be back to normal. Maria is in the garden with her scissors cutting flowers for Nannie's funeral. The old woman had helped grow all the flowers in the garden and raise all the children in the household. What I take to be the planned end of the story reads: "Maria quietly and hopelessly wondered what bargain she could make with what Power to have Nannie and Bud [here probably Hasty] off her conscience." And Porter wrote the story to bear "witness, not only against his murderers, but to the shame of those who believed they were his friends."

For many reasons "The Man in the Tree" is not a publishable manuscript. The very title I use is my choice among the several possibilities Porter suggests to herself on these pages. If these notes were to be published as an old order or Miranda story by Porter, violence would have to be done to them. The problem is of the kind that faced the editor of the Hemingway manuscript that became *The Garden of Eden*. First of all the manuscript was not finished by the writer, i.e. we do not know what revisions would have brought in the way of perhaps drastic changes. Secondly, and perhaps even more seriously, Porter's pages are unnumbered, so the very structure cannot be determined. It would not be enough to list the events as before, during and after the lynching, for much of the story is seen through Maria's mind, and she does not see the lynching. In most versions she has to find out what happened from the children and the servants. And it is a further complication that Porter seems to have planned to start with Maria's going to old Nannie, which is also the final scene of the story.

If we are honest, there is no reason to try to edit and publish "The Man in the Tree." But its existence should not be forgotten, and scholars should be allowed to quote readily from the text so full of hideous images of racism, especially from the passages that dispel any accusation of racism against Katherine Anne Porter.

1. The manuscript is on deposit with the Special Collections Division, McKeldin Library, University of Maryland at College Park. The Katherine Anne Porter Collection, Series 2, Subseries 1, Box 9, marked: *The Southern Story*.

2. In February 1915, W.E.B. DuBois published an editorial in *The Crisis* which numbered at 2,732 the registered lynching in the USA from 1885-1914. During Porter's childhood years in Kyle from 1892 to 1901, the national total of lynchings was 1,157. See Phyllis R. Klotman, "'Tearing a Hole in History': Lynching as Theme and Motif," *Black American Literature Forum* 19 (Summer 1985) 55-63.

3. Joan Givner mentions this manuscript briefly in *Katherine Anne Porter: A Life* (New York, 1982) 288-89. Givner does not fully grasp Porter's experimentation with different names for the same character, so some of her information on this manuscript is misleading.

4. Cp. Porter's letter to Andrew Lytle of 15 September, 1947. Porter Collection. Quoted below.

5. Individual passages are numbered. The passage Porter thought of as "Newspaper Row" is numbered pages 1 to 4. Whereas the passage about Hector, a great Dane, has four pages marked "1," a fact that reflects Porter's work on this part of the manuscript.

6. The parallels between these characters and members of the Porter family and servants are obvious. See Katherine Anne Porter's letters in the Porter Collection to her older sister Gay Porter Holloway of 30 July, 1919 and 21 July, 1924. Loute was a black girl of fourteen of that name who took care of Katherine Anne Porter when the writer fell ill during a visit to her sister in Dubach, Louisiana.

    Gay visited Katherine Anne in Shreveport in 1916 and brought her three-year-old daughter, Mary Alice, who was named for her grandmother. The girl died early in 1919. The correspondence implies that she was the inspiration for the character of Gabrielle in this manuscript. See also Porter's letter to Glenway Wescott of 30 July 1956 in which she wrote: "imagine having the Negro Question bounce back into my life after I left my native land to get away from it!"

7. Malcolm Cowley, *The Faulkner-Cowley File: Letters and Memoirs, 1944-62*, New York, Viking Press, 1966, p. 111.

8. See Porter's holograph notes to Faulkner's "That Evening Sun" in the Porter Collection, The McKeldin Library.

CHAPTER SEVEN

In a Run-Away Buggy:
Ralph Ellison's Bi-Racial America

I had been a regular G.I. in the 42nd Armor, U.S. Army, 1962-65, and I felt rather strongly about civil rights for black Americans. After I began my studies back in Denmark, my first academic essay was eventually published. It was on Ralph Ellison's Invisible Man. *It appeared in* Six American Novels: From New Deal to New Frontiers, *eds. Jens Boegh and Steffen Skovmand, published by Aarhus University Press in 1972. When I went to Charlottesville to do graduate work at the University of Virginia, 1973-74, it was natural that I should take Houston A. Baker's class on the contemporary black novel. We were two students in the class, one black and one white, both male and about thirty, and Baker worked us hard. He introduced us to Ralph Ellison's short fiction. One of my papers for the course was the origin of my "Protest and Affirmation in "And Hickman Arrives","which Claude Richard published at Montpellier in his successful periodical called* Delta, *in 1984. Chapter seven is a revised version of the* Delta *essay.*

In a Run-Away Buggy

In the interview with Richard Stern that opens the collection *Shadow and Act* Ralph Ellison points out that already at a very early age he wanted to be "more fully a part of that larger world which surrounded the Negro world" into which he was born.[1] In spite of the negative connotations of the heritage of all African Americans, Ellison's values were neither "white" nor "black" – what he considered truly valuable was an integral part of the mosaic that makes up the American experience. In 1963 he wrote, in "The World and the Jug," "While I am without doubt a Negro and a writer, I am also an *American* writer."[2] He thought it significant that the "American Negro" fights for a fuller participation in the society he shares with whites, and this may also be the message in the famed epilogue of *Invisible Man*. The year after the publication of his successful novel, Ellison said that he was unable to reject America: "It is a big wonderful country, and you can't just turn away from it because some people decide it isn't your country."[3]

He even found it necessary to rebel against the protest-centered fiction so he could choose his subjects without thinking of the identity imposed upon him by the general idea of what you would expect from a black American novelist. He did not want to be reduced to being a pamphleteer on race relations. He made sure that his character Ras, who wants an all-out race struggle, is spectacularly ineffective in the novel. The violence started by the black leader causes more deaths and misery among blacks than among the white enemy. The total focus on race proves to be disastrous. Ellison resisted the temptation to interpret black American experience solely in terms of race. Ellison transcended race, as Jean Toomer had done in *Cane* (1923), and used a full scale of values to communicate the peculiarly human in one black man's identity crisis.[4] He told us that the problem of black Americans has more to do with a historical invisibility than with civil rights. And he advised his fellow Americans never to lose sight of the American chaos against which they must create their identity.

Although American democracy is described as a comic nightmare in *Invisible Man* and, in spite of all the narrator's grievances, the novel finally seems to disregard the harshness of everyday living in order to affirm a continued belief in the *principles* of American democracy. The epilogue of the novel complements the prologue, but offers little new. After the surrealistic passion of the Harlem riot, Ellison finishes the invisible man's memoir on a moral and positive note. The narrator suddenly believes that his grandfather's "yes," with which white

Americans are to be overcome, must be a yes affirming the principles the country is built on. Is the belief in the principles of American democracy really what the novel amounts to? Ellison certainly thought so. He wanted to write of the African American struggle and saw it as a part of a universal quest for self-knowledge. And in this sense he spoke for everybody, at least "on the lower frequencies."

On one low frequency Ellison even spoke for the South and about the values that had been left behind during the great migration. In *Invisible Man* the characters Mary Rambo and Peter Wheatstraw come to personify the black American heritage. They remind the invisible man of all he left behind in the South: the folklore, the stable family, and the still authoritative religion. In the chaotic world of the North folk wisdom was discarded, the black family disintegrated, and the church lost much of its influence. The regret for the loss of original values is obvious in Ellison's fiction from the beginning. In "King of the Bingo Game" from 1944, Ellison was certainly writing dramatic protest fiction, and the protagonist is almost an archetype. He is a victim of social injustice and the author's indignation is obvious: for a whole group of Americans life is like a bingo game and their lives, or death by starvation, are decided by pure chance. And it is a white man who runs the game. As it turns out, the main character realizes that his only chance of survival is to keep the bingo wheel moving. For once that wheel of fortune stops it will become a fact that he has lost. He knows this because he has been running right in front of a destructive racial train, with spinning wheels, ever since his early childhood. What is foreshadowing Ellison's later thoughts is that even in the heavy-handed early protesting there is a measure of affirmation in the values that make up the "king's" identity.

One way of escaping the eternally "pursuing train" of racial prejudice is to affirm the uniquely black heritage and values of African Americans. Ellison did not think black writers had done enough in this respect. He said, "This is not to denigrate what we have done, but in all *candor* we haven't begun to do what we can do or what we should have done."[5] Ellison also tried to explain what it was he tried to capture in his fiction: "There is a body of folklore, a certain sense of American history. There is our psychology and the peculiar circumstances under which we have lived. There is our cuisine, though we don't admit it, and our forms of expression."[6] The black aesthetic values that Ellison wanted to affirm are definitely present already in the story from 1944. When the bingo king has a nightmare, two others in the black audience bring him out of it and offer him a drink of whisky. To him his helpers remind him of the kind people from his home who have been on his starving mind: ""If this was down South," he thought, "all I'd have to do is lean over and say, "Lady, gimme a few of those peanuts, please ma'am," and she'd pass me the bag and never think nothing of it." Or he could ask the fellows for a drink in the same way. "Folk down South stuck together that way; they didn't even have to know you."[7] The unnamed king of the bingo game demonstrates the values of optimism, cunning, natural sexuality, love for his family, and a fighting spirit. He is indeed "one of the chosen people," and it is ironic that it is the white man with the microphone who tells us this about him. The black man's ordeal on stage takes place against a background of a singing and handclapping audience. They sing:

> Shoot the liquor to him, Jim, boy!
> Clap-clap-clap
> Well a-calla the cop
> He's blowing his top!
> Shoot the liquor to him, Jim, boy!

The value is in the rhythm, the poetry, and the humor. These are black values, Ellison indicates, that must not be sacrificed as the price of integration. The protesting is an affirmation of a belief in the values that make up identity. The lesson of the story is harsh. The king cannot win. At the end of the story he has not gotten any money, and his Laura will have to do without medicine. All he can do is stall for time by keeping control of the wheel of fortune. But as he controls the wheel, it controls him by keeping him in the same spot. When uniformed men move in on him, the long black cord of the bingo wheel is his only potential weapon. The cord *can* be used as a weapon. Just as cultural nationalism and separatism *are* possible. But if he pulls too much at the long black "umbilical" cord, the American bingo wheel will stop, and everything that has been gained will be lost. It is significant that he does bingo in the end. When the wheel finally stops it rests at double-zero, or twice nothing, and that is exactly what he gets.

In both the early story and his famed novel Ellison excelled in pointing out problems. His fiction heralded the explosion of black protest and prophesied the integration battles of the late 50s and the 60s. It could be asked: what are the alternatives Ellison would accept? The search for an identity and the acceptance of one's identity are obviously necessary. But how is the black American, even with an identity visible to himself, to go about forcing white America to accept him for what he is? Is there an alternative to violence? It is obvious that such questions preoccupied Ellison for the rest of his life, and some of the possible solutions are suggested in stories that were potential chapters toward a new novel.

"And Hickman Arrives" was the first fragment of his long projected novel that Ellison published. This was in 1960. Seven other stories that seem to be potential fragments have been published and many years have passed since then, but the long awaited second novel has not appeared. "And Hickman Arrives" remains the longest and the most interesting fragment, especially if we try to divine the nature of Ellison's planned novel. A close reading of the first fragment indicates that the topics are protest and affirmation, but not necessarily the protest or the affirmation that we have come to expect in African American fiction.

"And Hickman Arrives" is set in Washington D.C. and somewhere in the Deep South.[8] The time is three years before "the shooting"; only later do we learn that this refers to the assassination of Senator Sunraider (pp. 16-17), who is senator of a New England state (p. 12). The events in the Deep South are described as a flashback experienced by the senator (pp. 19-43), and the story ends with Rev. Hickman's confession (pp. 43-49). – The fragment begins with the arrival of forty-four elderly blacks in Washington, D. C. They are Southern men and women. Ellison dresses them as if they were on an outing: the women wear little white caps, they are deaconesesses, and carry palm-leaf fans. The air-conditioners of Washington are placed in an explicit opposition to the old-time palm-leaf fans. The fans serenely defy the droning air-conditioners (p. 6). The women also carry picnic baskets, which contain fried chickens and sweet-potato pies, elements of a cuisine which is innately African American.[9] The men are dressed in army-like uniformity and wear old-fashioned black suits and Panama hats. They look like Yoknapatawpha County in its Sunday dress.

Reverend Alonzo Zuber Hickman, affectionately nicknamed Daddy Hickman, is singled out for an individual portrait: he is tall, broad as "a carriage in a state ceremonial parade" and distinguished looking. He is known as "God's Trombone," which echoes the title of James Weldon Johnson's collection of gospel lyrics. A. Z. Hickman attains heroic stature in Ellison's portrait of him. His name indicates that from A to Z he is the American man. And his last name obviously stems from the grass roots of America. Ellison has to build him up as a truly religious American leader to give the story its full impact and validity. Hickman's sincerity must be beyond doubt.[10] Rev. Hickman is firmly in control of the group at all times. This is not difficult as his congregation has a strong sense of group identity, and it is more than just externally motivated.[11] Their motivation is their religion, language, social background, regional roots, music, race, cuisine, folklore, behavior patterns, and their common aim in coming to Washington.[12]

We are quickly informed of Senator Sunraider's extreme racism. Significantly, his ante-room is equipped with a bust of pre-civil-war Vice President Calhoun and a live secretary from Mississippi. We are informed that the only "colored" the Senator knows is "the boy who shines shoes at his golf club" (p. 7). Sunraider is considered the most vehement enemy of black people in either house of Congress (p. 8). In "It Always Breaks Out," another novel fragment, Senator Sunraider has the floor of the Senate when he proclaims that so many black citizens drive Cadillacs that the trade mark should be changed to the *Coon Cage Eight*.[13] In rebuttal a black man burns his expensive Cadillac on the senator's lawn. The authorities cannot accept this as a justifiable and courageous rebuttal, for a black man who burns his own Cadillac must be "crazy." So the former Cadillac-owner is held in the observation cell of a hospital.[14]

In view of the senator's behavior in the Senate, the events in his ante-room are not surprising. The secretary thinks she knows all the "tried-and-true techniques" for quickly getting rid of blacks. She is astounded when her techniques fail, and even more so when the blacks treat her as if she were invisible. She finally calls the guards, and forty-four elderly blacks are evicted from Senator Sunraider's admission room. The reader's admiration for the group is enhanced by their stoic calm in facing the guards. For no apparent reason, they are searched by the guards. In the face of this humiliation, their "obviously religious" patience is even more impressive.

Their behavior during the incident reads as a complete rejection of militancy. The composure, tolerance, understanding, and serene dignity of the group triumph over the violence of the senator's guards. It is not that the group lacks the strong, almost violent emotional life that Ishmael Reed sees as the major difference between whites and blacks, e.g. in *Mumbo Jumbo*. Sunraider's Senate speech provokes a significant emotional reaction[15]: "It was then that a tall, elderly woman wearing steel-rimmed glasses arose from her chair and stood shaking with emotion, her eyes flashing. Twice she opened her mouth as though to hurl down some retort upon the head of the man holding forth below, but now the old preacher glimpsed her out of the corner of his eye, and, without turning from the scene below, gravely shook his head" (p. 11). The non-Reed element Ellison demonstrates here is that at times control of emotions is a better weapon than letting yourself go. The incident in the Senate confirms our impression of the blacks as a well-organized group with a strong leader.

Their foremost weapons in trying to achieve their objective in Washington are their persistence and optimism in the face of adversity, their vivacity in spite of their age[16] and their trickster knowledge. This knowledge is especially interesting. How do they know where the senator has his secret suite ? How do they know that Sunraider is in danger? How does Hickman know the name of Sunraider's assassin? (p. 17). It is implied that a certain Janey, who wrote a letter to Hickman, knows that the senator is in danger.[17] But that is the closest we get to an explanation in this fragment. We do learn, however, why the blacks not only care about but also feel responsible for the senator's fate.

It is perhaps significant that the liberal press in Washington gives Hickman even less of a hearing than anybody else. Ellison's quick rejection of Northern liberals recalls the rejection of Messrs. Norton and Emerson, Jr. in *Invisible Man*. Later in this fragment, however, Ralph Waldo Emerson is praised by Hickman as a man who" knew that every tub has to sit on its own bottom" (p. 24). The belief in non-violence and belief in an innate moral sense even in whites indicate that Ellison reevaluated the New England Transcendentalists and accepted many of their ideas. Only a publication of the entire manuscript can show how far he was willing to go in his reevaluation.

Hickman's congregation prays within the Lincoln Memorial from late afternoon to early morning. From the Memorial they go peacefully to the visitor's gallery of the Senate. This course of action is a very strong affirmation of

Ellison's ultimate belief in American principles, past and present. After all, the group had just been rejected by white America in the form of a Southern secretary and the liberal press of the North. Not even the Senate experience reads as a total rejection of white America. When Sunraider makes his mocking comments about black Americans "a few whites departed, some angrily shaking their heads over the Senator's remarks" (p. 12).

Even the rejection of Sunraider is not total. His speech reads, in Hickman's interpretation, as a typical Fulbright speech. "He has to play the game so he can stay and play the game...." (pp. 14-15). If the senator can give foreign aid to Africa and Asia, the people there will stop criticizing the United States particularly for its racial politics. But it is no easy matter to sort out what is good and what is bad in Sunraider. "What I mean is, he's complicated," says Hickman.

As we learn that Senator Sunraider imitates Rev. Hickman's oratorical technique in detail, the most exciting idea of the plot is revealed, i.e., the close identification of Hickman with Sunraider. We learn that in the past the senator was called Bliss, and used to be the child apprentice to Hickman, when the preacher was a traveling tent-revivalist in the South.[18] At the time of the events in the South, the senator was six years old (p. 25). Hickman has every reason to worry about the future senator's fate; he is partially responsible for what the senator is and therefore partially responsible for the assassination. Hickman is the "sun" Bliss raided. But first Bliss had been exploited for several years in the minister's revivals. If we can understand Hickman's reaction to Bliss' death, we will probably understand the story better: "Bliss!," he cries, "you were our last hope, Bliss; now Lord have mercy on this dying land !"(p. 18).

The past relationship between Hickman and Bliss was almost a father-son relationship. Bliss is white-looking, but significantly his race is uncertain. Bliss grew up with and was trained as a revivalist by Hickman. The emphasis in that training was on the boy's linguistic development:

> I say do you see, Bliss?
> Yessuh.
> Say Sir !
> Sir.
> Good. Don't talk like I talk; talk like I say talk. Words are your business, boy. Not just the Word. Words are everything. The key to the Rock, the answer to the Question.
> Yes, sir. (p. 23)

At the conclusion of the story, Hickman is still teaching his Bliss/Sunraider: "I mean "box"; it ain't actually a coffin till it holds a dead man" (p. 43). Hickman's talk of "Good Book English" is ironic, as Sunraider's success as a politician is due partly to his rhetorical skill. Ellison clearly implies that without the contribution of black Americans there would be no American dialect of English.

Daddy Hickman, known as black Garrick, is the supreme campaigner and the great performer of the Lord's service. He teaches Bliss the rhetorical importance of the personal approach. He teaches the boy to exploit religion: "You got to look like you feel it, Bliss" (p. 24). Hickman does not tell him that he *should* feel it. If Hickman does have heroic stature in the story, he is certainly not impeccable. With the assistance of some ice-cream, he tries to convince Bliss that he should not be afraid of the dark in a "box." The boy lies in the dark in a white suit with his white Bible. He breathes through a tube, until he – night after night – must appear slowly from the coffin, which is placed in the middle of the revival meetings, to cry: "Lord, Lord, why hast thou forsaken me?" In the description of the boy in the coffin, Bliss's identification with Hickman is stressed. The boy even believes that he would not be able to emerge from the coffin, if Hickman should breathe while preaching: "If he stops to breathe I'll die. My breath will stop too. Just like Adam's if God had coughed or sneezed" (p. 29).

Ralph Ellison says that Hickman is "unsure whether he was simply exploiting the circus side-show shock set off by the sight of a child rising out of a coffin, or had hit upon an inspired way of presenting the sacred drama of the Resurrection."[19] That he is uncomfortable with what he makes his young apprentice do, is obvious in his conversation with the boy. Ellison uses considerable space to show how the boy's psyche is warped as the revival is repeated in every church in the circuit: "In the dark, trembling in the dark. Lying in the dark" the boy learns to hate the hypnotic music and the rhythmic hand-clapping of the revivals. The boy's *Angst* is offered as an explanation for the mature Sunraider's racism.[20] It is, however, equally important to note the contents of a typical Hickman sermon. He preaches that "man was born to suffer and to die for other men!" Here we find Ellison's message of Christian love through integration, and integration through Christian love: "Oh, we must dare, my little children.... We must dare in our own troubled times to be our father's own" (p. 37).

The later Senator Sunraider loses his Christian "ballast" on the night his biological mother struggles with the revivalists. When Bliss feels the redheaded woman's arms lock around him, the Bible slips from his fingers and falls "irretrievably away" (p. 39). The role of Bliss's mother is crucial. She claims that the "gypsy niggers" have robbed her Cudworth of his birthright. From being Bliss, the boy is now reduced to the value of a cud, a cud for her pride. The big freckled woman tries to regain her child in order to take" him home to his heritage," which clearly means his European heritage.

It is in the surrealistic scene that Ellison makes his main point: Sunraider/Bliss/Cudworth will never be able to escape the mixed heritage implied by the multiplicity of his names. The heritage will be "with him night and day" throughout his career and even in his death. We should also note that the blacks refuse to give up the Bliss they have helped create. They react as if someone is trying to rob them of their religion, and "nothing makes our people madder and will bring them to make a killing-floor stand quicker than to have white folks come bringing their craziness into the church" (p. 44). The congregation does not welcome white people in its church, and it certainly does not plan to give up the little white-looking boy who has become a part of their divine service. Ignoring the probable white reprisals the provoked members of the black congregation fight to keep the boy: "Their faces, wet with wrath, loomed before him [Bliss] ... their dark, widespread hands beginning to tear at his body ... ; lifting him screaming clear of earth and coffin and suspending him there between the redheaded woman who now held his head and the others who had seized possession of his legs, arms, and body" (pp. 42-43). This is vintage Ellison in his often repeated role of cultural assimilationist. The fight between the redheaded woman and Sister Susie Trumball, and later six-foot Sister Bearmasher, symbolizes the futile struggle between white and black about a heritage which, if it is to survive at all, can only belong to both. In the present situation the redheaded woman controls the head and the black women the body, as a result the boy has lost contact with a normal life, as represented by earth and coffin. It is a serious issue depicted with much humor in Rev. Hickman's voice: "Talking about King Solomon, he didn't have but *two* women to deal with, I had seven. And one convinced that she's a different breed of cat from the rest. Yes, and the others chock-full of disagreement and out to prove it. I tell you, Bliss, when it comes to chillen, women just ain't gentlemen" (p. 44).

The main theme of "And Hickman Arrives" is the demonstrated futility of racism and segregation. But it would be a mistake to overlook the element of black protest in the story. Ellison was just as active in his protest as Richard Wright. This story proves the point. Ellison cannot in any meaningful sense be blamed for not having protested enough. It is great fiction writing, and it is harsh protest. And there is no dichotomy between them.[21]–The story is a protest against African-Americans being pushed aside as a quaint group that could have nothing of value to contribute to the common good. People like Senator Sunraider must understand that blacks "have arrived, because soon it might be too late" (p. 7). In this way Ellison claimed an American heritage for his black community already in 1960, which was before the riots and the political assassinations of the late sixties.[22] America must behold its invisible people or the old eagle will rock dangerously, as Ellison already stated in *Invisible Man*.[23]

The African-Americans in the story are old-fashioned, distinguished men and women from the South. It is important to note what they are *not*. They are not Muslims or Panthers from the big cities. They speak their own Southern vernacular and say things like: "These here folks don't understand nothing." They live by the Christian doctrines of love and have a religion that makes it possible to address God personally. To qualify for their "kiss" you must be a "churchmember."[24]

There are several instances of indignant protest in the story. Daddy Hickman is proud that they can line Bliss' coffin with silk instead of cotton, which to the Southern blacks is "something most folks have to work all their lives and wear every day.... Something that most of our folks never get away from" (p. 22). Hickman preaches that they must "stand up to their oppressors." He has not forgotten what his mother told him about run-away slaves and water cures. But Hickman believes man can move beyond mere pain with Jesus, who shines "like a prism glass with all the shapes and colors of man" (p. 35).

Toward the end of the story the protest becomes even more obvious. Hickman is only too aware "that one miserable [white] woman could bring the whole state down on us" (p. 43). So he does not "want to touch that woman." The black minister has plenty of reasons to be worried. He is, after all, responsible for Bliss' career as a revivalist. Hickman cannot explain his part in this "with that woman there to tell the sheriff something different – with her just *being* with us more important than the truth" (p. 47). But the other members of his congregation also have reason to worry. Whites often come out to laugh at the black revival meetings. The fear of the black people expresses itself in a rage against their situation, and it climaxes in a scream at the redheaded woman: "Who's the black man you picked to die?" Ellison implies that if Bliss is indeed the son of the redheaded woman, she may well be in a position to accuse a black man of rape. In other words, if a black man claimed he had shaped his part of the American future, he would not be praised, but punished.

The ending of "And Hickman Arrives" is a picture of black and white America fighting over their child in a run-away buggy. Only Rev. Hickman's Christian advice can prevent the buggy from crashing instantly. The black buggy, which is pulled by "snow-white horses," represents more than 300 years of American history. blacks and whites are, whether they like it or not, trapped in the run-away buggy together, and they cannot jump off. For the moment they seem safe in their buggy. It is obvious that neither the child nor the buggy would have existed without the contribution of both races. And now, in 1960, Ellison writes, the American buggy is rushing straight toward a burning barn: "It was too far to see if anyone was there to know about it, and it was too big for anybody except us not to see it; and as we raced on there seemed no possible way to miss it burning across the night" (p. 48). The burning barn symbolizes the destruction by fire of America, as predicted in the Bible and broadcast by James Baldwin.[25] The whole world except America can see the country heading for destruction. Yet Daddy Hickman manages to wheel around the burning barn by three Christian acts. First he prays for the wild redheaded woman. Then, almost in the fashion of S.T. Coleridge's ancient mariner, he asks the Lord to bless "the man" who owns the burning barn. And finally, Hickman accepts his part of the blame for the buggy's course and direction. He admits that he has forgotten to pray for Bliss, the American child, who is "the promise of our fulfilment, the guarantee of our mortal continuance" (p. 31).

Ellison never fails to see black religious values in a positive light. As a source of black culture, religion is only rivaled by folklore. In the story, however, he asks a very legitimate question: just how positive a value is a religion which prays for its own people only? Christianity is by definition pro-integration: "Why shouldn't they break the bread and sip the wine together?"[26] Ellison's buggy contains the past, present, and future of America. It is a result not only of "money-greed and show-off pride," but also of "sweat and dedication." Ellison offers it as one explanation why the future wandered off its course and became a racist and a raider of black values that the sweat and dedication were not accompanied by the prayer of the black community for the common American off-spring: "I left you out, Bliss, and I guess right then and there you started to wander."

[1] Ralph Ellison, *Shadow and Act*, London, Secker and Warburg, 1967, p. 3.

[2] Ralph Ellison, *Shadow and Act*, p. 125.

[3] Ralph Ellison, "Sidelights on Invisibility: An Interview," *Saturday Review*, 35 (March 14, 1953) 49.

[4] Cp. Ralph Ellison's idea of the novel in an *American Scholar* forum: "What's Wrong with the American Novel," *American Scholar* 24 (Autumn 1955) 476.

[5] J. A. McPherson, "Indivisible Man: An Interview with Ralph Ellison," *Ralph Ellison: A Collection of Critical Essays*, ed. John Hersey, Englewood Cliffs, N. J., Prentice Hall, 1974, p. 54,

[6] Ralph Ellison, "A Novelist Who Sometimes Teaches," *New York Times Magazine* (Nov. 20, 1966) p. 179.

[7] Ralph Ellison, "King of the Bingo Game," *Dark Symphony: Negro Literature in America*, eds. J. A. Emanuel & Th. L. Gross. New York, The Free Press, 1968, p. 272.

[8] All page references are to "And Hickman Arrives," *The Noble Savage* (New York, 1960) pp.4-49. Other fragments of Ellison's planned novel are: "The Roof, the Steeple and the People," *Quarterly Review of Literature*, 10/3 (Sept. 1960) 115-28. "It Always Breaks out," *Partisan Review*, 30/1 (Spring 1963) 13-28." Juneteenth," *Quarterly Review of Literature*, 13/3-4 (1965) 262-76. "Night-Talk," *Quarterly Review of Literature*, 16/4 (1969) 317-29. "A Song of Innocence," *Iowa Review*, 1 (Spring 1970) 30-40. "Cadillac Flambé," *American Review*, 16 (Feb. 1973) 249-69. "Backwacking: A Plea to the Senator," *Massachusetts Review*, 18 (Autumn 1977) 411-16.

[9] Cf. "A Novelist Who Sometimes Teaches," *New York Times Magazine* (Nov. 20, 1966).

10. See Also John Hersey, "A Completion of Personality: A Talk with Ralph Ellison," *Ralph Ellison: 20th Century Views*, ed. John Hersey (Englewood Cliffs, N. J. 1974) p. 11. Ellison mentions "the old man searching throughout the years for a little boy who ran away."

11. Ellison would disagree with Donald B. Gibson's statement: "Negroes, ... , only feel a defensive externally motivated sense of group identity." "The Negro: An Essay on Definition" (1968), *A Galaxy of Black Writing* (Durham, N. C., 1970), p. 92.

12. Ralph Waldo Ellison: "Folks down South stuck together that way," in "King of the Bingo Game," *Dark Symphony* (New York, 1968), p. 271.

13. *Partisan Review*, 30/1 (Spring, 1963) 13-28.

14. There is additional information about the planned novel in John Hersey's interview with Ralph Ellison: "A Completion of Personality." See note 10, above.

15. A rich emotional life is displayed by the full participation in the service in the revival tent. The crowd "boiling in the heat of the Word" is particularized in a holy jumper, Brother Pegue (p. 38).

16. "the old ladies giving their skirts a whirl as they turned in their flat-heeled shoes." (p. 8).

17. A Miss Janey is mentioned in "A Coupla Scalped Indians," as the guardian of one of the boys. *Black Literature in America*, ed. Houston A. Baker, Jr. (Charlottesville, Va., University of Virginia Press, 1971) p. 324.

18. The name has echoes of Bliss Proteus Rinehart of *Invisible Man*, who preached as "a lil-ole twelve-year-old boy, back in Virginia" (Penguin edition, p. 399).

19. "A Completion of Personality," *20th Century Views*, p. 6.

20. Bliss comes to identify the darkness with Deacon Wilhite, who is Rev. Hickman's assistant.

21. Cf. Ralph Ellison, *Shadow and Act* (New York, Signet, 1964), p. 170.

22. Ralph Ellison's second novel was to have been set around 1955, "A Completion of Personality," *20th Century Views*, p. 6.

23. *Invisible Man*, p. 464.

24. Cf. Aunt Mackie's question in "A Coupla Scalped Indians," p. 329.

25. Cf. James Baldwin's, *The Fire Next Time*.

26. Ralph Ellison, "No Apologies," in "Letters July 1967," *Harper's Magazine*, p 18.

CHAPTER EIGHT

"A Good Man with a Good Voice": A Visit with Martin Luther King, Sr.

On Auburn Street in Atlanta, "Sweet Auburn" as the local people call it, there is one of the big tourist attractions in the American South: The Ebenezer Baptist Church. The church became known world-wide as Martin Luther King, Jr.'s point of departure. Today a memorial for the civil-rights martyr is located next to the church, complete with a pool, shaped like "The Reflecting Pool" in Washington, where Dr. King, Jr. gave his most influential speech, "I have a dream," on August 28, 1963. Now an eternal flame burns on Auburn Street to remind us of the murder on April 4, 1968, of the most beloved black leader of our time.

But Dr. King, Jr. is not only remembered through symbols. Down the street is the headquarters for the powerful civil rights organization, "The Southern Christian Leadership Conference," which became synonymous with his name. Across the street from the church there is "The Martin Luther King Center," which has meant much for Atlanta's black youth. The center is being led by Coretta Scott King, the widow of Dr. King, Jr.

The King family have been ministers in Georgia at least since Dr. King, Jr.'s great grandfather. And a grandfather became the first leader of Georgia's branch of the NAACP. – It is, however, Dr. Martin Luther King, Sr., the father of the city's famous son, who more than anybody has decided developments on Auburn Street. He pastored Ebenezer when the SCLC was founded there in 1957 to support non-violent social change. "Daddy King," as his friends call him, has become a legend in his own time. Although he now only preaches on special occasions, it is difficult to imagine an Ebenezer Baptist Church without him. He is 79 [1978], not tall, but powerfully and solidly built, and he has a voice that can awaken even the hard-of-hearing. He has always been actively involved with the struggle for civil rights. It is partly his achievement that black teachers receive equal pay in Georgia.

Dr. King, Sr. is obviously a determined and effective leader, and he is also an open and friendly man. It is not apparent that his recent years have been full of personal tragedies. Besides the famous son, and co-minister at Ebenezer, who was shot in Memphis, the old preacher lost another son in tragic circumstances. And it must have seemed totally absurd to him when his wife was shot in Ebenezer by a mad-man, who may have been aiming at Dr. King, Sr., himself. The June 11, 1977, escape from Brushy Mt. Prison, Tennessee, of James Earl Ray, the man convicted of the murder of Martin Luther King, Jr., his recapture, and repeated professions of innocence; the racially divided reception of the NBC film on King, Jr. in the fall of 1977; and the mixed reactions to the issue of a stamp honoring his son on January 15, 1978 are just some of the events that are constantly on King, Sr.'s mind at the time of the interview below.

Today he is the only one left in a position of power on Auburn Street. He is influential among America's black voters. Thousands take his advice when it is election time. For years he has been the friend of Jimmy Carter. By actively campaigning for him Daddy King helped the former governor of Georgia to many black votes during his campaign to become president. In August 1976, when Carter was nominated, King led the Democratic Convention in New York City's Madison Square Garden in the final singing of "We Shall Overcome." And he conducted a special service to mark Carter's inauguration on January 20, 1977. The old parson in the Ebenezer Church is one of the few men in the U.S.A. who can always reach the President.

After I had tried for a long time by phone and letter to get to talk to Dr. King, Sr. and all my efforts had been ignored, I mentioned my problem to a friend in Atlanta, Jack Etheridge, a white judge and professor of law. "Oh," he said, "would you like to have his private number? – Or, maybe I'd better call Daddy King to introduce you." His phone call worked like magic, and I was invited "to come to the Ebenezer Baptist Church to see Dr. King." The time of my visit with Dr. King, Sr. was right after President Kaunda of Zambia had received the Martin Luther King Peace Prize on May 23, 1978. The campaign to make Dr. King Jr.'s birthday a national holiday had begun and so had the efforts to reopen the investigation of the assassination. But Dr. King, Sr. wanted to talk of other things, subjects uppermost in his mind.

Interview with Martin Luther King, Sr.,
in his office in the Ebenezer Baptist Church, Atlanta, June, 1978.

A Good Man with a Good Voice

[The interview has been published in Danish only. It appeared in the national paper *Jyllands-Posten*, December 24, 1978.]

Gretlund: In the South the rivalry among the Protestant denominations is keen. Doesn't the competition among Methodists, Presbyterians, and Baptists do more damage than good for the Christian faith?

King: I have now found the man who is going to take over, after me, as minister of my congregation. I have been looking for a good human being with a good voice, a man who will be respected by the congregation. And the new minister for the Ebenezer Baptists has been raised and educated as a Presbyterian. As you see, we know very well that various affixed names are inessential. It is the human being and his Christian temper that count.

Gretlund: Your son became famous as a Southern minister and as a civil rights activist. Are you now satisfied with the progress after the segregation days? Or was your son's sacrifice in vain?

King: During the 60s many white people joined our church. But today we only have two white families who attend regularly. The others were also good people, but were forced to leave the congregation by pressure from their "friends," neighbors, and employers. But still, the racial situation here in Georgia has improved much since the 50s. I don't think my son and his friends have worked in vain. The good results of their work are everywhere about us. Black wages have gone up, the housing situation has improved, and our children get a better education. – But there is still a lot to be done.

Gretlund: Are there still members of your congregation who "go North" in search of the land awash with milk and honey?

King: No. – The great exodus to the North began in 1917, and continued all the way into the 60s. But today our sisters and brothers are coming home. Why should they prefer the North? Wages were the original reason why they went North. But now the pay in Atlanta is about the same as the pay up North. So now they are coming home by the thousands. There are many in the North who now see the South as the land of golden opportunities. And it is true, of course, that the South has everything. The oil wells are here, in Texas and in Oklahoma. Atlanta, New Orleans, and Houston are the future, and the American Negro wants his share of that future. That is why they are returning from the big cities in the North. All Chicago, Detroit, and Boston can offer today are economic problems and racism.

Gretlund: Do you feel that white people still divide black Americans into "good" *or* "bad" blacks?

King: It seems to me that the image of the black American in literature, and also in magazines and newspapers, is positive on the whole. I don't read everything, of course; it is difficult to keep up at my age. Both white and black publishers send me a great many novels, which I don't have time to read at all. But I read my son's books on non-violence, again and again. And I also keep up with the many new actors and writers who work for TV, like Alex Haley. But I do not have time to keep up with all the new literature.

What the white part of the population really thinks of their black neighbors? It is not for me to say. TV transmissions from our civil-rights demonstrations created the popular opinion that finally gave us the civil-rights legislation. I am convinced that today most white people have a positive opinion of integration. – But not all – far from all.

Gretlund: It seems to me that most black people exclude all whites from their everyday lives.

King: It is the task of the Church to teach everybody about neighborly love. I have just told you how difficult it is for a white person to remain in our congregation. The Church has failed, also the black Church. The racially most segregated hours in Atlanta are still Sunday mornings. You can invite people to come to church, but even if they do come, you can't force them to seat themselves next to each other. – You can lead a mule to water, but you can't make it drink. We cannot force people to like each other through legislation. But it is the job of the Church to show the congregation that it lacks in basic neighborly love.

Gretlund: In many big cities black citizens live in separate sections of the city. Are you living in an integrated part of Atlanta?

King: Yes. – At this time there is housing enough in Atlanta, and only little discrimination even in the best housing sections. If we hear about an area that is not integrated, we will help the NAACP integrate it. – But right now we do not receive many complaints.

I still remember my first protest actions in this town. One of the first was to integrate one of the lifts in the courthouse. It was Fulton Court House, which had three lifts for "Folks" and one for trash and black people. The sign said: "Garbage & Colored." But we have changed all that.

As a black American you can today travel from Atlanta to New York, Chicago, or Los Angeles and be treated like everybody else. But on the way you pass a lot of small societies, where absolutely nothing has changed in the relations between the races since the War [i.e. the Civil War]. Racial prejudice is today first and foremost a problem in local areas in the country. So the the next goal of the civil-rights movement is to integrate all those rural societies. In spite of court orders and legislation almost nothing has changed in the country.

Gretlund: Is there a tendency toward militancy among the young blacks in Atlanta?

King: The young black people of today know and understand more than my generation did. When our young demonstrate they do so together with young white people. I am convinced that the young will solve the old problem. But once in a while I fear that the young lack a clear sense of direction. Violence is certainly not the answer to anything. But violence is the result of the greatest problem of the young: the high rate of unemployment. Our young people are in the worst situation. It seems that nobody needs them. There are three times as many unemployed blacks as there are whites. It makes the young bitter – and violent.

Gretlund: Is it possible for educated blacks to find a job in Atlanta?

King: People come from Chicago and Detroit in big buses to visit the Ebenezer Baptist Center. And often they don't want to go home again, even though they just came here as tourists. This is also true of some the well-educated. In such cases we help them find temporary places to live. And at the moment we can also help find some jobs.

Gretlund: Are you satisfied with the pace of integration in Atlanta's school system?

King: Most people in Atlanta know very well that we have only a token integration of our school-system. I think that busing is still a necessary evil in the effort to integrate the schools. But the great problem is, in the school as in the church, that even if we do manage to get the children into the same school, and into the same classroom, we still cannot force them to like each other and become friends.

We also force people into the same neighborhoods, but to make them see each other socially ... ! As I said earlier, the Church must do more to make the races love each other.

Gretlund: Are black school children in Georgia today offered an education that can equal that of white children taught here?

King: The reason I talk of token integration is that white people resist integration of schools in every possible way. The situation is that white parents are desperately trying to escape to the suburbs, out to the expensive houses and private schools! The scandal is that now that we, thanks to legislation and busing, have succeeded in integrating the public school system, almost only black children are in the public schools. It is the pattern for most of the large cities in the South. It goes without saying that the best teachers are hired where they make more money. – The whole thing demands a real change of mind.

[Through a window I see a group of tourists move about in the church, all dressed in colorful African costumes.]

Gretlund: Are the Baptists in Atlanta in touch with nationalist movements in African countries?

King: It seems that many from Africa identify with my son's non-violent philosophy. In any case, when they come to the US, Atlanta is the first city African students head for. More African students are in Atlanta than in any other American city. – The African politicians also come here. The President of Zambia has just visited the church and the memorial.

Gretlund: Do you see a future cooperation between Africans and black Americans?

King: Our problems are in America, and they must be solved by Americans. But we are certainly not blind to the value of international connections. As Americans, we have to think of where raw materials are going to come from in the future. We can't just hand Africa over to the communists.

Gretlund: Other minorities in the US feel they are treated unfairly. Does the NAACP ever work together with American Jews, locally?

King: We try, and have often tried to. But our problems are not quite the same. We the American blacks have the power of eloquence, but no financial power. Jews have "green power." If they are treated badly in a hotel, they simply buy the hotel!

Martin Luther King's facial expression shows that he considers his last statement a joke. Our conversation has lasted for about an hour, interrupted by several phone calls, and Dr. King chooses to end our session. "Would you like to see the church?" he asks politely. After a quick tour of the church with the mementos from the great civil-rights battles of the 50s and 60s, Dr. King escorts me to the church door and takes his leave: "I hope you were satisfied with my answers." Dr. King's ringing "Good-bye" must have been audible at the other end of "sweet" Auburn. He is indeed a good man with a good voice.

Walking down the street from the Ebenezer Baptist Church I realize how lucky I had been to be granted an interview with the extremely busy, highly influential, and obviously over-worked black leader. I wondered why my Atlanta friend had been able to set up my visit with Daddy King after just one phone call, when all my other efforts to see him had met with nothing but silence. After some questioning my friend the judge admitted evasively that he had relied on a long-established connection between the Kings and the Etheridges. His uncle, Paul Etheridge, had many years ago employed a young yardman named Martin Luther King, who stayed around and married the maid; and that had been the start of life-long friendships. That is also the biracial South.

CHAPTER NINE

Eudora Welty's Reaction to the Killing of Medgar Evers

My love of Eudora Welty and her fiction has been constant for more than twenty-five years. I have written more about her fiction than about any other Southern writer. I first met her at the inauguration of the Center for the Study of Southern Culture at the University of Mississippi in the fall of 1977. I was granted interviews with her in the spring of 1978 (twice) and again in 1993. Most of my work on her fiction was published in Eudora Welty's Aesthetics of Place, *which appeared in 1994 by Odense and Delaware university presses. A second revised American edition appeared as a paperback from University of South Carolina Press in 1997. I have, with Karl-Heinz Westarp, edited a collection of essays* The Late Novels of Eudora Welty, *which appeared from University of South Carolina Press in May 1998. The essay on her story "Where Is the Voice Coming from?" has its origin in "Hometown Violence," which was a talk I gave at the meeting of the American Literature Association in Baltimore in May, 1993.*

Eudora Welty's Reaction to the Killing of Medgar Evers

In some of her stories Welty enumerates highly poetic names to bring to life the flora of her native state. She often uses the exotic sounding names of flowers, bushes, and trees to detail a setting and to specify the time of year and the chosen location. In one passage from "The Demonstrators," Welty's story from 1966, she mentions roses, perennials, crape-myrtles, redbuds, dogwoods, Chinese tallows, pomegranates, pear trees, and a falling wall of Michaelmas daisies (*CS*, 621). The object of the poetic passages is always to prevent generalizations by using specific names and to create a vivid and localized setting. The poetic prose is not invoked as a mere indulgence in the color of a scene. Welty describes a place in detail because she is writing about human beings. To understand and define them, it is essential in her aesthetics of place to locate people through details of their world. "Their meaning must always bear on and be defined by what they came out of," as Welty put it in an interview (*C*, 281). This is, of course, also true of the artist who celebrates a place and in turn is defined by it.[1] People are not the same, nor are the places where they live, and this matters in fiction, as Welty shows in "Place in Fiction."

In important respects we are products of our native place, its history, its atmosphere, and its essence of place. The specific place could be one of the many houses so carefully described in Welty's fiction, e.g. old Mr. Marblehall's two houses in Natchez, the double-house "across the street" in "The Winds," the Shellmound Mansion of *Delta Wedding*, the MacLain House of *The Golden Apples* with its side "like a person's," the Renfro-Beecham Farmhouse of *Losing Battles*, or the McKelva House of *The Optimist's Daughter*. The specific narrative value of these buildings is what they convey about the people who live in them, which is a good deal about their background and about the lives they live. Their houses reflect their ambitions and disappointments. A description of a building may be even more evocative than any direct statement about the people living there. The houses are probably indicative of the economic background of the occupants, and every segment of society may be represented by their specific house. This may sound like simply the stock tool of most authors, but Welty's use of place also suggests an acceptance of the heritage of a place.

I do not see Welty as "fundamentally an historian," but she is also that.[2] In 1980 she made a public statement about her native Mississippi and the importance of the state's history for the local writer: "Heroism and shame have lightened or darkened pages of [our history]. It is filled with extremes – some of it is tragic, some it ugly beyond bearing. But in order to be good writers, we need to face and encompass all we are – no human action is too good or too bad to forego being understood. We must not disown any part of our heritage, ..."[3] When we consider Mississippi's history of stubbornly obstructing integration for more than a hundred years before the 1960s, we understand why Welty had to make such a statement and had felt obliged to write "Where Is the Voice Coming From?" Welty lives up to her own words from that speech, when she unflinchingly faces a tragic, ugly, and shameful part of her heritage as a native Jacksonian.

It is not always easy to show where a voice comes from. The disturbing character Welty created for "Where Is the Voice Coming From?" is clearly a lower-class white Southerner. Apparently, he has not always lived in Mississippi, but near the state, if we judge by his reference to what is going on "in Mississippi." He is a poor man, who is jealous of a black man's success. And he is a product of a society with a long history of oppressing of blacks, by force when necessary. By placing us in his mind for long passages and by making us listen to the story in his own casual tone of voice, Welty shows us just where this man's voice comes from.

The tragic event that inspired the story was the killing of Medgar Wiley Evers in Jackson, Mississippi, on June 12, 1963. The sit-ins, marches, and voter registration drives organized by CORE, SNCC, and the NAACP had been going on in Jackson since 1961, and had led to numerous arrests. Early in 1963 Evers had filed an unsuccessful suit against Jackson's all-white public schools, demanding that they comply with the 1954 Brown vs. Board of Education of Topeka decision of the U.S. Supreme Court.[4] June of 1963 was a time of great racial tension in Jackson. During the first days of the month blacks had demonstrated for integration and called for a boycott of the downtown businesses. The protest marches became violent, and hundreds of black people found themselves detained in cattle pens at the fairgrounds.[5]

On Monday, June 12, at 12:20 a.m., upon returning from an NAACP rally, Medgar Evers, state field secretary of the NAACP, was shot in the back with a 1917 Enfield army rifle. Ironically, the murder was committed on the night of President John F. Kennedy's nationally televised address on integration in the South, which Evers had watched. Kennedy said: "If an American, because his skin is black, cannot enjoy the full and free life all of us want, then who among us would be content to have the color of his skin changed and stand in his place?"[6] The situation *was* beginning to change rapidly in the South. On the day of the murder Governor George Wallace finally admitted two black students to the University of Alabama. But Evers would not see the results of his labor.

Evers, a son of a minister in the Church of God in Christ, a strict Pentecostal denomination, had attempted to register to vote in 1946, and he tried to enroll in the Law School at the University of Mississippi in 1954, but was denied admission on a technicality.[7] As a field secretary his NAACP job was to investigate and publicize violent crimes against blacks in Mississippi. Evers became well-known when he pledged the resources of the NAACP to James Howard Meredith's efforts to integrate the University of Mississippi during the fall of 1962.[8] During the desegregation campaign in Jackson, Evers emerged as an able spokesman for black people. He encouraged the black people of Jackson to demonstrate "till freedom comes," and he helped organize a campaign to integrate the municipal work force.

As one of his fingers had left a print on the rifle, which was found in a nearby honeysuckle thicket, Byron De La Beckwith was charged with the murder of Evers. Beckwith grew up on a dilapidated Greenwood plantation, rich in its Southern heritage, and he claimed that his grandfather rode as a colonel in the Confederate cavalry. Greenwood had added a chapter to the state's bitter history of race relations in 1955, when Emmett Louis Till, a fourteen-year-old boy had been killed there for "wolf-whistling" a white woman. Two men were arrested for the murder, but found not guilty in court.[9] At the time of the murder of Medgar Evers, Beckwith was living in the decaying family home in Greenwood, where he was an active member of the Citizens' Council.[10] During the administration of Governor Ross Barnett, 1960-1964, these councils received $193,500 from public funds, although they were privately organized.[11] The citizens' councils commanded considerable popular support in the state and practically "ran the state on matters racial."[12] The murder of Medgar Evers meant a new low for Mississippi's reputation, and the state "reached the ultimate in closedness."[13] Roy Wilkins, executive director of the NAACP, expressed the national public opinion when he reacted to the murder: "We view this as a cold, brutal, deliberate killing in a savage, uncivilized state, the most savage, the most uncivilized state in the entire fifty states. There is no state with a record that approaches that of Mississippi in inhumanity, murder, brutality and racial hatred; it is absolutely at the bottom of the list."[14]

Fortunately, the murder of Medgar Evers became a turning point for Mississippi. During the summer of 1969 when the NAACP held its Sixtieth Anniversary Convention in Jackson, the delegates noted that all hotels, restaurants, and public facilities were now desegregated. Without incident the convention unveiled a six-foot marble tablet dedicated to the memory of Medgar Evers.[15] In 1964 two Mississippi trials of Beckwith ended with all-white juries deadlocked on verdicts; mistrials were declared, and the colonel's grandson was not sentenced. But he was not found innocent, which is perhaps more surprising considering the general racial climate of the time. In December 1990 the now 70-year-old white supremacist was facing a new indictment for the same murder. On February 5, 1994, Beckwith was finally convicted of the murder of Medgar Evers.

As it turned out, the man charged with the murder is not of a poor white family, as Welty had anticipated in her story – which only goes to show that fanatic racists exist in all classes of society. That fact does not detract from Welty's achievement in transforming an actual event into an imagined one while observing a clear distinction between fact and fiction. Criticism of the social and political problems of her region is not usually the purpose of her stories. She sees it as her job to show in fiction what the world is like, not to question that reality. In her "Must the Novelist Crusade?" Welty makes it clear that her fiction is not a platform for political opinions. And the essay is also her reply to those who questioned her silence on racial issues in the early 1960s.

The strong stand against the use of fiction for political crusading should not obscure the fact that Welty's fiction is built upon a moral basis. As Katherine Anne Porter pointed out there is, "an ancient system of ethics, an unanswerable, indispensable moral law, on which she is grounded firmly."[16] Welty seems to expect her fiction to cause her readers to ask questions also about their own moral stance, for in the same essay she maintains that it is the writer's obligation "to convey what we see around us, whatever it is," even when the events are "wrenchingly painful and humiliating" (*ES*, 154-55). The statement may be read as Welty's justification for breaking her silence on racial issues by publishing "Where Is the Voice Coming From?" Her attitude to the artist's involvement with current events is close to that of Chekhov. In a letter of October 27, 1888, Chekhov warned his friend A. S. Suvorin not to suppose that the artist's duty to offer a correct presentation of a problem implies an obligation for the artist to also suggest a solution to the problem: "The court is obliged to submit the evidence fairly, but let the jury members make the decision, each according to his own judgment."[17]

If "Where Is the Voice Coming From?" does appear to be closer than Welty's fiction in general to the actual event that inspired it, the reason is probably the quick transmutation of fact into art. The first version of the story was written on the night of the murder of Medgar Evers (*C*, 265). The story was created out of Welty's emotional reaction to an act of perversion in her hometown, and she had no time to reflect on the murder in tranquility. I suppose the killing in Jackson upset Welty's psychological security in her identity as a Jacksonian. Her anger had been provoked for some time. It went back at least as far as the racial crisis in Little Rock, Arkansas, almost six years earlier. On September 25, 1957, she wrote Diarmuid Russell: "I feel like emigrating from the whole country. Bayonets!"[18] Such an outburst is the product of great disappointment, with both the North and the South. And it seems mixed with some nostalgia for her childhood days when a town like Jackson seemed like one big neighborhood. It was, however, a racially motivated murder right in her beloved "neighborhood" that forced Welty to question her native sense of group identity in fiction. The publication of the story made it clear that her idea of place involves more than memories of times past. Welty's "place" is time made visible, and this is also true of the unpleasant present of June 1963. In her preface to her *Collected Stories* of May 1980, Welty explains that "Where Is the Voice Coming From?" is unique "in the way it came about":

> That hot night when Medgar Evers, the local civil rights leader, was shot down from behind in Jackson, I thought, with overwhelming directness: Whoever the murderer is, I know him: not his identity, but his coming about, in this time and place. That is, I ought to have learned by now, from here, what such a man, intent on such a deed, had going on in his mind. I wrote his story – my fiction – in the first person: about that character's point of view, I felt, through my shock and revolt, I could make no mistake. (CS, xi)

The reason why Welty had to react is reflected in her aesthetics of place. If a murderer's meaning bears on and is defined by what he came out of, he is also a product of where he lives. And in this case the site of the crime happened to be Welty's hometown.

In the sense that all values are aesthetic, as argued by philosophers as diverse as George Santayana in his *The Sense of Beauty*,[19] and A. J. Ayer in his *Language, Truth and Logic*,[20] and perhaps already implied by Baruch de Spinoza in his *Ethica*[21] (although the term "aesthetics" had not yet been coined by the 1670s), Welty's aesthetics of place will reveal her ethics. She has decided to avoid all crusading in her fiction, but a distinction between her moral and aesthetic values cannot be final. A sense of place involves a sense of the people who live and lived in the place. To live among them in the small town, on the plantation, in the hills, or in the city means to be a part of a community, and to find one's identity in relation to it by sharing in or rebelling against its values. Like everybody else Welty's characters learn that living with yourself and others means that existential choices have to be made. The decisive factors for the existential choice are not abstract, but values with origin in the community of the place, past and present, and in the emotional and imaginative experience of the individual. The choice takes its point of departure in the individual's imaginative sense of place and has consequences for the ethics of the individual and therefore for the community.

In his essay "Dodging Apples" Reynolds Price argues that all artists create because they believe in the "value and urgency" of what they see and attempt to understand. His point is that "all works of art came into existence to change something," "to cause some action," "in the hope of altering, literally causing movement" in the writer himself, his reader, and "the world at large."[22] The aesthetic look at a place and its people in Welty's fiction often becomes a humorous and satirical view of everyday life. Like Balzac and Chekhov she implies the existence of an inherent norm of decent human behavior.[23] Through its existential implications the aesthetic impression becomes by necessity an ethical evaluation. How obvious this is in her fiction is finally a question of emphasis.

Welty's fiction is not usually read as the product of an ethical or a didactic purpose, nor is "Where Is the Voice Coming from?" Her experience of the town at that time and her idea of its values were different from that of the assassin who tells the story. Yet, she could not ignore the fact that their aesthetic experiences co-existed within the framework of the same historical experience and in the same place. This is what made it necessary for Welty to show that in the situation of June 1963 in Jackson, her aesthetic experience had implications for what she could accept in her community. If she had tried to detach herself from her native town by ignoring its time of crisis, she would only have managed to diminish her own integrity.

Like her fictional characters Welty has to see her life in context. She is finally measured against the enduring identity of her place, which means against all that has happened in Jackson and against all the human relationships that have been experienced there. The history of the town is an ever-present commentary on today's events. In this way the past of Jackson is integrated with its present, and contemporary Jacksonians participate in a drama of place that began before they were born and will end after they are dead. I believe that this is what C. Hugh Holman meant when, in an essay on Ellen Glasgow, he included "a sense of place as a dramatic dimension" among characteristics that set the best Southern writing apart from much American writing in this century.[24] Welty could not disown her native town, for she loves it. But their relationship has a dramatic dimension which generated the story "Where Is the Voice Coming From?" It first appeared in *The New Yorker* on July 6, 1963. The galleys for this publication are dated June 26, which is just two weeks after the assassination of Medgar Evers.[25]

The problems that preoccupy Welty in this story are and have been particular to the place she describes. They echo an era when "ancient rituals demarcated the separate spheres of racial life," and they echo a time when individual black men "were made sacrifices to a sacred concept of white supremacy."[26] But the problems of this community are finally universal in that the subject is our basic sense of right and wrong. The universal is brought to the story through the troubled mind of the main character. It is the very convincing presence of his thoughts that saves the story from being mere propaganda. The situation speaks for itself without any crusading on the part of the author, and the story never becomes a tract of social protest. "Where Is the Voice Coming From?" demonstrates how Welty, even in the thick of the racial upheavals of the 60s, managed to write fiction that is "stone deaf to argument." If there is any message in this story, it goes beyond the political subtext and beyond the usual attack on conservative political and social traditions still ruling in the early 1960s within some areas of the South.

Welty also implies a rejection of the distortions and stereotypes aggressively imposed upon all Southern whites during that period. As I read "Where Is the Voice Coming From?" the story also demonstrates Welty's resentment of the arrogance of those who wanted to change her native state into their own image, while ignoring individual differences and time-honored characteristics. Welty did not consider her state "savage and uncivilized." In 1972 she summed up her reason for writing the story, in an interview: "I had been having a feeling of uneasiness over the things being written about the South at that time, because most of them were done in other parts of the country and I thought most were synthetic. They were perfectly well-intentioned stories but generalities written from a distance to illustrate generalities. When that murder was committed, it suddenly crossed my consciousness that I knew what was in that man's mind because I'd lived all my life where it happened" (*C*, 83).

The voice of this man is one among many in the town of Thermopylae, but his voice is fully individualized. His is the voice of a weary man who defends himself without much conviction. While the complexity of the situation and the emotions involved become the focus of the story, the political issues remain implicit. But finally the existence of evil is more important in the story than the dramatic events on a certain day in a Southern town. In this way the story becomes art. The desired universality eventually has to be abstracted from the details of the life of a specific individual in a particular place, a man who uses the identity of a place to measure himself. The universality is achieved through the specifying and particularizing. The important question for the writer must be: what do the thinking, acts, and fate of this man, who deliberately kills, mean to readers of another time and place? In this sense character is a more profound subject in the story than situation and even more profound than place. But place can have important and even dramatic significance, as it does in this story, in which it is almost a character. It remains an "almost," however, for Welty's interest in place leads to a more profound interest in the human being of that time and place. To understand that the murderer fails and tragically goes "down, down, down" as a human being is ultimately more important than knowing where the murder was committed. And the murderer knows he has failed completely, hence the unchanging and ever-present elegiac note of his story.

In this short story Welty's aesthetics of place encompasses central concepts such as race, class, history, and religion. It would be too much to ask to have all of these in the same paragraph, but most of the passages in "Where Is the Voice Coming From?" bring out at least one or two of these central concerns through simple descriptions of place. One of the early paragraphs reads:

> So you leave Four Corners and head west on Nathan B. Forrest Road, past the Surplus & Salvage, not much beyond the Kum Back Drive-In and Trailer Camp, not as far as where the signs starts [sic] saying "Live Bait," "Used Parts," "Fireworks," "Peaches," and "Sister Peebles Reader and Adviser." Turn before you hit the city limits and duck back towards the I. C. tracks. And his street's been paved. (CS, 603)

The voice we hear is that of a man who is on his way to a part of his hometown of Thermopylae to commit a murder. He has the kind of "feel" for the place and familiarity with the town which it takes long to acquire, and which can only be absorbed through the experience of long residence. The reality offered by the town is, of course, a selective reality and just one individual's sense of place. What Welty means when she claims that place delicately confines and defines character becomes clear even in such a short passage (*ES*, 122). The character of the Voice is moulded and even given meaning by the town he drives through. In his mind he goes over his route, and he seems to take pleasure in his detailed knowledge of this part of town. Every detail is fully realized and its reality accepted. The details are "chosen, specific, pertinent, and thus revelatory," and in this way the story lives up to Welty's own criteria for good fiction (*P*, xvi). What is revealed is the nature and anxiety of a potential killer. He is certainly not retarded, or even "half-demented" as Peggy Prenshaw calls him.[27] He does not appear to be unbalanced on the night of the murder. Instead he seems cold-blooded, callous, and fully aware of what he does. It does not mean, of course, that he fully understands why he is getting ready to kill. If his actions were accidental and the results of a disturbed mind, we would have no reason to ask where such a voice comes from. It is essential that he seems as sane as most people.[28]

The places in town that the killer notices and enumerates tell us about his daily environment. It is a town where peaches are sold; it is possible to fish in the area; some people live in a trailer camp; at least two shops sell second-hand articles; it is a town serviced by the Illinois Central railroad; there is enough superstition for a fortune teller to make a living; fireworks (for the July 4th celebration) can be sold here, probably unlike some more restrictive community near by; and it is a place that has honored Nathan Bedford Forrest by naming a road for the General of the Confederate Cavalry. After Appomattox Forrest started the Ku Klux Klan (originally as a resistance movement), and his name therefore brings white supremacist ideas to mind. Forrest's presence is perhaps emphasized by the words "Fireworks" and the "No Riders" sign in the truck, which the killer believes does not refer to him. Although the passage is first and foremost a listing of what the Voice considers landmarks worth noticing, it also informs us about the town and the social situation there.

In one sense the man and his town are one, and their vocabulary and grammar are one: the sign saying "the Kum Back Drive In" and his thought "the signs starts saying" are phrases of a kind. His lack of grammar, his vocabulary, his colloquial expressions, and his pronunciation, which is reflected in the spelling, tell us that he is Southern, of the working class, without much education, and probably from a rural area.[29] The Voice knows his way so well because he lives not too far from his victim, a black civil rights leader. It is implied that the black neighborhood is where white men go to visit whores. It is obvious that the Voice takes comfort in knowing the area so well. But he does not live in the same neighborhood, for the housing districts are not integrated.

It is clear that the locality is not just a setting for a plot in a short story. It is first and foremost an integral part of the motives inciting the main character. The jealousy of the Voice and a part of his motivation are obvious in the last sentence of the quoted passage. He recognizes that the black couple in some financial, social, and emotional ways are better off than he is. But his innate conviction of white supremacy makes it impossible for him to accept the role as inferior to black people in any respect. Leonard W. Doob summarized white attitudes as of the 1930s and 40s in these words: "... all whites retain this stereotype concerning his [the Negro's] low intelligence, his brute strength, his unquestioned immorality, etc. Negroes must be kept in their place, a place quite different from that enjoyed by every white man, including the poor ones. No one dares question the dictum that a Negro must be killed occasionally in order that the rest may remain docile."[30] It is the killer's main problem that in the early 1960s, he still thinks about blacks along these lines. He is outraged: why should the street in a black man's neighborhood be paved when some whites, including the Voice, still live on dirt roads. He is white and poor, and he becomes aggressive when he thinks about the social advancement and the political power that pave streets in black neighborhoods. So in one short paragraph describing a part of a town, we learn about the social and racial situation in Thermopylae, and its historical background is implied. The rest of the plot is foreshadowed through General Bedford Forrest's name and the mentioning of the paved street. Later we read that Roland Summers is shot and drops to "his paved driveway."

Welty makes sure the story is thoroughly located by mentioning that the rifle was fired from near a sassafras tree (a sweetgum in an earlier manuscript version) with a mockingbird busily mocking the assassin right up until the crack of the shot. In this way the locality, in all its sensuous and yet ordinary detail, stamps itself upon the plot. The constant presence of a specific place imposes its own conditions on the story, and it finally produces a powerful effect peculiar to place and story. The murder is committed at night between 3:45 a.m. and 4:35 a.m., and the temperature never drops below 92. The Voice sees both time and temperature on the sign of the local Branch Bank. His wife is sure that he was bit by "the skeeters." The scorching heat of the night is in the rifle, the pavement, and everything else. The heat is used to describe the relation between the man and his wife and, by implication, the relation between the assassin and the community in Thermopylae.

The Voice is a self-centered man who questions his own motives, but when his spiteful and mocking wife tries to analyze his doings, he does not like it. He seems to be thoroughly henpecked by his Lady Macbeth. He wants his wife's praise and acceptance. But she is always in judgment of him, mainly for his lack of faith in himself. She wants to know why he has dropped the rifle at the scene of the crime: "And I told her, 'Because I'm so tired of ever'thing in the world being just that hot to the touch! The keys to the truck, the doorknob, the bedsheet, ever'thing, it's all like a stove lid. There just ain't much going that's worth holding on to it no more,' I says, 'when it's a hundred and two in the shade by day and by night not too much difference. I wish *you'd* laid *your* finger to that gun'" (*CS*, 606).

Through the emphasis on the suffocating heat in Thermopylae, Welty manages to express the feverishly frustrated state of the assassin. Appropriately, "thermo" means "heat" in Greek, and the full name of the place means "hot gates." The town's name may appear ironic as it evokes the year 480 B. C. in Greek history and an image of badly outnumbered soldiers that defended themselves bravely against the enemy. But seen from a Southern point of view, the associations are not necessarily ironic. The Voice has been trying to "hold on to something," but he is finding that it was not worth the effort. He obviously sees his wife as an extension of the society that in the media has called for the killing of the black leader and has brought the racial situation to the point where it is too late to turn back from a confrontation. The Voice thought he was acting out the will of the community, but he finds that the community does not necessarily identify with his efforts to deny blacks all social mobility. The community is divided, and not everybody feels as negatively and passionately about race as the Voice does. The acquiescence of those with social and official power can not be taken for granted, which the Voice might have known if he had read the fact of the "paved street" correctly. It is a community which will not, as the Voice learns, celebrate its assassin. The coveted "pat on the back" from the governor remains an unrealistic product of a daydreaming mind.

The Voice, who must be middle-aged, is deeply envious of people who live in North Thermopylae in houses with watered lawns, own their cars, have garages with a light burning all night, and appear in the news. In his influential study of Indianola of the mid-30s (a Mississippi town that in the 1960s became the birthplace of the citizens' councils), John Dollard pointed out that it is often the "visibility" of a black person "that tells the prejudiced person whom to hate and makes easy and consistent discrimination possible. Real competition gives an added reason for hostility and exploitation of the group against which one is prejudiced."[31] The Voice has to borrow Buddy's, his brother-in-law's, truck to get to the black neighborhood. The following day when he walks under the mimosas that, as he puts it poetically, hang "them pones of bloom like split watermelon," it looks to him as if the town is on fire already. He knows that potential violence is in the town and in its people: "watch TV long enough and you'll see it all happen on Deacon Street in Thermopylae."

In its fear of change the town may choose to live up to its name and be a Thermopylae against the forced school integration of the time. But even though he speaks of "us white people," the Voice does not necessarily see himself as simply a pawn of whites who want to protect the old caste system and their status. Why is he able to dominate the situation during the assassination, but unable to come to terms with his situation after the killing? His resentment is not limited to the blacks in town. It includes anybody that is better off than he is. His motives for the murder are probably his own social and racial prejudices. But he would, I think, reject any talk of personal motives and claim he was forced to shoot by circumstances beyond his control. Is it possible to argue that when he sets out that night, he is "simply caught up in the formed pattern of his life" in Thermopylae, and therefore not fully responsible?[32] Is it possible to see his behavior as a result of a long history? As if living in the town has preconditioned the assassin, he seems so sure of the purpose and of the communal significance of his act that the murder itself comes to seem predictable and even ritualistic.

It is only after the killing, perhaps from the moment he decides to drop his rifle at the scene of the murder, that the Voice begins to consider his situation. It is possible to see his disgust with himself and the town after the killing as a result of his realization that the situation in town had dominated him and determined his actions. Throughout the story Welty brings the town to life by portraying the community through the killer's thoughts about columnists, TV, hundreds of cops, "nigger children," American flags, Birmingham, Harlem and Chicago, Governor Ross Barnett, "that nigger Meredith," who Caroline [Kennedy?] is supposed to want to marry when she grows up, and through his remarks to himself that "it's still a free country," that "them Kennedys," and "even the President so far, he can't walk in my house without being invited." The killer's stream of consciousness echoes the old poor white mistrust and even fear of outside authority. On the night that Medgar Evers was shot, John F. Kennedy made his strongest speech on civil rights. He pointed out that, "Those who do nothing are inviting shame, as well as violence, those who act boldly are recognizing right, as well as reality."[33] If the killer of Evers heard it, he chose his own twisted interpretation of the speech.

What makes Welty's story art is not the perfect evocation of a place, of a changing community, and a historical period, nor is it the obvious political comment. What makes it art is the analysis of the nature of the murderer with all his serious flaws and total wrongheadedness. Time is his enemy, and the changes wrought by time make it hard for him to love the place where he lives.[34] Welty's analysis of him comes from the memory and the imagination of a writer who has lived almost all of her life in the town she describes. Her material is "the relation between the artist and the people around her," as Robert Penn Warren put it.[35] The insight into the killer's mind is thoroughly informed by Welty's intimate sense of a place and its people. He killed, as she writes, for his own "pure D-satisfaction," he killed for bitterness and despair in an attempt to turn loose the load placed on his shoulders by others. And this is where the voice really comes from. As a critic has pointed out "the voice comes from me, from such as me, from such as I know, from the character of the culture we all live in and have helped to create."[36]

The target for Welty is our calm complacency and smugness. We are "the comfortable homebodies with our names on the mailbox out front," we are insured against medical bills and natural catastrophes, but, as Welty said in her final tribute to Walker Percy, there is no insurance against the intrusions upon our calm through the imagination of the artist. We are forced to realize and recognize, because the truth shown to us is that the voice is our voice. As the story proves, Welty's fiction is more than enchantment; it is also discovery and, hopefully, recognition.[37]

In his internal monologue on what happened the night of the murder, the Voice is sensitive and creative like an artist. His grammar and syntax may often be incorrect, but in his creation of images and metaphors he is an artist. To himself he describes the immediate effect of the fatal shot in these words:

> Something darker than him, like the wings of a bird, spread on his back and pulled him down. He climbed up once, like a man under bad claws, and like just blood could weigh a ton he walked with it on his back to better light. Didn't get no further than his door. And fell to stay. (*CS*, 604)

The poetic paragraph, which invokes the American eagle, has caused some consternation among the best Welty critics. In an early statement Peggy Prenshaw found that his narration "detracts from the credibility of his characterization."[38] And Ruth Vande Kieft found that "the killer seems suddenly too sensitive to his victim's vulnerability." She admitted that she was "unwilling to believe that a man cowardly enough to shoot his helpless victim in the back would be capable of thinking of that victim humanely."[39] These are serious reservations indeed, for they argue the very heart of Welty's fiction. I believe that it is exactly because it is so hard to accept that she wants to show the humanity of the assassin.

Even though Welty could not have found him "more alien or repugnant," she still felt the obligation of the artist to enter "into the mind and inside the skin" of the character. She demonstrates her empathy even with him. If we deny him all human features, we will be repeating what he did in order to be able to kill. In order to be able to hate the black leader enough to commit his crime, the Voice denied his victim all humanity and considered him inferior by reason of race: "Never seen him before, never seen him since, never seen anything of his black face but his picture, never seen his face alive, any time at all, or anywheres, and didn't want to, need to, never hope to see that face and never will. As long as there was no question in my mind" (*CS*, 604). As long as he can keep the shooting completely impersonal by de-individualizing his target, he has no doubts about what he must do. To argue that the Voice is less than human would defeat the purpose, or at least reduce the effect of Welty's warning in the story. Her warning is against the consequences of man's dehumanizing of man. Only by accepting that even a killer is a human being, can we begin to understand that his voice is a part of our voice, and therefore also our responsibility.

The killer of "Where Is the Voice Coming From?" has great existential problems. For a while he manages to convince himself that he would be satisfied if only he had what his victim enjoyed: a loving wife, a new white car, a good house with green grass and a paved driveway, a sense of achievement, and the applause of the world. In his interior monologue the Voice is, of course, revealed as a mass of prejudices. His thoughts are a study in frightening pride and nauseating vanity. But he is also a lonely and complex individual who longs for recognition and acceptance. The place he lives never granted equality to his social class. It has endowed him with an identity that made him a killer, but the community has changed and rejects him and his ways of thinking. What the Voice learns the hard way is that black advances in Southern society are no longer, in phrases used by Bertram Wyatt-Brown to describe the 19th century South, considered a "departure from accustomed servitude," nor are they today seen as a development "endangering the white man's honor."[40]

The fact that he has time enough to wander around downtown the day after the murder may indicate that the killer is unemployed. But he wants to be "on top of the world." If the community and state, i.e. the upper social class, will "credit" him with the murder, he is willing to become the instrument of society, at least for a moment. He is even willing to risk capture. In an early version of the story he states: "I ain't going to shy if they do come after me."[41] When he leaves the rifle behind, he seems rather melodramatically to invite arrest. He is a man who boasts that he has never once dropped, forgotten, lost, or pawned his guitar for good, but now he asks his wife to believe that he has accidentally dropped his rifle at the scene of the murder. He has, it seems, left his weapon as a clue, so he can be sure to be credited with this act of national importance. He is a product of the general pursuit of fame and fortune, the revered values of modern society, but so far they have escaped him. Now he hopes for recognition and perhaps popularity through the murder of a carefully selected victim, a civil rights leader, who can serve as a scapegoat for both the town and himself.

The Voice calmly anticipates the possibility of frying in the electric chair for his crime. When a $500 reward is offered for the arrest of the murderer, he is flattered by the attention, although it was a very small sum even in 1963. He is a man who is tired of being a "no count" that never even had his photo taken. Now he wants the attention that has eluded him his whole life (except once when his mother told him to come home through an ad in the county weekly, a memory which he treasures). His parents, who might have given him the attention he yearns for, are merely memories of the past, his wife does not think much of him, and although he appears to be, or to have been, a church-going man (from the way he remembers a shouting preacher's eyeballs), he does not go there now that he needs help. There *is* a thin streak of humanity in the assassin. In spite of his deep-seated hostile feelings towards the town's established class, whose values have always made him feel inferior, he still wants to be recognized, accepted, credited, identified with, or just noticed. Even if he has to commit a murder to earn the attention. But as his wife points out, the joke is on him.

The fact that the dominant race has once again asserted itself through an act of violence is not an occasion for great celebration in the community. The news is still full of pictures of his victim, whereas nobody knows the Voice, and he gets no publicity. The local seller of roasted peanuts tells him: "They'll never find him." Finally the Voice is convinced that everybody is still better off than he is, and he has a clear sense that he "can't win." When we last see him, he is alone and not even a hero to himself. He remains an onlooker and a victim of history. The community endures, but it has changed and left him behind with an obsolete identity. In his isolation he tries to take comfort in his knowledge that he is "evermore the one." *He* has seen his victim sink down, he knows it – but he has no satisfying sense of triumph. He brings out his guitar and starts playing the blues, monotonously and depressively. His separateness has become his curse, and finally he is the one who is "down, down, down. Down."

Place offers identity, and the killer of "Where Is the Voice Coming From?" has an identity that is shaped by Thermopylae, and the people and history of that town. His restless existential search for acceptance, however misguided and atrocious, is finally of any place and of all time. In a speech at the inauguration of William Winter as Governor of Mississippi, Welty explained: "Regardless of how fast society around us changes, what remains, at any time, is a relationship in progress between ourselves and the world. Our subject remains humankind, and we are part of it. When we write about our people as we know them in our here and now, if our work is worth doing, we are writing about everybody."[42] It is only through Welty's familiarity with the particular place that the particular voice becomes universal.

The manuscripts of the story, which are on deposit with the Mississippi Department of Archives and History in Jackson, offer thirteen other working titles. They span from "ask me my daddy's name," "find me," and "it was me" to "where is the racket coming from?" and "voice from an unknown interior." A fairly complete manuscript is called "from the unknown," which seems to have been Welty's favorite title for some time. The choice of the final title, which is a question to the reader, is a marked improvement over the others. As indicated by some discarded titles: "a voice from the Jackson interior" and "from my room," Welty chose not to use the word "unknown" in her final title because she knows very well where the voice comes from.

The story reads as a broad accusation. Welty slowly lets her reader discover that the whole population of Thermopylae, past and present, is responsible for the death of the black civil rights leader. The story aptly demonstrates what Welty means by the following sentence from her essay on "Place in Fiction": "Location is the ground conductor of all the currents of emotion and belief and moral conviction that charge out from the story in its course" (*ES*, 128). The voice is not unknown to the author or to us, we hear it all of our lives. It is an interior voice of petty jealousy, paranoid prejudice, and violent inhumanity to others – that we listen to now and again. We know the voice and its heritage well. It is an everyday presence in our neighborhood, and this fact is what makes Welty's final title so appropriate. The author knows the voice. Her moral conviction, shaped by *her* place, charges out in the course of the story against its inhumanity.

[All references to Eudora Welty's Works are to the first editions. *C = Conversations* (1984), *CS = Collected Stories* (1980), *ES = The Eye of the Story* (1978), and *P = Photographs* (1989).]

[1] William Ferris, "Introduction," *Local Color: A Sense of Place in Folk Art*, ed. Brenda McCallum, New York, McGraw-Hill Book Company, 1982, p. xvii.

[2] Albert J. Devlin, "Eudora Welty's Historicism: Method and Vision," *Mississippi Quarterly* 30/2 (Spring 1977) 214.

[3] A Copy of Welty's untitled speech for the inauguration of Governor William Winter on January 21, 1980 is in The Welty Collection. The quotation is from the manuscript, p. 4.

[4] George A. Sewell & Margaret L. Dwight, *Mississippi Black History Makers*, rev. ed., Jackson, University Press of Mississippi, 1984, p. 121.

[5] Alan Huffman, "Dixie Dynamite," *The Oxford American* 3 (1993) 20-26.

[6] George Brown Tindall, *America: A Narrative History*, 2nd ed., New York, W. W. Norton & Co., 1988, vol. II, 1370.

[7] Gayle Graham Yates, *Mississippi Mind*, Knoxville, 1990, p. 266, p. 74. See also George A. Sewell & Margaret L. Dwight, *Mississippi Black History Makers*, rev. ed., 1984, p. 119.

[8] See Neil R. McMillen, "Development of Civil Rights 1956-1970," *A History of Mississippi*, ed. Richard A. McLemore, Jackson, 1973, II 161-62. James Meredith was admitted to the University of Mississippi on September 30, 1962.

[9] Gayle Graham Yates, *Mississippi Mind*, p. 66. See also Neil R. McMillen, *The Citizens' Council: Organized Resistance to the Second Reconstruction, 1954-64*, Urbana, Ill., University of Illinois Press, 1971, pp. 217-18.

[10] *The Clarion-Ledger*, Jackson, Mississippi, Dec. 18, 1990, p. 9A. For some of the information about Byron de la Beckwith's background I am indebted to Nancy D.

Hargrove's "Portrait of an Assassin: Eudora Welty's "Where Is the Voice Coming From?"," *Southern Literary Journal* 20 (Fall 1987) 74-88.

[11] Neil R. McMillen, *The Citizens' Council*, Urbana, Ill. 1971, p. 337.

[12] As pointed out by Hodding Carter III in 1986 on the PBS program "Mississippi: Is This America?" in the series *Eyes on the Prize: America's Civil Rights Years 1954 to 1965*. See also Neil McMillen "Development of Civil Rights 1956-1970," *A History of Mississippi*, ed. R. A. McLemore, II 159-60.

[13] Waldo W. Braden, *The Oral Tradition in the South*, Baton Rouge, Louisiana State University Press, 1983, p. 109. The expression "a closed society" was first used by James W. Silver in his *Mississippi: The Closed Society*, New York, 1966.

[14] Interview with Roy Wilkins rebroadcast on the PBS program (1986) "Mississippi: Is This America?" in the series: *Eyes on the Prize: America's Civil Rights Years 1954 to 1965*.

[15] George A. Sewell & Margaret L. Dwight, *Mississippi Black History Makers*, rev. ed., 1984, p. 122.

[16] K. A. Porter, "Introduction," Eudora Welty, *A Curtain of Green and Other Stories*, New York, 1947, p. xvi.

[17] The letter is quoted in Aleksandr Pavlovich Chudakov's *Chekhov's Poetics*, trans. by Edwina J. Cruise & Donald Dragt, Ann Arbor, Ardis, 1983, p. 194.

[18] Quoted in Kreyling, *Author and Agent*, p. 189.

[19] In his chapter "The Nature of Beauty," George Santayana argues that "the philosophy of beauty is a theory of values," and that "all values are in one sense Æsthetic," i.e. all values are ultimately intrinsic. *The Sense of Beauty: Being the Outlines of Æsthetic Theory*, New York, Charles Scribner's Sons, 1896, p. 14, p. 28. See also Heinrich Straumann's chapter "The Realm of the Imagination," *American Literature in the Twentieth Century*, 3rd rev. ed., New York, Harper & Row, 1965, pp. 130-78. I am indebted to Straumann for the references to Santayana and Ayer.

[20] Alfred J. Ayer wrote "our conclusions about the nature of ethics apply to Æsthetics also. Æsthetic terms are used in exactly the same way as ethical terms." *Language, Truth and Logic*, London, Victor Gollancz, Ltd., 1936, p. 170.

[21] Baruch de Spinoza, *Ethica Ordine Geometrico Demonstrata*, (1675) "Pars Quarta," Proposito VIII, & Proposito XIV. And also "Pars Quinta," Proposito XLII. *Opera – Werke*, 4 vols., Darmstadt, Wissenschaftliche Buchgesellschaft, 1967, II 84-556.

[22] Reynolds Price, "Dodging Apples," *Things Themselves: Essays & Scenes*, New York, Atheneum, 1972, pp. 7-12.

[23] See Sean O'Faolain's discussion of "romantic" versus "realist," *The Short Story*, Cork, The Mercier Press, (1948) 1972, pp. 125-26.

[24] C. Hugh Holman, "Ellen Glasgow and the Southern Literary Tradition," *Southern Writers: Appraisals in Our Time*, ed. R. C. Simonni, Jr., Plainview, New York, Books for Libraries Press, (1963) reprt. 1969, p. 123.

[25] Suzanne Marrs, *The Welty Collection*, Jackson, 1988, p. 50.

[26] Bertram Wyatt-Brown, *Southern Honor: Ethics and Behavior in the Old South*, New York, Oxford University Press, 1982, pp. 402-403.

[27] Peggy W. Prenshaw, *A Study of Setting in the Fiction of Eudora Welty*, Ann Arbor, University Microfilms International, 1970, p. 100.

[28] In making this point I find myself in agreement with Charles Clerc's "Anatomy of Welty's "Where Is the Voice Coming from?"," *Studies in Short Fiction* 23 (Fall 1986) 390.

[29] Nancy D. Hargrove, "Portrait of an Assassin," 85-86.

[30] Leonard W. Doob, "Poor Whites: A Frustrated Class," "Appendix I" in John Dollard, *Caste and Class in a Southern Town*, 2nd ed., New York, Harper & Brothers, 1949, p. 470.

[31] John Dollard, *Caste and Class in a Southern Town*, 2nd ed., 1949, p. 443.

[32] David Kranes, "Space and Literature: Notes toward a Theory of Mapping," *Where? Place in Recent North American Fictions*, ed. Karl-Heinz Westarp, Aarhus University Press, 1991, p. 20.

[33] Rebroadcast on the PBS program (1986) "Mississippi: Is This America?"

[34] Welty: "Man can feel love for place; he is prone to regard time as something of an enemy." "Some Notes on Time in Fiction," (*ES*, 164).

[35] Robert Penn Warren, "Foreword," Brenda McCallum, ed., *Local Color*, 1982, p. xi.

[36] Noel E. Polk, "Continuity and Change in Eudora Welty's "Where Is the Voice Coming From?" and "The Demonstrators"," *Turning Points, Mississippi Mindscape*, Jackson, Mississippi Committee for the Humanities, 1986, p. 8.

[37] Eudora Welty, untitled contribution to *Walker Percy, 1916-1990: Memorial Tributes*, tributes read in Saint Ignatius Church, New York, on October 24, 1990, Farrar, Straus & Giroux, 1991, unpaginated.

[38] Prenshaw, *A Study of Setting*, p. 101.

[39] Ruth M. Vande Kieft, ""Where Is the Voice Coming From?": Teaching Eudora Welty," *Eudora Welty: Eye of the Storyteller*, ed. Dawn Trouard, Kent, Ohio, 1989, p. 200.

[40] Bertram Wyatt-Brown, *Southern Honor*, New York, 1982, p. 436.

[41] Eudora Welty, "From the Unknown," in John Kuehl, ed., *Write and Rewrite: A Study of the Creative Process*, New York, Meredith Press, 1967, p. 12.

[42] Copy of Welty's untitled speech for the inauguration of Governor William Winter, ms, p. 5.

CHAPTER TEN

Silencing the Voice of the Past in Southern Fiction

This chapter represents my latest work on Madison Jones's fiction. I have long felt provoked by the inability of critics and readers to distinguish clearly between author and narrator, and also by the common unwillingness to admit the vanity of applying today's criteria for political correctness to historical situations and people long dead. I gave a version of this chapter called "Silencing the Voice of Iago in Southern Fiction of the 1990s" at the European Southern Studies Forum meeting on "The Contemporary South and Its Background" on the Island of Ærø, Denmark, in August, 1997.

Silencing the Voice of the Past in Southern Fiction

The South is a most fertile ground for fiction writers. Fiction has completely replaced moonshining as the favorite domestic activity. But maybe we have reached a saturation point? My latest count revealed at least half a million short story writers and novelists in the old Confederacy. It can be home-wrecking when so many people spend more time with their word processors than with their families. But everywhere you go in Dixie new writers are creeping out of the woodwork. If you give a talk on Southern fiction at South Middle-Georgia Northern University or at East Southern Mid-Tennessee Western Community College (institutions that are likely to ask me to speak), there will after your talk be a row of highly talented people waiting, not to discuss the topic of your talk, but to ask you to read their fiction. The fevered creative writing activity has also left its mark on academic publishing. For what good is writing, if your work does not appear in print? So new literary magazines arise daily to cater to the new Southern talent and their urge to publish. Can we today do without publications (that are likely to consider my work) such as *The Southern Possum Review of Mountain Metaphysics and Literature; The West-North-Central Alabama Journal of Self-Deconstruction; The Sad Hill Intellectual Literary Quarterly; The Nanawaya Bogalusa Tallapoosa Creek Commentary Magazine;* or *The Flunk River Rafting Review of Arts and Letters* ?[1]

Surprisingly, one of the subjects that now seem excluded from Southern fiction is race. If we judge by the fiction of the industrious contemporary black and white writers, it is possible to travel through broad stretches of the South and find scarcely a black face in sight. The awareness of the issue of race as a problem is not really reflected in much of the fiction I have read. There are reasons for that fact. In an interview Josephine Humphreys, a true daughter of a prominent Southern family, told me:

> I didn't know any black people until – really until I was an adult. There were black students at Duke when I went there, but not many. I mean there were three girls in my class that were black, they were the first ones. But then when I came home [to Charleston] in my twenties I taught English at the Baptist College for seven years, and that's where I got to know black people well.... In college I avoided studying history. I had never been interested in the Civil War, in reading about the battles. I was not inter-

ested in the family history, because it was used the wrong way! It was used to defend segregation. It was used to make the South into something that I thought it wasn't, and to glorify something that no longer existed, and I just didn't want to have anything to do with it.... But now you can read about real people, I mean historically real people: women, blacks, and poor people. From that point of view history becomes a living thing, a real thing, and an important thing.... Obviously there are a lot of good changes that have been made, but all of America is still quite racist in terms of how white people think about black people in general, and in terms of what doors are open to black kids. (1993, unpublished)

When asked about race problems and her fiction, Kaye Gibbons, who has an entirely different Carolina country background, told me:

In *Ellen Foster* (1987) [which has now been filmed for a Hallmark Hall of Fame adaptation, reset in an urban setting!] the race issue was between two children. Then on the last page Ellen Foster moves it out into society. In the other books the racial issues are brought out inside the household. And it is how the domestic help is treated. In *Sights Unseen* when one woman is called "a Nigger," she is defended by all the members of the family. I believe with Miss Welty that the writer should not crusade. I never set out to crusade, but I would like to teach small lessons through stories ... I get letters from people who have read *Ellen Foster* all the way through and think she is black. Ain't that pitiful? ... But in the South, more so than in any other place in the world, black people and white people grew up so closely together, grew up on the same farms together, that we have the same foodways and folkways. We do share a lot of the same beliefs, and certainly the same religious background. I guess it doesn't surprise me at all that people would become confused by race in the books. (1996, unpublished)

But few of the younger Southern novelists agonize over blacks. One of Barry Hannah's latest books is called *High Lonesome* (1996), (like a country music record by Randy Travis).[2] Hannah has little to say on race in the book. I cannot imagine that he thinks much of academic convocations to examine race relations. He seems preoccupied contemplating his existential problems. One of his characters – note: *not* Hannah but one of his characters – is thoroughly disgusted by "a little man who had followed the civil rights struggle and written several books about it, a white man. He had a name of esteem, but in the hall I attacked him for being a civil rights junkie with his eye on the main chance, a part of the modern university industry where all the grants and prizes were. I accused him of living off the grief of better men" (p. 75). The character admits that he holds "no brief for the universal holiness of African-Americans that goes down as commandment in much of the press today" (p. 113). For him the expression "the burden of history" is the nickname for a mentally reduced

Rambo-like Vietnam veteran. But he admits that he likes watching rhythm-and-blues musicians, "I loved them for their bellies. They'd been having it for a long time, on much good collards, fatback, and cheap whiskey" (p. 113).

The writers who still agonize over race are older writers, such as Ellen Douglas, Madison Jones, Maya Angelou, and Mary Ward Brown, who have *lived* the recent history of the South. In their fiction racial differences are seen as a part of a rich and varied heritage. C. Vann Woodward's "burden" of racial guilt has disappeared and so have the Faulknerian characters who used to take up page after page brooding over the hurts inflicted by history. If we judge by the fiction, Southern racial history does not weigh heavily upon the consciousness of contemporary Southerners, they have finally escaped the past. If prejudice is voiced, it is usually through monologues exposing characters on the political right, who among others complain that the women at Duke University are being paid "to kill off" dead white males (see Clyde Edgerton's *In Memory of Junior*).[3] It is hardly ever the basic black-white problem that is in focus. Even Maya Angelou, Alice Walker, Toni Morrison, and Dori Sanders (at least in the novel *Her Own Place*)[4] seem more interested in the black community and in the community of women, than in the black and white community.

Clyde Edgerton's *Killer Diller* (1991) exposes the racial, religious, and social hypocrisy at Ballard University, a Southern school. The misguided students at Ballard are only saved from the sins of the past by their common love for the blues. The music of the black and white band becomes a mediator between the races. Holister Jackson, a stoic, poor white mechanic, thinks to himself: "In music, race don't matter."[5] The music is a powerful force that seeks to subvert Ballard's established world, for if the blues music is accepted, played by an integrated band, it would no longer be possible to distinguish between "them" and "us." It is refreshing that Shanita, a black girl, is by far the most unregenerate racist in the novel. She "does not like the bass player, Wesley Benfield, or the lead singer, Sherri Gold. Because they are white" (*Killer Diller*, p. 22). When she meets a white radio personality by the name of Good Morning Charlie, she thinks of him as "You red-faced-queer-fag-honky-cracker shit" (*Killer Diller*, p. 97). In general the new white Southern writers have little to say on race. The subject is not significant in their fiction, it may be brought up, but it is not explored. Does this mirror the situation in society? Should it? Is it just wishful thinking that race should be so unimportant in today's South?[6]

Maybe we can take comfort in the fact that the black characters that *do* appear in the new fiction are not stereotyped? Albert Swan in Josephine Humphreys's *The Fireman's Fair* (1991)[7] and Ben Ashley in *Killer Diller* are fully developed individuals with full names and with little in common. They are not in the novels to be yardstick characters, which is just as well because we could not endure another black saint in fiction. The black people in these novels are not better, or worse, than whites, they are simply ordinary individuals. The progress is in the individuation. Their personal relations and shared experiences with whites are given space and attention, but the politics of rights and integration are not.

The debate about the correctness of imaginary characters that were created earlier in history has become increasingly important during the 1990s. Shelby Foote, Justin Kaplan, and William Styron went to New York in the Spring of 1997 to explain that Huckleberry Finn supposedly lived in the 1840s and that this is why his vocabulary is less than politically correct. The argument, broadcast on C-span, did not impress everybody in the audience. And in some places Mark Twain's book from 1884 is again banned in schools and libraries, because it is not politically correct by the standards of the 1990s. – Readers appear increasingly unwilling to suspend their convictions when they read fiction. Maybe because they are secretly convinced that all fiction is really factual confession. (But a confession of intimate family history, as is all the fashion today, exists for the writer's own peace of mind or wallet. The confession may be a boast, but mostly it is a cry for pity: "Real-Life Misery. Read All about It," as *Time Magazine* titled a column on the contemporary memoir explosion: "There are some 267 million stories in the naked U.S., all of them yearning to be told and sold."[8] The confessional mode is the true civilizing and embalming of Southern fiction. The true storyteller does not tell stories because she is eager to confess).

The ayatollahs of Iran are convinced that all voices created in Salman Rushdie's fiction are the voice of the author and hold him responsible, demanding his life. American readers are surprisingly unwilling to make allowances based on the time and place of the writing of a book. They seem anxious to convince themselves that ethical standards are fixed, permanent, and fundamental. It is good to know, they seem to think, that what is correct behavior and expression must always have been correct, even if people could not live up to our standards in earlier centuries. The line of thinking seems to be that if morality is *not* contingent, even writers of the past should not be permitted any poetic license, and therefore Huck Finn cannot be allowed to speak the way Mark Twain imagined he would.

If we think this way of reasoning is hard on the positive heroes in old fiction, think of what it will mean to books with bad and even evil characters. Should Iago voice his thoughts on Desdemona and Othello, on gender and race, in politically correct vocabulary? Or, is it that Iago should not have been created at all? The lesson seems to be that a writer may use his negative capability to create characters who are not himself, as long as they are not bad or evil characters. John Milton's Satan will have to go, for the existence of such negative forces in literature would be a corrupting influence on the young. And they should not be taught what scheming and vile people think. The presence of Iago will no longer be tolerated. It is indeed a severe limitation on writers, and fortunately most of them choose to ignore the correctness ideal.–Maybe

Shakespeare saw political correctness coming, Iago's last words in the play are: "From this time forth I never will speak word."

The suggestion that we exclude in order to be politically correct is not just a phantom of my European imagination. A personal experience brought the point home to me. In the Spring of 1996 I had been asked to speak at a community college in the South, and as they had many African-American students, I suggested that they read "Where Is the Voice Coming From?" by Eudora Welty.[9] I had used the story successfully before a large integrated audience of students at Mississippi State, where my interpretation of the story led to much debate. As you may be aware, the story in question is the one Miss Welty wrote as her immediate reaction on the night of the murder of Medgar Evers in Jackson, in June 1963. It was written and published before Byron De La Beckwith was first arrested. It is a very short story, and well-suited, I thought, for the students at the community college. And at first it was accepted as a good idea by the organizers.–But about two weeks before my planned visit, I received a letter from the main organizer stating:

> When I read "Where Is the Voice Coming From?" again, I realized that this story will not be an appropriate choice for us to put on reserve in the library and ask students to read. It simply would not be the politically correct thing to do because it would probably be perceived as our promoting offensive language of the sixties. Instead of your discussing this story, we would like for you to talk informally about your interest in ....

So thirty-three years after she wrote it, Mississippi's greatest living writer was censored for her great anti-racist story. And what was the offensive language used in the story? Well, it is hardly surprising. If you write a story that takes place exclusively in the mind of a racist so fanatic that he kills a civil rights leader solely because of his race, the vocabulary in the killer's mind *is* racist. He repeatedly thinks of his victim as "the nigger"–and any other word in the assassin's mind and mouth would be unbelievable.–When I protested that the story constitutes a powerful attack on all racism, I was informed that once they noticed the offensive word, the college students would not read the story. This was not my experience at Mississippi State and at other Southern schools, and it is probably a case of greatly underestimating the students at the college. But it presents a problem for all art. If evil characters are censored out of the arts (*excluded* in the age of total inclusion) because of what they say or do, how can we learn about the presence of the Roger Chillingworths and John Claggarts of the world? Will silence make the leeches go away? Can we have good *without* evil?

Are politically correct opinions necessary to create great art? Or, can you sport awfully incorrect ideas, politically, historically, and morally, and still write fiction of the highest grade? Madison Jones's successful novel *Nashville 1864:*

The Dying of the Light is different from Welty's short story, and yet very similar in its effect on the excluding forces in today's America.[10] Jones's novel has been severely criticized, not for the incorrectness of its language, but more for a passage of provocative interpretation of history, which implicitly questions the South's role as flawed exemplar in the national imagination. In the novel – his tenth–Jones tells us how a twelve-year-old Steven Moore and his slave-boy companion Dink become unintentional participants in the Battle of Nashville, one of the fiercest engagements of the Civil War. The Confederates were outnumbered by more than two to one, and the battle became the final stand of the Confederacy. Driven by desperate conditions at home, Steven and Dink have set out to find Steven's father, a captain in J. B. Hood's Army of Tennessee. The story of their walk across the field of battle encapsulates in miniature some of the greatest themes of American history and literature, including the burden of slavery and race, and the loss of old certainties, values, and integrity.

The memoir was supposedly completed in the year 1900, and only recently discovered by a grandson, who, provoked by moden histories, had it published. Steven Moore was a Southerner of his century and *not* of our time. But the victors' history of the war is now the established version, so can the reviewers accept a man with Steven's opinions on the war and its origin? Early in the novel there is an apology for the South of the 1860s. Moore informs us that the defection of the first slaves came as a surprise in the South, "a surprise informed by considerable disillusion," as most owners considered their slaves family "in a special sense." And he maintains that:

> It is only fair also to view the matter through the eyes of the slaveholders themselves.... Look at it this way: the institution of slavery was an inherited one, passed down from time immemorial to the first American settlers at Jamestown and hence to us. Until the latter Eighteenth Century, critics of the institution were hard to find, even among New Englanders .... Why the South did not continue in the apparent intention of that first generation of settlers to reject slavery is at least understandable. I assume that economics played the larger part, but there was much more.–The South was by no means alone in seeing the black slave as a primitive child of Africa requiring, if he ever was to be fully civilized, generations of schooling in the white world. In spite of recent Yankee historians and excepting a minority of loud Abolitionists, the North held much the same view. (pp. 18-19)

Moore then goes on to talk about Lincoln's ambiguous pre-war opinions on race, the killing of hundreds of blacks in the streets of New York in 1863, and the desperate political background for Lincoln's Proclamation. Moore then points out that few white people in the Confederacy ever doubted the justice of their cause, and that the invasion of Northern armies only strengthened the will to resist. And he ends by adding: "Given an educated choice between

Southern slavery and the wretched sweatshops then prevailing, many a Northern laborer might well have chosen the former" (p. 20).

Madison Jones talks to us because he is genuinely concerned about the human condition and has a story-telling bent. He tries to describe human identity, to outline how it was shaped, and to indicate the meaning of its history. The novel is really about "the dying of the light"–the vanishing of a civilization, and the focus is on the human concerns of all classical fiction. The whole apology for the Confederacy takes up less than three pages of the novel's 129 pages. Nevertheless, the reaction to it was predictable and unfortunate. I read the manuscript and advised Madison Jones to delete the passage. Not because of its contents, for I certainly accept that an old Confederate captain may have had these thoughts in the year 1900. And it is a part of the truth to hear these opinions voiced. I advised a deletion because stylistically the passage sticks out like a sore thumb, because it seems to be a glued-on disquisition and is a blot on an otherwise perfectly organic novel. The apology is not only superfluous, it also says the exact opposite of the novel as such. I advise the reader to trust the tale and not its narrator.

Madison Jones answered that he knows the passage sticks out, but that he wanted to risk it and added: "I want these things to be clearly said." But he promised to try to minimize the damage to the unity by adding a passage, making it clear that the apology is an aside and that "the narrator just for a moment assumes the role of formal historian."[11] Jones added two sentences: "Here I suddenly find myself digressing into the realm of polemics. I feel, however, in the light of the recent and growing tendency to factual distortion by historians and others, that certain things cry out to be said in our defense" (pp. 17-18).

The addition was too little, too late, the damage was done even before the novel's publication. *Kirkus Review* praised the novel for its "raw power and harsh originality," but complains that it is "so entirely partisan," finds the power of the book diminished by "Steven's rhapsodic celebration of the Confederate soldier, and his defense of slavery," and ends by asking for "some authorial distance" (March 15, 1997). *Publisher's Weekly* complained: "Jones attempts to put a redeeming spin on the ignominious end of the slave-holding agrarian South, advancing the romantic image of a benign, paternalistic Confederacy.... In the end, we get a boy's-eye view of an old man's sanitized image of the gentility of the old South" (April 14, 1997). Notice that in the review "agrarian" is here as bad as "slave-holding," and what is worse, no attempt whatsoever is made to distinguish between the author and the voice he has created: In the review Steven Moore has been totally replaced by Madison Jones. Steven Moore is *not* accepted as a fictional creation or as a man of his own times.

The novel has actually little to do with our view of the old slave-holding South, or even with the Battle of Nashville. To be fair to the reviewers, some of them, especially Jonathan Yardley of *The Washington Post* (May 28, 1997) and

Robert Benson in the *Sewanee Review*,[12] have recognized that the book is about something completely different and has complex human dimensions. Like Eudora Welty's short story it is about insight, recognition, and truth. It is about man's inhumanity to man, a boy's comprehension of it, and his loss of all romantic notions of class and race. The central passage of the novel has Dink and Steven witness the Rebels ambush a whole regiment of Yankee troops: "Shifting my stance for clear sight through the trees, I watched them come on, closer and closer, the hot blood mounting in my veins. There was something strange. Suddenly, "Them's niggers!" Dink's pitched voice had said it. "Shh," I said, with a glance at his astonished face. A minute more and those black troops would be in easy musket range.... I remember thinking how perfect it was, how brilliant at every step: the black Yankees caught with their backs to the cut and the long jaw closing in" (pp. 74-75).

The result of the ambush is that the ground is littered with wounded and dead black soldiers. The boys try to leave, but Dink, who earlier had told a black Yankee soldier that he was "a Confederate," now speaks in a new strange tone of voice and wears a gloomy and sullen expression. When Steven leaves, Dink follows, but "not up close anymore." Steven tries to find words to comfort Dink and bring him out of his persistent sullen silence. He wants to say "Black or white, they were Yankees," but he does not. After a long time, Steven bursts out: "They were Yankees too, come to take our country away from us. We got to fight back." After a brief silence Dink says: "They was niggers just like me." Nothing more came from him, nothing to comfort his companion's distress (p. 80).

From the moment that Dink meets the black Union soldier, who is also the first free black man he has seen, to the moment when the slave boy identifies with the dead black soldiers, Steven is feeling uncertain and troubled. He is slowly coming to recognize and accept Dink's humanity, his race, his pride in it, and his certainty in his new-found allegiance. The thoughts that it was not Dink's fight, and that he should not have been brought into the battle, come as Steven's discomforting realization. When he was led into danger, Dink had acted against his own will and in Steven's behalf. "No matter the bond of real affection between us, this was what it meant to be a slave" (pp. 56-57). The parallel to Huck's recognition of Jim's humanity is unmistakable in Steven's rejection of slavery and acceptance of Dink's identity as a black human being. Steven's loss of innocence, sense of frustration, failure and defeat, and his sudden awareness of limitation, responsibility, and guilt transcend the Battle of Nashville, December 15-16, 1864. The novel does not deserve to be excluded.

As the history of Southern literature documents: to apprehend the South, and be nourished and sustained by it imaginatively, is not enough to be able to see it, and certainly not to be able to see beyond the region. In order to gain the necessary perspective and vision, a journey of self-discovery is required. Madison Jones's new novel constitutes such a journey from one boy's discovery of his racism to the reader's self-questioning on the issue of race. To apprehend the South you have to *include* not only Jimmy Carter but also his brother Billy, not only Elvis Presley but Jerry Lee Lewis, not only Rev. Jesse Jackson but Rev. Jimmy Swaggart, and not only Leontyne Price but also James Brown. If you *exclude* the others, there is no South.

---

[1] James J. Thompson, Jr. inspired my invention of these "periodicals." See his "Getting Out from under Eudora Welty," *The World & I*, (May, 1989) p. 375 (pp. 375-80).

[2] Barry Hannah, *High Lonesome*, New York, The Atlantic Monthly Press, 1996.

[3] Clyde Edgerton, *In Memory of Junior*, Chapel Hill, Algonquin, 1992, pp. 175-77.

[4] Dori Sanders, *Her Own Place*, Chapel Hill, Algonquin, 1993, pp. 134-35.

[5] Clyde Edgerton, *Killer Diller*, Chapel Hill, Algonquin, 1991, p. 159.

[6] Cp. *In Memory of Junior*, pp. 139-42.

[7] Josephine Humphreys, *The Fireman's Fair*, New York, Viking, 1991.

[8] Paul Gray, "Real-Life Misery. Read All about It," *Time Magazine*, April 21, 1997, p.106.

[9] Eudora Welty, "Where Is the Voice Coming from?" *Collected Stories*, New York, Harcourt Brace Jovanovich, 1980, pp. 603-607.

[10] Madison Jones, *Nashville 1864: The Dying of the Light*, Nashville, J. S. Sanders & Company, 1997.

[11] Letter to me of December 5, 1996.

[12] Robert Benson, "All Flinders Now," *The Sewanee Review* 105/4 (Oct.-Dec. 1997) cxxii-cxxv.

The Existential South

CHAPTER ELEVEN

Southern Silence?: A. R. Ammons, James Dickey, and Donald Justice

The chapter has its origin in a paper "Southern Silence?: A Development in Southern Poetry" that I gave in a workshop on silence and literature at the meeting of the European Association for American Studies in Luxembourg in March 1994. A version of the essay was published in Semantics of Silences in Linguistics and Literature, *eds. Gudrun Grabher and Ulrike Jessner, Heidelberg, Universitätsverlag C. Winter, 1996.*

Southern Silence?

The traditional entertainment in the South is talking. Due to politics the nineteenth century Southern mind was mostly turned inward towards its own self-destructive society. But it was a community attitude and did not reduce the noise level of everyday life. Silence was considered a terrifying state to be in. The threat of silence to a mind such as Edgar Allan Poe's was a threat of chaos loosed upon a world sustained by words. In 1827 Poe wrote a story he called "Silence – A Fable." It contains a description of a man who is caught in a place without "any shadow of sound":

> And mine eyes fell upon the countenance of the man, and his countenance was wan with terror. And, hurriedly, he raised his head from his hand, and stood forth upon the rock and listened. But there was no voice throughout the vast illimitable desert, and the characters upon the rock were SILENCE. And the man shuddered, and turned his face away, and fled afar off, in haste, so that I beheld him no more.[1]

Southerners have always lived in a "world of words," as Poe wrote in his poem, "Al Aaraaf," with neither quiet nor silence. The sound of silence has always startled the Southern ear. Silence is experienced as an unnatural absence. Exactly a hundred years after Poe's comments on silence, Allen Tate voiced a similar fear of silence in "Ode to the Confederate Dead" (1927):

> You hear the shout, the crazy hemlocks point
> With troubled fingers to the silence which
> Smothers you, a mummy, in time. (ll. 53-55)

The smothering is made obvious in the two last lines by the missing or "silent stress," as Philip Davies Roberts called it.[2] The shout heard by the man at the cemetery wall is both that of rebels charging during the Civil War and his own shout of desperation. He is a typical man of our time, and in his isolation he is smothered. Without anyone to talk to, he is reduced to the state of being "a mummy, in time." In the presence of the silence of the dead Confederates even time dissolves.

Southerners have always talked – continuously, and given the slightest opportunity they still speak to the source of their pleasure in the world. It is an oral and aural culture rather than a print culture. The everyday life is more public and interactive than private and reflective. Southern society is loud. Silence does not have much of a chance among the Confederates of today. Instead words are welcomed and savored like old friends. Words are the joy and possible escape from reality. The mere recitation of a poem may work as an exorcism of all that could possibly be a threat. The sound is used to impose unity and reassuring familiarity on everything that suggests change, contingency, and the passing of time itself. Whereas silence would serve only too obviously as a reminder of time passing. Poems, stories, and talk impose order and direction on the apparently accidental nature of an often disappointing existence. Sound seems to be a means to improve the quality of life for a while. The constant chattering away fills the void with sound and may serve to dissemble, to mask, to hide, so the individual does not have to reveal her true self by saying what she really thinks. The sound may offer oblique communication only, but at least it sounds like communication and participation.

Our identity is by necessity relational. We need someone as a mirror in our attempt at defining ourselves, so we listen and identify with our listeners. It seems that the only thing that gives our existence a momentary individual existence is the uttering and repetition of sound. Only in the identification with the group, and in the repeated exposure to the sound of the group, is the hope for immortality. We may then question whether we are mastering our present through sound, or really trapped in and mastered by sound. George Steiner thought the latter is the case. He asked if we "are not writing too much, whether the deluge of print in which we seek our deafened way is not itself a subversion of meaning.... In how much of what is now pouring forth do words become word – and where is the silence needed if we are to hear the metamorphosis."[3]

In the South silence is not accepted as having the redeeming qualities of sound. This is apparent in the Southern literary tradition. Southern writers seem to have been worried about allowing even a moment of silence in their compositions. Traditionally they have chosen to include obviously meaningless words, empty words, and superfluous lines rather than allowing a moment of silence to creep in on the reader or listener. A reason for it is, of course, that knee-high in tall tales, narrative poems, family legends, sentimental pastorals, family legends, or just personal memories most Southerners know that what they communicate is not only entertainment, but also instruction. The ceaseless flow of sound is the process by which a sense of the past is integrated with the sense of place. In general Southerners know they can deal better with experience, and do more justice to reality, by reading a poem out loud, or by telling a story (which may be the same) than by discussing problems, dreaming up silent plans, and proposing abstractions. In his essay, "Solzhenitsyn as Southerner," Marion Montgomery sums up the lingering Agrarian argument in these words: "storytelling becomes for the Southerner his homage to the largeness of reality, as well as a means of resisting deformations of reality by abstractionism."[4]

This is the everyday tradition and reality. But if we look at changes in Southern literary history during the last thirty years, we will see an interesting development. Since the 1920s the South has been the center of American literary activity. Its poetry and fiction prove beyond doubt that good writing is preeminently provincial and springs from a definite period and a specific locality. If we define renaissance as "an impressive flowering of letters," it seems to me that the Southern literary renaissance has gone through at least three phases. The first began in the early 1920s with the famed "backward glance" and can be said to have ended with Mrs. Rosa Parks' refusal to go to the back of the bus in December, 1955. Most of the literature from the period showed a struggle to arrest the disintegration of memory and history.

The first phase was the result of social and economic change in the South. The second phase came when the South was caught up in social upheavals precipitated be desegregation efforts. After 1955 the South was exclusively preoccupied with civil rights questions, and so were Southern writers. In *The Death of Art*, Floyd C. Watkins demonstrated that most of the literature written in the South between 1955 and 1968 was one-sided, narrow-minded, and often sentimental. Blacks and whites could not be seen as human beings in the literature of the period. Today it is difficult to believe the many portraits of Christ-like blacks and satanic whites, or vice-versa. The static of the chattering voices is overwhelming.

The Vietnam War was not good for anything; Southern literature is a possible exception. When the trend of the headlines all over the world shifted from racial issues to the Vietnam War, it became possible for a generation of Southern writers to write quality literature again. The third phase of the renaissance left the sociological focus behind. The social and political topics suddenly seemed outdated. Instead the focus shifted from the community to the individual. The general tendency in Southern literature after 1968 has been a concern with loneliness and the disintegration of minds, lives, marriages, families, relationships, and communities.

The shifts in emphasis from the shared preoccupation with history and myth to racial politics, and then to the relative silence of isolation and existentialist concerns are manifest in the poetry of A. R. Ammons, James Dickey, Donald Justice, and Robert Penn Warren.[5] (In parenthesis let me add that I consider the third phase over by 1982. We are now in the fourth phase which takes its point of departure in women's politics. And Southern literature is once again caught up in propaganda for "a worthy cause.")

Real people abound in James Dickey's poetry, often named and always felt as *physical* human beings. He is a positive poet from Georgia (for many years he has lived in South Carolina) who sees existence as a workable proposition. Beginning with the celebrated poem called "The Performance," collected in *Into the Stone* (1960), Dickey wrote several poems, among them "Falling" (1967), in which he tries to establish a connection with dead people, such as a pilot beheaded by the Japanese and a stewardess who at thirty thousand feet falls out of a plane. The subject did not lead Dickey to a use of silence in his technique.

But certain things are left unsaid in unmarked gaps in the poems. In "The Performance" gaps occur in connection with changes in perspective.

Dickey's vision is of the pilot, he calls him Armstrong, making a handstand beside his grave. It is a final performance in the face of a grotesque death. The personal extinction that threatens him seems for a moment unimportant as Armstrong expresses his own nobility in making a perfect handstand (for the first time). The act is graceful. Performed for its own sake it becomes a value in itself. Armstrong's last stand has a strong impact because his performance (on his hands) shows a calm acceptance of death.

The poem is made up of only five sentences that can be grouped in three sections. The first section (ll. 1-16) is an account of the narrator's last sight of Armstrong. Then there is an obvious "Leerstelle," as Wolfgang Iser would call it, as the perspective changes. The second section (ll. 17-25) states that the very next day Armstrong was beheaded and buried in a grave he had dug himself. As it is the tradition in the classic ballad much information is withheld and the narrative seems gapped. The section reads as a lacking reconstruction made from available random information. Yet, it reads as fragments of someone's eyewitness report. The third and final section (ll. 26-48) comes after another gap in the poem. The perspective changes back to the original narrator. But if the first section was observed, and the second based on months-old information, the third section is the work of the secondary imagination. The few known facts of the execution itself do not give meaning to a life cut short in this manner. In order to put the inhumanity of war into perspective Dickey needs to rewrite Armstrong's death so it will transcend the limitations of time. In the poem the pilot transcends death by making an impression on the executioner, the pilot makes the encounter a personal one (ll. 37-42). In the same way James Dickey establishes a bond of humanity with the dead performer through his own performance, which is the writing of the poem.

When the poem is read aloud by the poet, which I have heard, it is obvious that the text is much less stable than it appears to the silent reader of the printed poem. Dickey makes pauses, some unexpected, that imply meaning and interpretation. The apparently simple and straight-forward poem changes meaning with the changing distribution of silent – or heard, or read – gaps in "The Performance."

It is, of course, a bit of a paradox that the Southern celebration of the oral tradition, or just the spoken word, is now mostly seen and not heard. The poetry we encounter is mostly written down, and a part of the effect on us is the visual impression of the lay-out of the print. And the visual impression creates meaning. The ceaseless stream of sound, the luxuriant spillage of things in the world, is now held, fixed by black type on a white page. The disadvantage is the absence of sound and the meanings inherent in breath pauses and modulations of sound. The advantage of poetry as a written art is the instant recognition of conventional forms and with them long traditions in the history of poetry. The visual format "functions as a poetic effect," as Richard Bradford has put it.[6] And the reader has a better chance to interact with the written poem, simply because it remains present in front of us. – Apparently, the most obvious difference between the vocal and the visual pattern is the seeming finality of the printed word. Supposedly the meaning of the spoken sound is changing and not finally determined. But attention to a number of silent and unmarked gaps in Dickey's poem makes it clear that the printed poem is finally just as unstable as the poem in oral performance. We do not see or hear the same poem.

Unlike James Dickey, Donald Justice has only recently become recognized as an important poet. He now lives in his native Florida. His *Selected Poems* (1980) won him a Pulitzer Prize. He has published little. As he admits in "The Telephone Number of the Muse," – the muse:

> Rebuttoning her nightgown, says:
> "Sorry, I just have no desire, it seems."
> Sighing? "For you, I mean." Long silence. Then:
> "You always were so serious."

The muse is right. But the poem is proof that when Donald Justice calls his muse, she still knows his voice. Even though he "can hear, / Beyond the music of her phonograph, / The laughter of the young men with their keys." Justice's characteristics are a sense of form and a tone of understatement. But not everything is understated. In "Unflushed Urinals" (*Selected Poems*, 1979) he wrote:

> Seeing them, I recognize the contempt
> Some men have for themselves.
> This man, for instance, zipping quickly up, head turned,
> Like a bystander innocent of his own piss.

Justice's subjects are basic emotional themes, far removed from Dickey's dramatic world. Justice writes about love and friendship, grief and loss. He is especially concerned with the loss of his childhood world, which is the topic of "First Death" (*Selected Poems*). The poem appears to have only few gaps. So it is predictable, and maybe even boring. Its forty-eight lines are easily paraphrased. June 12, 1933, a boy sees his grandmother die. The mystery and rituals of death terrify him. He feels isolated. The next day he hides in an abandoned Ford and tries to escape the present through the use of his imagination. On the third and final day of the poem, the boy participates in the burial. The boy feels oppressed by the heat, the ritual, and the fact that the service does not seem to comfort or console anyone.

The poem is a narrative with a beginning, middle, and end. It has all the characteristics of a short story. Events in the poem have been selected from many other omitted events. The silence on the implied events enhances the poem, so the emphasis can remain on the child's reactions to his first encounter with death. In general the poem does not need any explication. Complication is apparent when religion is allowed to intrude on the boy's sensibility: "The Void grew pregnant with the Word" (l. 8). The line seems to offer a disjunction open for interpretation. But if we decide to fill the gap (there is no need to fill all gaps – except for Southerners) this cannot be done subjectively, as the obvious structuring of the whole forces us to see that the line simply refers to the adding of the grandmother's name in the family Bible.

The only two lines that indicate a void crying out to be filled are the last lines of the second section:

> And when I touched the silent horn
> Small mice scattered through the corn. (ll. 31-32)

It seems strange that the mice should react to the silence of the "dead" horn, as if it were a frightening noise. The lines bring out the boy's suppressed emotional turmoil. It is the only place in the poem where the significance of the absent expression of his grief is indicated. He may simply be projecting his own terror on to his surroundings. But such an explanatory reading is simply this reader's attempt at filling a gap. – Maybe we should be more reluctant to do that and with Susan Sontag pay more attention to silence, let it speak, and work as a purifying and positive agent.[7] The last lines of the poem read:

> There was a buzzing on the sill.
> It stopped, and everything was still.
> We bowed our heads, we closed our eyes
> To the mercy of the flies.

Donald Justice has also written poems that belong much more obviously to the existentialist phase of the Southern renaissance, e.g. "Fragment: To a Mirror." In the poem he looks at the world – of which he is a fragment – in a mirror and discovers that everything has come "To a sudden inexplicable halt." The persona's reaction is a question which ends the poem:

> Tell me,
> Is this the promised absence I foresee
> In you, where no breath any more shall stir
> The surface of the sleeping pond,
> And you shall have back your rest at last,
> Your half of nothingness?

I read these lines as Justice's rejection of an afterlife that promises to be nothing, just nothingness. If death is meaningless, so is life. It will be a parallel (a mirror) of our present existence in a dead world. Life is nothing, so dying would just be like adding our "half of nothingness" to the one that awaits us, and there will be nothing to reflect. In his poem "The Missing Person," Donald Justice suggests that what we may finally see in the mirror is our own missing person emerging from a room furnished only by darkness. Justice says it will be years before we can trust ourselves to the light in our "last disguise."

Both James Dickey and Donald Justice write in the Southern tradition of perpetual sound. They may be slow noise makers at times, but they are hardly ever really silent. This is not necessarily true of North Carolina poet A. R. Ammons. It is true that he has made the extended movement a characteristic of his poetry. He regulates his verse by the colon, a mark he has made his, as Emily Dickinson made the dash hers, and Walt Whitman at the beginning of his career made the ellipsis his. Ammons's colon connects and joins what may appear to be separate phenomena so that closure seems perpetually suspended.[8] But in spite of his use of the colon, Ammons is much more likely than Dickey and Justice to express himself by suppressing, suspending, and dissolving time through silence.

Talk that allows language to get too far from "the concrete" usually allows it to die within itself. In the poem written on a calculator strip of paper, "Tape for the Turn of the Year," Ammons admonishes himself: "get out of boxes, hard/ forms of mind:/ go deep:/ penetrate/ to the true spring," which illustrates the impulse behind his best poetry. It is only in his choice of topics that Ammons seems severely limited. Almost no people appear in his poems – no other people – therefore the range of emotions is also limited, mostly, to the emotions of the poet. We read about his joy, his disappointment, and his fears. But where are the passions that involve other people, such as love and pity?

Ammons's "Hardweed Path Going" is a traditional initiation poem. It is about a boy who grows up, also emotionally. At hog-killing time he has to accept that a measure of callousness is necessary to survive among adults. This is the hardweed or grown-up path that everybody must walk. – It is a straightforward narrative poem told as a memoir. The boy's desperation when the cold weather comes, and the killing of his favorite hog is imminent, is not articulated fully. It is most obvious in the ruptured lines:

> Doom caving in
> inside
> any pleasure, pure
> attachment
> of love. (ll. 41-45)

This is one of those moments in poetry when the irony of anyone hoping to find more significance in sound than in silence becomes obvious.[9] Why should noise convey the inexpressible emotions better than silence. Ammons's lines state that in the grown-up world no pleasure exists that is not doomed to cave in. Maybe Ammons also says that this is even true for "the true attachment of love." The lines seem to hide more than they communicate, they represent the necessity of the boy's withdrawal into silence. The words come from a boy who feels he will now "go dry in [his] well" and "will turn still." The suppression of his true rage against the bitter knowledge of adulthood is brought out in the typography and could not be expressed better than Ammons does in reducing language to a minimum. In poems such as "Visit" and "Unsaid" Ammons is further from the preoccupations with memory, and more an existentialist poet of the third phase of the Southern renaissance than he is in "Hardweed Path Going." In "Visit" he talks of the "dense reserve/of silence we can poise against/ conversation": – and Ammons's "Unsaid" seems to have been written for this chapter. It opens with these lines:

> Have you listened for the things I have left out?
> I am nowhere near the end yet and already
> > hear
> > the hum of omissions,
> the chant of vacancies, din of
> silences: (ll. 1-6)

On the other hand Ammons points out that we should really hear him *when he is silent*. That is the time to "gather the boundaried vacancies." It is not because "words *cannot* say/ what is missing: it is only that what is missing/ cannot/ be missed if/ spoken" (ll. 25-29).

With the growing realization by modern writers from Anton Chekhov to Samuel Beckett of the difficulty of effective verbal communication, silence has become an obvious presence and a necessary function in contemporary literature. In spite of the Southern fear from Edgar Allan Poe to Allen Tate of the absence of sound, silence has, as a means of communication, gained the status of meaningful speech in poetry by questioning modern Southern existentialists.

1. Edgar Allan Poe, "Silence – A Fable," *Collected Works of –*, ed. Thomas Ollive Mabbott, Cambridge, Mass., Harvard University Press, 1978, pp. 195-200.

2. Philip Davies Roberts, *How Poetry Works: The Elements of English Poetry*, Penguin, 1986, pp. 22-23.

3. George Steiner, "Silence and the Poet, *Language and Silence: Essays on Language, Literature, and the Inhuman*, New York, Atheneum, 1967, pp. 53-54.

4. *Why the South Will Survive, by Fifteen Southerners*, ed. Clyde N. Wilson, Athens, Ga., The University of Georgia Press, 1981, p. 177.

5. Ammons, A. R. *Collected Poems, 1951-1971*. New York, W. W. Norton & Company, 1972. James Dickey, *Poems 1957-1967*. London, Rapp & Carroll, 1967. Donald Justice, *Selected Poems*. New York, Atheneum, 1983.

6. Richard Bradford, *Silence and Sound: Theories of Poetics from the Eighteen Century*, London, Fairleigh Dickinson University Press, 1992, p. 180.

7. Susan Sontag, *Styles of Radical Will*, New York, Delta, 1978, pp. 3-34.

8. Stephen Cushman, *Fictions in American Poetry*, New Jersey, Princeton University Press, 1993, p. 186.

9. Cp. J. A. Ward, *American Silences: The Realism of James Agee, Walker Evans, and Edward Hopper*, Baton Rouge, Louisiana State University Press, 1985, p. 9.

CHAPTER TWELVE

Eudora Welty's Existential Statement

The chapter is on Eudora Welty's existentialism as it is expressed in her novel The Optimist's Daughter. *It seems to me that Miss Welty gives pretty good answers to Allen Tate's despairing questions in his "Ode to the Confederate Dead," which was the subject of my first chapter. The basic idea in chapter twelve was already present in my talk "Eudora Welty and Flannery O'Connor," which I delivered at Old Salem College, North Carolina, in the spring of 1978. The immediate predecessor of this chapter is "Old Mount Salus Blues" in my* Eudora Welty's Aesthetics of Place *(1994; paper 1997).*

Eudora Welty's Existential Statement

> *The headstones yield their names to the element,*
> *The wind whirrs without recollection;*
> Allen Tate "Ode to the Confederate Dead"

The first forty-five pages of *The Optimist's Daughter* take place in New Orleans, but that city is "out-of-town" to all the characters of the short novel. A New Orleans hospital is experienced by Laurel McKelva Hand as "a nowhere." She looks out of a hospital window and sees what could have been "the rooftops of any city." She sees a "dull" bridge in the distance, but the river itself is not visible (*OD*, 3, 14). Laurel approaches her problems and tries to focus on them through her sensory, in particular her visual, experience of place. At a critical moment for her father, who is a patient, she looks out of the hospital window and sees "the whole Mississippi River Bridge in lights." It is at night and she cannot see the river, which is what she needed to see to restore her sense of place and sense of reality. Although three full weeks of the action, most of the plot time by far, have been placed in New Orleans during the Mardi Gras Carnival, the novel is psychologically never of the city.

Scenes of small-town life in Mount Salus, which is Laurel's hometown, dominate *The Optimist's Daughter*. The *salus* of the town's name is the name of an old Roman goddess often associated with the Greek Hygieia, who personified health. And, as Welty wrote in a review of a book on place-names, "what facts are closer to people, more revealing of people's hearts, than the names they bestow?"[1] Just how healthy Mount Salus is, or is not, is one of the questions the novel raises. Laurel now lives and works as a textile designer in Chicago. To her old friends in Mount Salus, the city she now calls home seems remote and even somewhat unreal. Laurel has come south because her father Judge McKelva is hospitalized, seriously ill with an eye disease. After three weeks he dies in the hospital. His body is brought back on the New Orleans-Chicago train through the black swamp, past the cypresses outside the crescent city, and across Lake Pontchartrain to be buried in Mount Salus, Mississippi.

As Reynolds Price pointed out when it was first published, the novel demonstrates an "apparent lack of concern with Mississippi's major news at the time of the action – the civil rights revolution. Its apparent absence is as complete as that of the Napoleonic wars from Jane Austen."[2] Price emphasizes *apparent* because forms of dimmed vision and blindness are examined in the novel. Welty makes sure that Tom Farris, Mount Salus's blind piano tuner, is on hand for the open-coffin scene in the McKelva House and for the service in the cemetery. He attends all funerals in town. Blindness is an appropriate metaphor for much that was going on at the time of the composition of *The Optimist's Daughter*, and the novel won Welty a Pulitzer Prize. The early version of the novel appeared as a long short story in *The New Yorker*, March 15, 1969. It had been worked on during 1967, the year of great racial riots in American cities. The following year Dr. Martin Luther King, Jr. was assassinated in Memphis, and racial riots broke out again in the cities. Racial issues are nevertheless quite unimportant in *The Optimist's Daughter*. There is little about blacks and their situation in the novel. Missouri, a black domestic, behaves with the loyalty Laurel expects, and she gets little attention. At the funeral "Black Mount Salus had come too, and the black had dressed themselves in black." But Laurel seems to take this for granted and is not particularly grateful to them for their tribute to their old benefactor.

A much longer version appeared as a novel in March, 1972. This was when Haiphong and Hanoi were being bombed, and when the Vietnam War had been the burning national issue for at least seven years. War as such is unimportant in the novel. When Welty mentions a war in *The Optimist's Daughter*, it is not the Vietnam War, but the war in the Pacific during WW II. As in most of her fiction no political crusading appears in the novel. Although the problems that surface in Mount Salus have little to do with major political topics of the day, the town is there as a container of all that was ever experienced in that place, including the prejudice and blindness that lead to racism and war. In that sense history is always present in Welty's fiction. In "Place in Fiction" she puts it in these words: "place in history partakes of feeling, as feeling about history partakes of place" (*ES*, 122). Welty's concerns in writing about Laurel Hand in (imaginary) Mount Salus, Mississippi, are as eternal and universal as those of Jane Austen writing about Elizabeth Bennet in the (imaginary) village of Longbourn in Hertfordshire.

Mount Salus is a town where families have known each other for generations. The town seems to be bigger than the town of Clay, which is the setting of *The Ponder Heart*. Mount Salus is probably about the size of Morgana in *The Golden Apples*, and like Clay and Morgana it houses a tradition-oriented and class-conscious community. The McKelvas are of the upper-class in Mount Salus. Among their ancestors they count a Confederate general and a Presbyterian missionary to China. It is significant that Dr. Nate (Nathaniel?) Courtland, who operates on Judge Clinton McKelva's slipping retina in the New Orleans hospital, is of the Courtlands of Mount Salus. He is clearly evaluated as a doctor on his family background. The Courtlands' cowshed could be seen from the McKelvas' backyard. The seventy-one-year old patient tells his new wife Wanda Fay that he is in good hands and adds: "I know his whole family" (*OD*, 11). Dr. Courtland is a guileless man. Laurel observes that "the Mississippi country that lay behind him" is all in his face (*OD*, 9). Judge McKelva had helped finance his education in medical school. Dr. Courtland promises Laurel to give her father "extra-special care," and Welty shows that he makes a special effort for his old friend, the former mayor of Mount Salus. The doctor had also treated Becky Thurston McKelva, Laurel's mother, who died ten years earlier. The portrait of Dr. Courtland is complex. He loses his patient, but seems more interested in evaluating the success of the operation.

Laurel, who is now in her mid-forties, no longer feels at ease as a member of the Mount Salus upper-class. Among her old friends she senses the unspoken accusation: why did she leave for Chicago after her mother's death when Judge McKelva needed her in Mount Salus? After all she was "The Only Child," which was the title of an early manuscript of this novel.[3] Ironically, it is Fay, her new stepmother, who in her dislike of Laurel voices the general accusation: "Oh, I wouldn't have run off and left anybody that needed me. Just to call myself an artist and make a lot of money" (*OD*, 28). This is echoed by the slightly drunk Major Rupert Bullock during an open-coffin scene. He silences Laurel's objections to the exaggerated stories about her father by telling her, "Honey, you were away. You were sitting up yonder in Chicago, drawing pictures" (*OD*, 80). After her wedding in the Mount Salus Presbyterian Church, built by the McKelvas, Laurel had left town for good in order to live her own life with her husband Phil Hand, who was an architect.

In her hometown Laurel has come to feel that she is an outsider. She has severed herself from her native place and has ambivalent feelings about it. The McKelva House is no longer "home" in the sense that it provides the foundation of Laurel's identity, and Mt. Salus no longer furnishes her with an identity as a member of the community. These feelings and the sad occasion for her visit are the reasons why she has no sense of homecoming upon seeing Mount Salus again. Her father had also married a stranger. Twice he had gone away and brought home a wife, but he always lived in his hometown. One of the unwritten laws of Mount Salus life seems to be that when you marry and move out of town, you not only marry a stranger, but also a new place; especially if your new home is out-of-state. And Laurel's marriage has been brief and not belonging to Mount Salus. Phil Hand, who served on a mine-sweeper in the Pacific during WW II, was killed in a *kamikaze* attack just six weeks after he had married Laurel. Her tragic loss of a husband gets little attention in her hometown. These events also get little space in the novel. But her loss of Phil is a constant presence in Laurel's mind.

Now that she is a widow, people in Mount Salus cannot understand why she does not return immediately to her house, her past, and her town – back where she belongs. Mount Salus would like to reabsorb her. By mentioning the old rose bush Laurel's mother once planted by the McKelva House, Miss Tennyson Bullock tries to convince Laurel to return to Mount Salus: "You still might change your mind if you could see the roses bloom, see Becky's Climber come out." Laurel responds, "I can imagine it, in Chicago," but Miss Tennyson argues that the roses, whose root is a hundred years old, cannot be smelled there (*OD*, 113-14). As Miss Tennyson is not answered, except possibly by the obvious connotations of her name, Welty seems to support her argument. Mount Salus can only be imagined in Chicago; and Mount Salus would not even consider imagining Chicago.

In a subconscious realization of her emotional vulnerability Laurel has cut herself off from her native community by not facing the past, both her own and that of her parents. Her period of finding her own self in Chicago has made her so self-related that her communion with Mount Salus has been lost. She is as alienated and estranged from the past and mortality as the man at the gate in Allen Tate's poem "Ode to the Confederate Dead." The wall that separates Laurel from the dead is her own inability to accept the "arrogant circumstance," the convictions, that made her parents live and die the way they did. She is in despair without fully realizing it.

The past is "immoderate" in that it devours Laurel's present. Although the troubled woman intuitively knows the whole truth about her parents and herself, i.e. has "knowledge/ Carried to the heart," she is not ready to accept that knowledge. In her isolation, alienation, and emotional poverty Laurel is very much a woman of our century. Welty seems to answer the question Allen Tate raised: is it possible for a solipsistic sceptic of today to draw any strength from her history and tradition by defining, reviving, and repossessing the past?[4] At the end of the brief visit to her hometown Laurel pins "her hair up for Chicago," steps back into her high-heeled city shoes, says good-bye to Mount Salus, probably for the last time, and heads back to a life in a South Side apartment and to her job. Her present project is to design a theater curtain.

At its best the novel becomes a part of Welty's aesthetics of place by questioning one of the old verities of the Southern community: does the past live in the present, and if so, does it enrich present lives? *The Optimist's Daughter* is about the difficulty of being honest and unsentimental about the past and the people who represent it. It is about the necessity of coming to terms with the past, both the public community myth of the past and the immediate private family past. This discussion presupposes that a community is still in Mount Salus, but that is uncertain in the novel. The town still has a framework of accepted codes that makes even death tolerable. As the present mayor of Mount Salus points out, a lot is done in town to show Judge McKelva respect: the "bank's closed, most of the Square's agreed to close for the hour of services, county offices closed. Courthouse has lowered its flag out front, school's letting out early" (*OD*, 69). The mayor adds that he has modeled himself on the deceased and calls the judge a "noble Roman." This phrase, which is obviously meant as great praise, invokes the old Stoic South.

The Greco-Roman tradition of Marcus Aurelius, Seneca, and Epictetus was the main ethos of the well-educated planter class of Mississippi up to WW II.

A Stoic will do "the right thing" in most situations, not because he expects to be rewarded for his efforts, but because he has to consider his own integrity. Virtues like honor, honesty, truthfulness, and justice are considered ends in themselves. The Stoic elements in Judge McKelva's mental make-up were demonstrated when he helped others in the community by paying for their uniforms, church, or medical education, or by protecting and even hiding them, without regard for race, creed, or social standing. His actions as a leading citizen of Mount Salus make him appear a patriarchal, stoic gentleman in the Mississippi tradition of William Alexander Percy, as set forth in his bestselling autobiography *Lanterns on the Levee* (1941).[5] In theory it makes the judge the natural antithesis of the materialistic, uncultured, self-serving, poor-white Chisoms.[6]

A community of mourners seems to be waiting to bury Judge McKelva, but the youngest generation is not present. The old Mount Salus community, as it is presented, consists of the surviving contemporaries of Laurel's parents, who still live near the McKelva House, and a few of her own school friends. Many of the latter have moved to the new parts of town. Their children have left Mount Salus to go to school, or have left town for good. One of Laurel's friends, one of her bridesmaids, has a son of fifteen who is still at home. But he lives there as if he were a stranger in the house. The young man has a girlfriend, and his life is not oriented toward collective community values. He has no interest in attending public events. He seems unaware of any connection between individual and community identity, and he does not come to Judge McKelva's funeral.

When Laurel was growing up in Mount Salus, the physical setting still shaped social interaction. The relationship between place and social place has weakened considerably in the town she is visiting. For the young generation there is now a dissociation, so that their behavior is no longer determined or defined by their physical presence in the town. Welty seems to suggest that the next generation will grow up without a feeling for place and without the steadying point of place to focus their minds. The community is changing rapidly, and it is becoming fragmented. A sense of self is no longer necessarily ingrained with a sense of community, and in as far as a social order is present, it is becoming impersonal and increasingly technological. As Joshua Meyrowitz has shown in his *No Sense of Place*, the physical location is hardly ever the social place in our world of electronic media.[7] There is no sense of a continuity between the past and the present of the community, and knowledge of the past does not inform and give meaning to the present. Personal relations in the Mount Salus community are obviously decaying, and family relationships are weakening. That this is representative of a national trend is, surprisingly, brought out in the description of the disintegration of Becky's idealized West Virginia mountain family. Becky's brothers "moved down the mountain into town, into the city, and the banjo player ... had turned into a bank official"

(*OD*, 152). And only one of her brothers had come for Becky's funeral in Mississippi.

Judge Clinton McKelva is buried in the new part of the Mount Salus Cemetery with an excellent view of the new interstate highway and the trucks roaring by. What is probably more important to the widow is that her husband is buried in a choice plot, if you want people on the road to notice the grave with its indestructible plastic Christmas Poinsettias. Laurel and her Mount Salus friends had no doubt that the judge would be put to rest under Chandelerii Elegans, his favorite camellia, next to Laurel's mother in the old part of the cemetery and with the other McKelvas. But his widow Wanda Fay McKelva, née Chisom, insists on burying her husband in the new part of the cemetery.

Although Laurel is met by some of her parents' friends and some of her own old schoolmates, she finds that her childhood home and her hometown have changed beyond recognition. Her disorientation and feeling of estrangement in Mount Salus are results of a general cultural displacement. The contrasting of city and small town does not mean, however, that the latter is seen in a positive light only. The ladies of the community are less than genteel in their outspoken censure of Laurel and her marriage. In such passages the novel becomes more than an excuse to indulge in a hilarious and touching tale of a Mississippi funeral. Welty outlines cultural change in the contemporary South and makes it clear that the disagreement over the choice of burial plot is just one expression of a profound disagreement between genteel and poor white Southerners about the past, traditions, and their importance for the present community. The reason why this becomes a vital part of the novel is that Welty criticizes and supports both parties in the discussion.

The Chisoms are from Madrid, Texas, where they operate a wrecking business. But like the Dalzells, a family Laurel observed in the hospital in New Orleans, the Chisoms are of "good old Mississippi stock," and proud of it. Fay's brother, called Bubba, wears a windbreaker throughout the ceremony. He seems to have come to the funeral to eat. Mrs. Chisom is loud and obese. The tow-headed, bony, feist-jawed, blue-veined, and country-blue-eyed Wanda Fay, who is younger than Laurel, initially claims that she has no family and has to depend on herself: "None of 'em living. That's why I ever left Texas and came to Mississippi" (*OD*, 27). Later when she sees all the friends of the McKelvas gathered in the house, Fay adds: "Well, it's evermore unfair. I haven't got anybody to count on but me, myself, and I" (*OD*, 54). But Fay has quite an extensive family, as Laurel finds out, and they are good Anglo-Saxon rednecks. Fay did not invite her family to attend the funeral of Judge McKelva, but her late husband's friend Major Bullock did, because the judge had requested it shortly before he died. And suddenly the Chisoms arrive in their pickup truck and are all over the McKelva House. Unlike the McKelvas, the Chisoms are not dying out.

Laurel is shocked by Fay's lie about her family and tells her so. She cannot accept Fay's ideas about family, and she cannot understand the pride Fay takes in being entirely on her own. Fay is convinced that everybody lies about their family, and lying them dead is not the worst lie she has heard (*OD*, 99). Laurel probably realizes that Fay is referring to the obvious lies told at the funeral to glorify Judge McKelva. As it turns out Fay is just as attached to her family as Laurel is to hers, maybe even more. After the funeral Fay feels the need to return to Texas with her family, so that for a couple of days she could be with people who talk her language – or maybe it is just to make sure that they leave. She knows that they will tell her if they do not want her to go back with them, because the members of *her* family are not hypocrites, she claims. The difference between Laurel and Fay has finally little to do with the way they feel about family. The difference is mainly in their social standing and in the way they feel about where they are and the past of that place.

A clash between social classes is important in several of Welty's communities and usually implies a fairly obvious social criticism. In *Delta Wedding* the class distinction between the Fairchilds and the Reids or Flavins gets some attention, in *The Golden Apples* the social difference between the Starks and the Mac-Lains is important in several of the stories, and in *Losing Battles* the Moodys clearly feel superior to the Beecham-Renfros. Class is certainly not a new topic in Welty's fiction, but it is in *The Optimist's Daughter* that the clash between social classes becomes a dominant theme. After the funeral it is Sis Chisom, the grieving widow's fertile sister, who tries to comfort Laurel by telling her that Judge McKelva had been "just plain *folks*." This is exactly what Laurel will not admit, not even to herself. Mrs. Chisom shocks genteel Mount Salus by proposing that the McKelva House be changed into a boarding house. The symbolism is heavy-handed. It is obvious that the Old South is being taken over by ill-bred poor whites, who have absolutely no regard for history and traditions.

On her last day in the McKelva House Laurel meets Mr. Cheek, the local carpenter. When Mr. Cheek observes that both of them are the last of their families and suggests that they "ought to get together," Laurel reacts to his good-natured small talk by angrily requesting Mr. Cheek's immediate departure (*OD*, 166). The carpenter observes that Laurel looks and sounds like her mother and makes his escape from the house. Laurel gets angry not only because Mr. Cheek lives up to the implications of his name, but also because he is insolent enough to suggest a connection between the Cheeks and the McKelvas, who are not of the same social class. The snobbish Laurel regards the mere suggesting of such a liaison as an insult. But there is more to this scene. I think Mr. Cheek's suggestion was primarily heard as a provocation because it served Laurel as a painful reminder that her father had married beneath him when he married Fay Chisom. Laurel has been brought up by her mother to be keenly aware of her social station in Mount Salus. When she returns for her father's funeral, she is not ready to accept the blurred class distinctions that she encounters. Laurel's comments on the Chisoms are not kind.

They seem to imply: this is what happens to you if you marry beneath you. But her comments seem ultimately to turn against herself.

We see both the poor white and genteel Mount Salus through Laurel's eyes, and her judgment is shaped by her existential problems and cannot be trusted. During her week-long stay in town we discover that she had been a poor judge of her father's taste. She decided to read Charles Dickens's *Nicholas Nickleby* to him during his final illness, but she comes to realize that she had read "the wrong book." (*OD*, 83). The judge would have preferred to hear her read from Edward Gibbon's *The Decline and Fall of the Roman Empire*, or even from Arthur Conan Doyle's stories of Sherlock Holmes, which are also in his library. She was wrong not only about her father's taste in reading. Laurel was shocked when he married a woman younger than herself, and she is incapable of understanding why he would pick somebody like Fay Chisom. The simplest explanation seems to be that the judge was not a snob, and not so much of a would-be spiritual aristocrat as his first wife and their daughter. It takes a bit of an optimist to marry a much younger woman late in life, and Judge McKelva obviously lusted for Fay. He seems to have been a man with a great appetite for life. And what Fay has to offer beyond her sex-appeal is vitality, spontaneity, and the desire to live fully in the moment.

Laurel finds it hard to accept her father's "common" inclinations. She has long banished certain characteristics of her father from her mind, blocked them from her consciousness, for it is a part of the Mount Salus past that she cannot accept. But, as John Edward Hardy puts it, "it is manifestly absurd to suppose ... that Fay entered the house uninvited, or changed anything in it to suit herself without her husband's approval."[8] The judge simply appreciated Fay the way she was. Just like Uncle Daniel Ponder in *The Ponder Heart*, who loved to indulge his young Bonnie Dee Peacock, the old judge "mightily enjoyed having him somebody to spoil." He let Fay have breakfast in bed, and he did not object when she redecorated the rooms in pink and peach colors and even quilted the mahogany headboard of the old McKelva bed in peach satin (*OD*, 59-60). Fay chooses "warm foolish pink" satin for the lining of her husband's coffin. Vulgar or not, Fay "gave a lonely old man something to live for," as Adele Courtland explains to the other ladies of Mount Salus.

Laurel's perspective offers a negative picture of Fay, not only as an individual with many egocentric comments on her husband's death, at least partly caused by herself, but also as an uncultured member of a lower class with "an awful taste." Laurel finds Fay common and lacking in decorum, dignity, integrity, and decency, and like many readers of the novel she remains puzzled by the flaw in her father that made him marry Fay. In a contest for the appellation "Welty's-most-thoroughly-vulgar-character" – for most readers Fay's only serious competition would be Leota, the beautician of "Petrified Man." It can be seen as a tribute to Welty's art that in his essay on the novel, Cleanth Brooks also ignores for a moment the fact that everything in *The Optimist's Daughter* is seen from Laurel's point of view – even if the story is told in the third person. Laurel's negative thoughts about Fay are so persuasive that Brooks is fully convinced. He labels Fay "a shallow little vulgarian," who may have come from "the Bronx or the Bay region of San Francisco," and he describes her as "cheap, self-centered, aggressive, and completely unmannerly."[9] Thomas Daniel Young calls her an "underbred," "crude and self-centered," woman, who is "oblivious of the past" and "as much unlike Laurel's mother (the first wife, Becky) as any human being could possibly be."[10]

In his essay on the novel John Edward Hardy unfairly sees Laurel's view of Fay as a change in Welty's attitude "toward the lower classes."[11] Hardy ignores the fact that much more than Laurel herself can realize is shown about her and the other characters. Laurel is far from being "an entirely 'reliable' central intelligence," as Ruth Vande Kieft calls her. (In fairness it should be emphasized that she undercuts her own statement through her use of quotation marks.[12]) What Laurel considers flaws in others may be flaws only when seen from her perspective and by her standards. She makes the dangerous assumption that Fay's "aesthetic inferiority necessitates moral inadequacy." Provoked by Fay's total disregard for all social conventions, critics make similar assumptions.[13] Most critics argue that even if Fay did not enter the McKelva House uninvited, she is there finally as Fay Chisom, "the negation," it seems, "of genuine emotions."[14] And it is, of course, true that no criticism of Laurel and her limited point of view will ever fully justify Fay and her ways. But it should be pointed out that Fay is as much a displaced person in Mount Salus as Becky McKelva was, or as Laurel has become. Little allowance is made by Laurel for the possibility that Fay is emotionally strained before, during, and after her husband's funeral. She is, after all, in a town that is blatantly hostile to her. She moves among people that show no inclination to allow her a sense of individual identity.

The novel is not a total condemnation of the Chisoms and their obvious lack of refinement. Welty tells us of the innocent and appealing toy-pistol-toting Wendell, Fay's seven-year-old nephew, and his Grandpa Chisom, who is as decent and as dignified as anybody in old Mount Salus. Old Mr. Chisom is genuinely sorry that Judge McKelva "had to go while he's so many miles short of home," and to comfort her he brings Laurel some Bigbee pecans, which he has hulled. What his grandchild Fay can offer is a zest for life. Unfortunately this vitality is not informed by any knowledge, or any desire for knowledge, of the place where she is or of its past. On the other hand her desire to live fully is not ruined or crippled by Laurel-like notions of the past.

The town gossip after the funeral reveals that the Chisoms are defended by at least one member of the community, i. e. Adele Courtland, who is the sister of Dr. Courtland, and originally of a poor background herself. She had known the judge better than most people in town and might even have hoped to become the second Mrs. McKelva. But she understands why the judge married

Fay. Adele Courtland sees the clash between two classes, but she is able to see something positive about the presence of the Chisoms. If it were up to the Mount Salus establishment, the McKelva House would probably become a public building, or maybe even a museum. But Fay is now the legal owner of the house, so it may be turned into the boarding house that Mrs. Chisom wants, and then it would at least be full of life. Welty offers no simplified truth, neither about the Chisoms nor about the traditionalists of Mount Salus.

Welty devotes much space in *The Optimist's Daughter* to the expression of an important Agrarian concern: the importance of the past for the present. It is clearly the main theme of the novel. The basic difference between Laurel and Fay comes out in their attitude to the past. Judge McKelva was the incarnation in Mount Salus of collective past experiences and of shared values. At the funeral Laurel is simply another mourner, although the judge was her father. She is an almost anonymous participant in the community's traditional rite venerating a prominent ancestor. He had known every mile of the county and everybody in the community. In his library he had kept civic papers from his years in office as mayor of Mount Salus, including those on the Big Flood. His own papers on floods and flood control are also there. His public office did not make him rich, and he did not inherit. He became free of financial worry when he came into "a little oil money" from a well on his old place in the country. He had loved the town and its people, but his town no longer studies his opinions. His writings are covered by dust, as Laurel observes. She concludes that the town did not deserve him, just as she is convinced that Fay did not deserve him. But if her father's values are not remembered, Laurel seems to be asking herself: whose values, and what values do the modern times go by in her native town? She obviously fears that the answer will depend on the Chisoms and their way of life.

The irony is that traditionalist Mount Salus is as unwilling to accept Laurel's new life as she is unwilling to accept Fay's ways. Laurel does not see the parallel. From the very beginning Fay makes it clear that she thinks little of the veneer of civility she is met with in Mount Salus. Ruth Vande Kieft claims that Fay "will destroy everything truly valuable in the house." Again, this means "valuable" seen from a traditionalist point of view.[15] In spite of the shallowness she demonstrates, Fay is not necessarily an unsympathetic character in her reaction against all that is imposed on her life as she becomes the second Mrs. McKelva. This is what makes the story of the confrontation between Laurel and Fay so unpredictable. Their motivations differ, of course, but Laurel and Fay do agree about one thing. They have no desire to become a new Becky McKelva and absolutely refuse to join the tradition-oriented, bridge-playing, garden-tending society of Mount Salus. Fay has no desire to become a custodian of a past that she does not consider hers.

Fay promises herself that the first thing she will get rid of will be the old McKelva clock in the parlor, which reminds her of passing time by striking every half hour. The clock had not been wound since Judge McKelva did it, but Laurel's bridesmaids, who apparently embody the continuity with the past, manage to wind it and start it again (*OD*, 93). When she brought her father's body to Mount Salus, Laurel was received at the station by her bridesmaids, and when she leaves town, on the last page of the novel, the bridesmaids are on hand to drive her to the plane. The six women exist in the novel as "the bridesmaids." Welty makes obvious their association with a fairy tale past by giving Becky McKelva's *six* brothers in her mythical account of her youth in West Virginia. As a girl of fifteen Becky had brought her father, who had suffered a ruptured appendix, by raft and train to Johns Hopkins Hospital in Baltimore, but she had not been able to save him. Laurel had been unable to do anything at all to save her father. She now feels she should try to preserve the memory of her father, as her mother had done through her stories for her father.

The new Mrs. McKelva has no interest in preserving anything of the past, not even the memory of it. By detailing the genteel version of the past in Mount Salus and by presenting this version as an intolerable burden on Laurel, Welty asks an unexpected question: should Fay be concerned about preserving the past? Fay's presence in the McKelva house is characterized by "the drops of nail varnish" she leaves on Judge McKelva's great-grandfather's writing desk, which was brought from Edinburgh when Mississippi was still a territory. As a true guardian of the past Laurel meticulously removes the drops of nail polish from the desk, and rubs and waxes the desk "until nothing was left to show of them" (*OD*, 123).

Laurel sees Fay's behavior as deliberate abuse of the house, the past, and the memory of Judge McKelva. In Laurel's mind the house and its objects from her childhood have become an accretion of sentiment, which makes up an important part of her identity. Her idea of self simply requires the past, as she sees it, in order for her to be able to deal with the present. Her passion for the past includes any tangible object that can support her sense of identity. She is enraged when she discovers that Fay has cracked walnuts with a hammer on a fine breadboard crafted by Phil Hand, as a "labor of love." The breadboard, which Laurel considers a repository of good memories, is now scored and grimy, splintered, full of gouges, gnawed, and blackened. Unlike the desk, the board cannot be rescued as a center of value. It is now a permanently defiled part of her past. The defaced state of the breadboard is, in Laurel's mind, the unmistakable proof that Fay is desecrating the house and the memory of the McKelva past. So far Laurel has spoken with a delicacy befitting her former station in Mount Salus, and she is not a violent woman, but at this point in the conversation she is tempted to hit Fay with the breadboard. Symbolically, she stops herself when she hears the McKelva clock in the parlor strike noon. She just holds on to the breadboard, as if it would "keep her from slipping down deep." The argument over the importance of the past is between genteel Mount Salus and its poor white newcomers. It is, as Robert Brinkmeyer has phrased it, between Laurel, who has been "a slave to the past," and Fay who is "a slave to the present" and unwilling to relate her present experience to anything in the past[16]:

> "I don't know what you're making such a big fuss over. What do you see in that thing?" asked Fay. "The whole story, Fay. The whole solid past," said Laurel. "Whose story? Whose past? Not mine," said Fay. "The past isn't a thing to me. I belong to the future, didn't you know that?" ... "I know you aren't anything to the past," [Laurel] said. "You can't do anything to it now." And neither am I; and neither can I, she thought, although it has been everything and done everything to me, everything for me. The past is no more open to help or hurt than was Father in his coffin. The past is like him, impervious, and can never be awakened. It is memory that is the somnambulist. (*OD*, 178-79)

This exchange starts a decisive development in Laurel's attitude to the past and to her own self. The crudity and meanness that come with Fay's willful rejection of family and community standards also descend on Laurel as long as she willfully blocks out an awareness of unromantic parts of her parents' past. She has been a stalwart guardian of the past with a monopoly in her own mind of a selective interpretation of it. In Allen Tate's words Laurel has "set up the grave/ In the house," and she finally realizes that it is a "ravenous grave."

Although McKelva's viewing is a public occasion in town, Laurel demonstrates an urban discomfort with a viewing and tries to keep her father's coffin closed. In the same way she is trying to keep her mind closed on the subject of the past. But when they invade the front parlor of the house, Mount Salus' mourners force her to open her father's coffin, so they can pay their last respects to their former mayor. The past she has been guarding so anxiously was not something evoked by her memory of life with her parents in Mount Salus, but rather a fixed and relic-like image that Laurel had chosen and willed to be the true representation of the past. It was a private "verity" that she had no desire to question. She kept it out of reach of her dangerous "somnambulist" memory, which is liable – if not controlled – to bring up disturbing details of subconscious knowledge. In this way Laurel's selective memory had helped falsify and distort the significant part of her own identity that is based on her memory of the past. As she had falsified the past, she had become unable to bring it to bear meaningfully on her present life.

The breadboard incident is the beginning of Laurel's growth towards an understanding of the meaning of the past. It is the start of her recovery of a sense of who she is. She learns that even though it is inextricable from the present, the past itself cannot be abused in the present. Her parents' house had always attracted and concentrated Laurel's thoughts of her childhood years, and she had endowed the place with remembered and imagined precious moments from the family past. But by the time she leaves for Chicago, she has understood that the McKelva House is not a shrine to the past and that she must cease trying to make it into one. She comes to realize that only a shrine can be desecrated, and that memory depends on somebody remembering for its existence and not on the physical possession of a breadboard or a house. Since "memories are motionless," as Gaston Bachelard puts it, they can be fixed securely in space and do not record concrete duration. Laurel's memory, localized as it was in the house of her childhood, could abide for ever in her unconscious without reference to present or future owners of the place.[17]

Towards the end of her stay Laurel catches a chimney swift in her father's house and sets it free. On returning to Mount Salus she has begun to realize that she is not benefitting in her life from her chosen version of the past. If she experiences the past as an ominous bird in her house, a bird that is so frightening that it is able to trap her in a small room deep in the house, that bird must be let out at once (*OD*, 132). The room is her mother's old sewing room. Caught in a place where she has spent so much time in her childhood, a true "gathering spot of all that has been felt," Laurel has to reflect on the past. She thinks of her mother and their relationship, and for the first time Laurel is not romanticizing the past but facing it – all of it.[18] Laurel's sweeping of the mines in her mind begins when she reads her grandmother's letters to Becky. She begins to realize that the past is not six brothers, or six bridesmaids, or (as she knew already) Major Bullock's rambling eulogizing falsification of Clint McKelva's life, or her own romanticizing of her late husband, his dramatic death, and his breadboard. So she willingly gives up the breadboard. She no longer has a family, except in her memory. She is now as independent and alone as Fay claimed she was when they first met.

The lesson Laurel learns about the past is that "memory lived not in initial possession but in the freed hands, pardoned and freed, and in the heart that can empty but fill again, in the patterns restored by dreams" (*OD*, 179). Together with the paragraph describing the regurgitating pigeons, feeding on each other as a family (*OD*, 140), this is the most often quoted passage from the novel. In spite of many excellent attempts at interpretation, it always seems to resist full explication, probably due to the emotion-loaded words: "pardoned and freed" and "heart" and "dreams." Welty seems to me to say that our *changing* feelings about the past, private and public, are valuable, and that we need to free ourselves every so often from the tyranny of the past by remembering that we cannot possess or control the past, but only recapture it through memory. Our memory is a product of our mental creativity. The word "memory" seems to represent a continuing mental process of exchange between our present and our past. Fortunately, it cannot be possessed once and for all. A living memory is, by definition, always unstable and inconclusive. It should not be forced to fit an already selected pattern. There must be room for detachment. In fact the past offers a choice of what we want to remember. This is limited only by our honesty and our ability to "freeze" and control memories.

Memory has always had a vital function in Welty's concept of knowledge. When she discussed Faulkner's idea of the past in "Some Notes on Time in Fiction" (1973), she added her own note on memory: "Remembering is so basic and vital a part of staying alive that it takes on the strength of an instinct of survival, and acquires the power of an art. Remembering is done through the blood, it is a bequeathment, it takes account of what happens before a man is born as if he were there taking part" (*ES*, 171). In a famous passage in his *Biographia Literaria* Coleridge links memory with the mental faculty he calls the fancy: "The Fancy is indeed no other than a mode of Memory emancipated from the order of time and space; while it is blended with, and modified by that empirical phenomenon of the will, which we express by the word CHOICE."[19] Coleridge emphasizes the element of choice and of volition in the use of memory. Memory is not really as accidental in its operation as fancy, because memory is not "emancipated from the order of time and space." It is not divorced from private experience in time and place unless we actively will it to be. We can confine and intensify our attention and give "vividness and distinctness" to any detail in our memory.[20] This is what Laurel did with her memory of the past, and her choice of what to intensify and preserve came to haunt her. But when she stops her willful concentration on ideal moments from the past and admits other, and perhaps less ideal, circumstances of the past into her consciousness, it is also memory which offers her emotional restoration.

Walter Sullivan is the Southern critic that in the 1970s most consistently expressed a deep pessimism about the future of Southern literature. He praised Welty for her aesthetic standard in *The Optimist's Daughter*, but he was disappointed in "the poverty of its conclusion." Sullivan went on to assert that the difference between the end of this novel and the end of *The Golden Apples* is not a change in the artist's ability, but a difference in "the circumstances under which she writes. The postmodern world with its loss of community and myth will no longer support her."[21] Is there any reason to join Sullivan in his vain search for "the rich comprehensiveness which enhances Miss Welty's earlier work," or any reason to feel disappointed with the ending of *The Optimist's Daughter*? From a starting point where Laurel was convinced that "some things don't bear going into" and denied the complexity of the past, she struggles on and comes to terms with the ghosts of the past and eventually accepts knowledge of the imperfections of both past and present. Sullivan says that if the present generation does not accept the old values, novel writing must degenerate. This is a traditional complaint. It is a sentiment, and therefore difficult to refute.

Curiously, Sullivan refuses to consider existential questions worthy of a novelist's attention. He claims that such issues have always been peripheral in great literature and continues "in the best of Faulkner, none of the characters asks himself, 'Who am I?' They all know who they are and even what they are...."²² But did such a happy breed of characters ever people Southern fiction? Would it not be more true to admit that generations of novelists in the South have sought their identity through fiction by asking: "Who am I?" This is the question Laurel asks herself, and she finds the wanted knowledge of self by facing her past. Ultimately, Sullivan's argument would lead to the absurd claim that nothing of value could be written in a less than homogenous society. At times quite the opposite seems to have been true. I do not accept the idea that good fiction cannot be created "in a society that has become unmoored," but only in a traditional community.²³ The yearning for the old times is not surprising, but it is hopelessly romantic.

We may question much that is seen from Laurel's point of view in this novel, but there is not, as Reynolds Price has pointed out, any attempt by the author to discredit Laurel's final vision.²⁴ Instead of being a load on her mind, the past should enable her to treasure her memory without a sense of guilt, so she can live fully in the present. It is when she tries to free herself from the domination of the past that Laurel begins to realize how much its influence depends on her memory of it. Only her memory can free her from her Mount Salus blues. This does not mean that Laurel shakes off everything that has ever happened in Mount Salus and goes to Chicago without it. She has been enriched by what she has gone through. Finally she does not look at Mount Salus "through the frame, or the knothole, of alienation" (which is a phrase that expresses Welty's complaint against some fiction writers of today (*ES*, 10)).

Laurel does not abandon anything. She takes everything with her. Her memory must recreate, unite, and reshape the past continually for it to live in her present. She is now able to be honest about the past, and the gained distance to it saves her from being a tragic character. She no longer lets the past devour her present, for she now accepts the past for what it was and is, both the public community myth of the past and her own private family past. What she has finally "raised up" "by her own hands" (*OD*, 154) is a past remembered, revived, rediscovered, and repossessed. Welty in this way gives a positive answer to Allen Tate's despairing question about the capability of the modern individual to overcome emotional stuntedness by reviving and repossessing the past. Laurel comes to a wall in a place she thought she knew well. She learns that she has to discover her hometown again in order to see what makes the wall within her and to be able to see over it. It is "a matter of vision," as Welty puts it in "Place in Fiction."

The essential difference between Fay and Laurel is finally not social, but a difference of sensibility. Fay demonstrates absolutely no curiosity about the meaning of her experience as a Chisom become McKelva, whereas Laurel is forever in anguish – desperately casting about for satisfying answers to questions raised by her past and present. Laurel suffers in her struggle to attain some vision that would encompass her experience. The novel ends, as Danièle

Pitavy-Souques has put it, "with Laurel's victory over time, it is a costly victory for the price is paid by her tender sensibility, but a certain joy is also born out of the triumph of the human spirit over its adversaries, mortality and chaos."[25] What Laurel finally sees is the subjectivity of her memory of the past, and in doing so, the subjectivity of her experience of the present. She realizes that human experience is a confluence, which in her mind she compares to the waters of the Ohio and the Mississippi flowing together at Cairo, Illinois. Laurel gains a new sense of the continuity of self, which in Faulknerian terms is a confluence of *what was*, now remembered and rediscovered, and *what is*, now discovered.[26]

Some important Welty characters, such as R. J. Bowman, Virgie Rainey, Eugene and Randall MacLain, and Laurel Hand struggle with a sense of alienation and a fear of paralyzed emotions. Welty shows how they try to find a way out of their psychological isolation by facing their past and accepting it for what it is and for what it can tell them about the subjectivity of life in their time and place. It is Welty's search for answers to the existential questions of life through an aesthetics of place that gives her fiction a place in the first order of world literature.

[All references to *The Optimist's Daughter* is to the 1st edition, New York, Random House, 1972]

1. Eudora Welty, "Place-names and Our History," *New York Times Book Review* (May 6, 1945) p. 1.

2. Reynolds Price, "The Onlooker, Smiling: An Early Reading of *The Optimist's Daughter*," including a "Postscript," *Things Themselves: Essays & Scenes*, New York, Atheneum, 1972, p. 133.

3. Suzanne Marrs, *The Welty Collection*, 1988, p. 45.

4. See chapter one above.

5. William Alexander Percy, *Lanterns on the Levee: Recollections of a Planter's Son*, Baton Rouge, Louisiana State University Press, 1984. This edition has an introduction by Walker Percy.

6. See Jan Nordby Gretlund, "On the Porch with Marcus Aurelius: Walker Percy's Stoicism," *Walker Percy: Novelist and Philosopher*, eds. Jan Nordby Gretlund & Karl-Heinz Westarp, Jackson, University Press of Mississippi, 1991, pp. 74-83.

7. Joshua Meyrowitz, *No Sense of Place: The Impact of Electronic Media on Social Behavior*, New York, Oxford University Press, 1985.

8. John Edward Hardy, "Marrying Down in Eudora Welty's Novels," *Eudora Welty: Critical Essays*, ed. Peggy W. Prenshaw, Jackson, 1979, p. 118.

9. Cleanth Brooks, "The Past Reexamined: *The Optimist's Daughter*," *Mississippi Quarterly* 26/4 (Fall 1973) 586n, 578.

10. Thomas Daniel Young, "Social Forms and Social Order: Eudora Welty's *The Optimist's Daughter*," *The Past in the Present: A Thematic Study of Modern Southern Fiction*, Baton Rouge, Louisiana State University Press, 1981, pp. 87-115.

11. John Edward Hardy, "Marrying Down in Eudora Welty's Novels," *Eudora Welty*, ed. Peggy Prenshaw, 1979, p. 108.

12. Ruth M. Vande Kieft, *Eudora Welty*, rev. ed., Boston, Twayne Publishers, 1987, p. 177.

13. See Patricia Meyer Spacks, *The Female Imagination*, New York, Alfred A. Knopf, 1975, p. 275.

14. Jane Hinton, "The Role of the Family in *Delta Wedding, Losing Battles* and *The Optimist's Daughter*," *Eudora Welty: Critical Essays*, ed. Peggy W. Prenshaw, 1979, p. 128.

15. Ruth Vande Kieft, *Eudora Welty*, 1987, p. 181.

16. Robert H. Brinkmeyer, Jr., "New Orleans, Mardi Gras, and Eudora Welty's *The Optimist's Daughter*," *Mississippi Quarterly* 44/4 (Fall 1991) 440.

17. Gaston Bachelard, *The Poetics of Space*, translated by Maria Jolas, Boston, Beacon Press, (1958) 1969, p. 9.

[18] The traditional idea is that a bird in the house is a foreshadowing of death in the house, as maintained by both Roxie and Troy in *Delta Wedding* (*DW*, 159).

[19] S. T. Coleridge, *Biographia Literaria*, ed. J. Shawcross, London, Oxford University Press, 1967, I, 202.

[20] S. T. Coleridge, *Biographia Literaria*, I 87-88. For a short summary of Coleridge's epistemological system see my "S. T. Coleridge: The Philosophy of the Poetic Imagination," *Proceedings from the Second Nordic Conference for English Studies*, eds. H. Ringbom and M. Rissanen, Åbo, Publications of the Research Institute of the Åbo Akademi Foundation, 1984, pp. 477-88.

[21] Walter Sullivan, *A Requiem for the Renascence: The State of Fiction in the Modern South*, Athens, Ga., The University of Georgia Press, 1970, pp. 56-57.

[22] Walter Sullivan, *Death by Melancholy: Essays on Modern Southern Fiction*, Baton Rouge, Louisiana State University Press, 1976, p. 90.

[23] I have tried to answer Walter Sullivan in my essay, "Novelists of the Third Phase of the Renaissance: Walker Percy, Madison Jones and Barry Hannah," *Aspects du Sud Aujourd'hui. Revue Francaise D'Etudes Americaines* 23 (Fevrier 1985) 13-24.

[24] Reynolds Price, "The Onlooker, Smiling," p. 134.

[25] Danièle Pitavy, "La Guerre du Temps dans *Losing Battles* et *The Optimist's Daughter*," *Recherches Anglaises et Américaines* 9 (1976) 196. My translation.

[26] Cp. Elizabeth Bowen's use of "confluence" in *A World of Love*, (1955) Harmondsworth, Penguin, 1983, p. 48.

CHAPTER THIRTEEN

Walker Percy: A Literary Correspondence

I first met Walker Percy on January 2, 1981, when I interviewed him in his home in Covington, Louisiana. With Cleanth Brooks, John Cunningham, and Lewis A. Lawson I had participated in a workshop on Walker Percy's fiction at the Modern Language Association at Houston, Texas, on December 30, 1980, and on my way back to Denmark I decided to stop by Covington. Walker Percy told me on the phone that he was going to New Orleans for a football game in the Superdome on New Year's Day, but promised to see me the next day.

After I had sent him a transcript of our first interview for comments, we began to correspond at the slow rate of a letter or a note about every six months. As we did not know each other's private and everyday life, we wrote mostly about our common interests: literature, religion, and philosophy. My letters were, of course, mostly longer than Percy's. It was an extremely productive period in his life. In the presentation of the correspondence most of my letters have been shortened, whereas Percy's are complete. I have never before or since kept my letters to anybody, but I kept the letters to Percy, save a few that I wrote from Vanderbilt University, 1984-85. I kept our correspondence because it was focused on literary subjects. Walker Percy's letters to me are all here except for one letter that I remember, but have lost. The value of these letters is that they show what Walker Percy was thinking about and reacting to, from the time before the publication of Lost in the Cosmos, *during the writing and reception of* The Thanatos Syndrome, *and during the writing of the essays: "The Diagnostic Novel: On the Uses of Modern Fiction," "The Fateful Rift: The San Andreas Fault of the Modern Mind," and "Approving or Disapproving Eyes."*

Covington
Feb. 13, 1981

Thanks Jan. It sounds pretty good, considering I wasn't paying much attention.[1]

Why don't you write an account of coming to Covington, putting up at the Mt. Vernon motel and going out to a New Year's Eve party with A. C. U. linemen?

Walker

P.S. Bunt says thanks for the lovely photo of me and Jack [a grandchild]. All the best to you.

WP

---

[1] My first interview with Walker Percy was first published in *The South Carolina Review* 13/2 (Spring, 1981) 3-12. Reprinted as "Laying the Ghost of Marcus Aurelius?" *Conversations with Walker Percy*, eds. Lewis A. Lawson and V. A. Kramer, Jackson, University Press of Mississippi, 1985, pp. 203-15.

The Existential South

Covington
Nov 25, 1982
Thanksgiving

Dear Jan

I most deeply appreciate the off print of your article "Contemporary Southern Literature"[1] – you were more than kind to me. Frankly however, I think pickings are pretty slim among current southern writers. I have difficulty finding talent among writers under 40.

Just finished a non-fiction book: *Lost in the Cosmos: the Last Self-Help Book.*[2] Out in May –

Best,
Walker

P. S. Have you ever heard of a Danish novel: *The Road to Lagoa Santa* by Henrik Stangerup?[3] I've heard good things about it and hope it has been translated into English. I think you'd be interested. It's about the spiritual journey of Kierkegaard's brother-in-law Peter Wilhelm Lund – Please look into this and let me know when it will be available.

W. P.

---

[1] "Novelists of the Third Phase of the Renaissance: Walker Percy, Madison Jones and Barry Hannah," *Revue Francaise D'Etudes Americaines* no. 23, X (Février 85) 13-24.
[2] New York, Farrar, Straus, and Giroux, 1983.
[3] Henrik Stangerup, *The Road to Lagoa Santa*. The Danish edition was published in 1981. The English edition was published by Boyars in 1984, and distributed by Scribner in the U. S.

Covington
Dec 27, 1982

Dear Jan

Well, you succeeded! I feel like a dummy looking at Herman's play – gazing at the pictures like a child. You'll have to come again and give me a right translation.[1]

I appreciate your information on Stangerup and shall be looking for *The Road to Lagoa Santa*.

I certainly have no objection to Lewis Lawson doing my biography,[2] though it is a meager subject. The only thing I dread and won't do is spend a lot of time talking to somebody about myself which would bore me to death.

Do Danes know that S. K. [Søren Kierkegaard] is the greatest philosopher-writer of the past 200 years?

Happy new year –

Walker

---

[1] Wladimir Herman, *Kierkegaards sidste dage* [Kierkegaard's last days], København, C. A. Reitzel, 1982.

[2] Lewis A. Lawson is writing a literary and psychological biography of Walker Percy.

The Existential South

Odense
Aug. 19, 1983

Dear Walker Percy

I have just read *Lost in Cosmos* and I want to congratulate you on its publication. I enjoyed reading it. I kept finding references to the novels and to *Message*, and it was like meeting old friends. You certainly manage to popularize and spell out a great many of your old themes ....

I saw the review in *NYTBR*. It seems to me that Francine du (solar plexus) Gray is mostly shadow boxing; if she has read your fiction, I do not understand why she is so surprised by *Lost in Cosmos*.[1] I much prefer Jack Beatty's review in *The New Republic*, but unlike him I do not want to leave it to you to listen to "the turbid music of my soul"....[2]

I find I have several quarrels with you. It is not so much the "survey of despair" that bothers me, for that is not how I see the book. I mean, if it were that, why is the author questioning and why is it the reader is interested enough to go on reading ... I am bothered by the selves you offer: nuclear physicist, radio repairman, divorcée, Catholic priest, etc. They are only types because we typecast them. Fortunately, nobody is just what we think they are .... The space travelers would probably *not* want to go their separate ways after eighteen years together in the 727. Dr. Aristarchus Jones may not want to leave the genetically defective children behind, (you load the dice here.)

I also think man is a much better reader than you do. The reader's pleasure is not based on temporary exaltation or escapism alone ... I read you not as escapism, perhaps not even with identification, and it is without accepting all your ideas.... For example, I do not believe that you have "to leave the world" to write about it. You may, as Miss Welty, live in it and write about it .... And I do not believe you can leave yourself to write about yourself.

In spite of such opinions I thoroughly enjoyed all your pages on re-entry, ... , I even formed opinions about re-entry problems: if you must leave to create, could you not re-enter through the enjoyment of the product of the process, yours or other people's ? – No. 7 (pp. 158-159): deep space (suicide) is clearly of a different category, as it is a final exit. – So I think the scientist after his discovery would head for home and join his family, as he always does. He now knows he is stuck with himself, ... , and he does not think that is too bad. And then we can leave God dangling on page 112, make love during the passing of Camille, improve, and not tell about it.

Sincerely,
Jan
Lost Cove

---

[1] Francine du Plessix Gray, *New York Times Book Review* (5 June, 1983) 9.
[2] Jack Beatty, *The New Republic* 189 (11 July, 1983) 38-39.

Covington
August 27, 1983

Dear Jan –

Cheers, Jan! – Always delighted to hear from you – from Lost Cove.
Thanks for the good words.
Right – you're right about the type casting – but see *L in C*, [*Lost in the Cosmos*] p. 126 (ff).
Disagree about Dr Aristarchus Jones. How could he, as a purely scientific scientist, justify taking the genetic-defectives along to contaminate the gene pool? I couldn't, if I were he – .
Re hurricanes and love-making: very well, but you better come back to Louisiana, we got one brewing in Gulf right now.
How did you like my print-out of the Swede from Örebro?[1]
What are you up to?

Sincerely,
Walker

* * *

Covington
Sept 7, 1984

Dear Jan –

Many thanks for your letter which was most cheerful and funny in your own inimitable way.
My best to Staffan Holmgren (I don't believe anyone sent me his translation but I'm glad you approve.)[2] You ought to encourage him to translate *Lost in the Cosmos* because the only prophecy in the whole book concerns a biology teacher (high school) in Örebro, Sweden. This should intrigue all Swedes.
If you can't find Dolly [Parton] in Nashville, I can put you in touch with a fellow who can.

All best
Walker

---

[1] *Lost in the Cosmos: The Last Self-Help Book*, New York, Farrar, Straus, and Giroux, 1983, p. 255

[2] Walker Percy, *De Yttersta Dagarna* [*The Second Coming*] trans. by Staffan Holmgren, Stockholm, P. A. Norstedt & Söners Förlag, 1984. Holmgren had translated *The Moviegoer* into Swedish in 1980.

The Existential South

Covington
Dec 14, 1984

Dear Jan –

It would be a pleasure to see you. Let's plan on lunch on Jan. 29.[1] Why don't you call me a day or so before and I will set up something.

Merry Xmas
Walker

* * *

Covington
Feb 14, 1985

[Postcard of Lt. Gen. "Stonewall" Jackson
Confederate States of America
Photo by Minnes.
Fredericksburg, April 1863.]

Lektor Gretlund

Thanks for lovely photos. It was indeed a pleasure seeing you again, and the very nice girl [Ann Ebrecht] made it even better.[2] I think you are going to be the Southern de Tocqueville – you know your stuff.

All best –
WP –

---

[1] The interview was published as "Difficult Times," *More Conversations with Walker Percy*, eds. Lewis A. Lawson & Victor A. Kramer, Jackson, University of Mississippi, 1993, pp. 103-107.

[2] Ann Ebrecht, a literary critic, was present for the conversation in the Percys' home in Covington, on January 29, 1985. Ann Ebrecht, who worked for the Louisiana Endowment for the Humanities, went to school with one of Walker Percy's daughters.

Odense,
Dec. 22, 1986

Dear Walker

I wish you and your family a happy new year. I hope *The Thanatos Syndrome* will be well received, much read, and understood ....

As I mentioned on the phone, I have just re-read "The Diagnostic Novel" in *Harper's* of June, this year.[1] As usual I agree with almost all you say, but I am still left with some questions. And I realize that they are all part of one question: why is it that I (as a prototype ex-Lutheran Dane), who should be in despair, am more optimistic about man and his future than you are? Even though you know you are in despair and on a search ....

In your "exploration of the options of postmodern man" you maintain that there has been "a radical impoverishment of human relations." It seems so obvious to you ... I consider it a romanticizing of the past to believe that human relations were ever better. I would be more prone to romanticize the present and say that human relations on this globe have never been better! ....

I do not believe that your diagnosis of man has proved that we live in a more deranged world. We have created a situation that is more dangerous than before in history. But man is, unfortunately, just as deranged or normal, as he was in the 17th century. And with this ... I enter the holiest place of all: I do not think man has an atom less sovereignty today than he did when he first walked the planet (though he was probably a better speller).

I hope my optimism will trouble you. I am, of course, looking forward to being set straight about this.

All the best,
Jan

---

[1] Walker Percy, "The Diagnostic Novel: On the Uses of Modern Fiction," *Harper's* 272 (June 1986) 39-45.

The Existential South

Covington
Dec 30, 1986

Dear Jan –

It is very good to hear from you – I am only sorry we couldn't have got together. But at least you got to Doe's in Greenville[1] – I am also happy you saw Jo Gulledge in Baton Rouge.[2] She is indeed a lovely gal and a good friend – SR [*Southern Review*] is publishing the first 10 pages or so of *The Thanatos Syndrome*.[3]

I don't know whether you are having sport with me in your report about the general euphoria of the western world – But maybe you are falling into a pseudonymous role like your compatriot S. K. [Søren Kierkegaard] and simply celebrating the delights of the esthetic sphere of existence – to which I reply: right on!

A psychiatric colleague of a writer friend (Don Barthelme) spoke to me about the paradoxical opposition in Denmark of the delights of the most secularized and materialistic culture in the west – truly delightful, best-looking girls, nicest people, a superior music, literature and food, an admirable social structure with a minimum of poverty and deprivation – And the highest suicide rate in the world[4] –

I am writing my publisher to send you a pre-pub copy of TTS [*The Thanatos Syndrome*] – I think you'll get a kick out of it.

Best for 87! I pray we see 88 –

Walker

P.S. Seriously Jan: in question my attribution of malaise to western society, aren't you taking on the entire post-modern European novel – American too? If it can be said that the main subject of western fiction since Flaubert[5] has been alienation of one sort or another, don't you find yourself in the position of claiming that these novelists are themselves neurotics in not realizing what a good time everybody else is having? (I'm not saying you are wrong.)

W.P.

---

[1] "DOES EAT" is a restaurant in Greenville, Mississippi, famous for its gigantic steaks.
[2] Jo Marie Gulledge, Assistant Editor of *Southern Review* in the mid 1980s, and a friend of Walker Percy.
[3] Walker Percy, "*From* The Thanatos Syndrome," *Southern Review* 23 (Spring 1987) 384-402.
[4] On the relation between "lewdness" and suicide, see Walker Percy, *The Last Gentleman*, New York, Farrar, Straus, and Giroux, 1966, pp. 345-46.
[5] Gustave Flaubert (1821-80).

Odense
January 15, 1987

Dear Walker

Thank you very much for your kind letter of December 30. I forgot to enclose my copy of *The Southern Register* from the fall ... I am sending it to you because of the two items on Mississippi-Russian relations. (And the page on Richard Howorth and his bookstore.)[1] I hope both you and Miss Welty will go to Russia. I know that Miss Welty is published in Russian, and if your novels are not out there yet, I am sure this would be a good occasion. In Denmark we are about one hundred miles from the East German border, which is enough to worry anybody. But we see the present as especially suited for endeavors to relieve some of the tension between East and West. On the other hand, if I had a similar invitation, I would leave a tape and a transcript at home of all I was going to say in public in Russia ....

It is true, of course, that with you I am the devil's advocate (appropriate terminology), but we are left with the fact that I do not have such a pessimistic view of the future as you do. This is probably because I have not yet graduated from the aesthetic sphere. I am trying to step into the ethic sphere and I find Marcus Aurelius appealing right now. Maybe one day I will even make *the* leap?

Most Danes never make the leap, this is true. But when you have the impression that Danes only leap out of windows or throw themselves before trains, I protest. Suicide here is not a stigma, a sin, a scandal that needs to be hushed up. In short whether you died from natural causes or committed suicide is not an issue – only death is. Is it any wonder that we have high statistics compared to countries that have a different view of suicide?

The other tradition I see in the fiction of the last two centuries is the desire to celebrate life. The Whitmanesque full enjoyment of life, which is there in Chekhov, and which is the backbone of Miss Welty's fiction. I see this as the tradition of Charles Dickens, the late Faulkner, and Dylan Thomas. In spite of all that is wrong with this life, it is great to be alive: let's celebrate it. This does not mean that I have overlooked the long list of novelists who felt the malaise more than the joy of living.

I thank you for the pre-publication copy of *The Thanatos Syndrome*, I appreciate it.

All the best,
Jan

---

[1] Square Books, Oxford, Mississippi.

Covington
1/27/87
[US Postal Card]

Dear Jan

Why are you trying to dump all this pessimism on me? If you take the trouble to read *Thanatos Syndrome,* you will see it is the opposite, a celebration of life + eros over death.[1]

    I think Shakespeare was right. You Danes like to have it both ways: being gloomy and enjoying it.

Walker

---

[1] I did not get my own copy of the novel until much later.

Odense
4 June, 1987

Dear Walker

What a fine novel, thank you for *The Thanatos Syndrome*. I came to it without having read a single review, so I could make up my own mind. It is good, very good, and I am happy for you. I know you have invested a lot of emotion and work, so it is gratifying to see that the novel succeeds .... I like the loose style, the talkativeness, the digressions, and emphasis on dialogue – all of which can be found in the earlier novels, but here there is more. The new delight is the suspense element of the thriller that keeps you reading.... The best feature is the way the river and the river country come alive, Louisiana, past and present, is there in living color, but without sentimentality. I also enjoyed the aside on the present state of fiction (349).

... It does bother me that I cannot find anything to disagree with this time. Comeaux and Van Dorn are just exactly as probable as you show, and Father Smith is correct in seeing the historical repetition by scientists in our own time, and it scares me, too. Yet, our hero is, of course, successful in stopping the "mad" scientists. So although this is the age of thanatos, it is also the time of an increased Percy optimism! (?)

On my favorite topics of stoicism and old Southern romanticism there was less this time. I did see it surface, 240-250, but it is less important. The ghost of Marcus Aurelius rests, which is no doubt good for the novel.... I like the way you bring in Flannery O'Connor, and tenderness that leads to the gas chambers, which supports Father Smith's "Confession" and footnote. These pages are for me the most rewarding, 239-257. And I can see why you wanted to place them where you did. But from a structural point of view they stick out like an extra thumb. I mean Tom More is anxious to get back to Belle Ame to save Claude Bon, but the urgency of this seems forgotten during Father Smith's confession.... The only other thing I could possibly criticize is that the funniest scene, and it is hilarious, seems to be too much of a movie-script, 311-323. I lose the sense of everybody as human beings in that scene, whereas only some of them have been reduced to primates.

I think the women characters, blacks and whites, are good. They are convincingly better than some of your earlier women. In short I celebrate the novel for the women, the out-of-doors, the action, and the necessity of the warning. What more can anyone ask for?

Please let me know how you feel about *Thanatos* and its reception. – By the way, Elisabeth Herion-Sarafidis, a Swedish scholar, gave an excellent paper on your humor at a conference I attended in Uppsala last week.

Sincerely,
Jan

Covington
June 13, 1987

Dear Jan –

I appreciate your letter more than I can tell you. Your reading of *Thanatos* was close and perceptive, as usual.

I am grateful that you liked it and freely acknowledge the faults. One fault was unavoidable – Fr Smith's "Confession" – even if it did stick out like a sore thumb. But I had to have it. It was central, my only excuse is that Dostoievski and Faulkner also took inexcusable licences and digressions –

The Marx-Brothers moviescript (311-323) was simply a self indulgence. I enjoyed it, mainly as satirical fun with certain semioticists, primatologists, and post-structuralist critics.

The reviews were mostly good – a couple of sour ones – e.g. *National Review*,[1] which I didn't expect, and *N. Y. Review of Books*[2] which I did. Surprisingly it has been on Times best-seller list for 9 weeks – me and Louis L'Amour and Stephen King! Actually I'm fed up with the book, and the interviews and can't stand to read it. I find myself turning to semiotics as usual, contemplating a book elucidating Peirce's "triadic theory"[3] (which I consider probably as important as Quantum Theory) toward end of reconciling it with people like Wittgenstein, John Poinsot (John of St Thomas) a 17th Century Dominican –

All best,
Walker

P. S. Sorry my publisher was so late – WP –
PPS – what are you up to?

WP

---

[1] Robert Royal, *National Review* 39 (May 22, 1987) 50.
[2] Robert Towers, "Danger Zones," *New York Review of Books* (June 25, 1987) p, 45.
[3] On Charles Peirce's philosophy, see for example Walker Percy, "Is a Theory of Man Possible?" *Signposts in a Strange Land*, ed. Patrick Samway, S. J., New York, Farrar, Straus, and Giroux, 1991, pp. 111-29.

Odense
2 July, 1987

Dear Walker

I appreciate your letter ... I suppose you never expected to find yourself on a best-seller list with Louis L'Amour and Stephen King. I would prefer to see you in the company of Dostoievski and Faulkner. I have just seen the review in the *New York Review of Books*, and I can see why you call it "sour."[1] It is the same old story, New York critics do not know what Southern writers are up to until the rest of the world tells them .... Alfred Kazin, whom I talked with in Copenhagen yesterday, is a good example. He has not read a single book from the 80s written by a Southerner: "the South is," he said, "just like the rest of the country now, so it does not interest me anymore."[2] .... When I read your comment: "I find myself turning to semiotics as usual" and heard of your plans for a book on Peirce's "triadic theory," I found myself thinking of S. T. Coleridge. In my youth I spent two years reading his prose works. I was fascinated with his attempts at proving the truth of his Christian faith by means of Kantian philosophy. His aim was really to prove that the Church of England does supply all the answers. For thirty-six years this was what he lived for. His attempt failed, of course, and we are left with some disjointed prose ... One of the best minds of the 19th century had brilliantly wasted his time. The Coleridge who is addressing the essential questions of life is surely Coleridge the poet. In the prose he lost the ability to apply the philosophy and communicate it by the creations of the imagination .... – I admire the essays of *The Message in the Bottle*, but Tom More is in my gut.[3] ....

In the first week of August we will have a conference in the of Jutland for critics who have published on your work. It is supposed to be a meeting of experts only. It will be along the lines of the meeting we had on Flannery O'Connor. The book you were kind enough to endorse is a result of that conference.[4] If you came, we could call it: Walker Percy faces his critics. You would enjoy my co-organizer Karl-Heinz Westarp .... He is working as hard as WAP [William Alexander Percy], or WP, to improve life for everybody around him.

Sincerely,
Jan

---

[1] Robert Towers, "Danger Zones," *New York Review of Books* (June 25, 1987) p. 45.
[2] At that time Alfred Kazin's most recent book was *An American Procession*, New York, Alfred A. Knopf, 1984. His best known book is *On Native Grounds*, 1942 & 1982.
[3] Tom More is the main character of Walker Percy's novels *Love in the Ruins* (1971) and *The Thanatos Syndrome* (1987).
[4] *Realist of Distances: Flannery O'Connor Revisited*, eds. Karl-Heinz Westarp and Jan Nordby Gretlund, Aarhus U. P., 1987. Percy's endorsement reads: "What a pleasure to see Flannery O'Connor recognized and acclaimed by such fine critics."

The Existential South

Odense
1 February, 1988

Dear Walker

... The good news from Denmark is that a publisher in Copenhagen is planning a Danish edition of *The Thanatos Syndrome* for this fall.[1] It is about time that another Percy novel made it into Danish, and I hope it will get better reviews than *Biografgængeren* was granted[2] ....

I just received John Edward Hardy's book on your work.[3] I have read in it. It looks like a good effort, and if I may rate him by his work on Katherine Anne Porter, it is probably very good.... I did read the note where he quotes our interview and gets awfully close to accusing you of fascist tendencies. In my review of his book I will address the problem.[4] It seems that he has not learned from "Father Smith's Confession." (It is always in the mind of the reader that true wonders occur. One student just wrote an immortal comment on Stanley Kowalski of *A Streetcar Named Desire*: "At first he is rude to Blanche, but eventually he rapes her.")

The planning of the Walker Percy Symposium at Sandbjerg is progressing. I enclose a few copies of the provisional program. Lewis Lawson, John F. Desmond, and Patrick Samway are interested, so we are off to a flying start. We have also had inquiries from Poland, Bulgaria, Japan, and Italy .... It would be great if you could turn up, but I do not really believe that you will come to stare down your critics, and I do not blame you. If you did, I could keep it out of the advertising and spring it on the critics, who would not have time to review their papers. It would be hilarious. You could do an essay on yourself along the lines of "Questions They never Asked Me."[5] ....

How are you these days? Are you writing? Is there still a long line of men and women making their way to the edge of the Bogue Falaya River to visit with the Sage of Covington?

Sincerely,
Jan

---

[1] This was dated news. *Thanatossyndromet*, København, Holkenfeldts Forlag, had appeared already in 1987.

[2] *Biografgængeren* [*The Moviegoer*] København, Gyldendal, 1964.

[3] John Edward Hardy, *The Fiction of Walker Percy*, Urbana, Ill., University of Illinois Press, 1987. Hardy wrote *Katherine Anne Porter*, New York, Ungar, 1973.

[4] Jan Nordby Gretlund, "Walker Percy's Art and Vision," *The University of Toronto Quarterly* 58/3 (Spring 1989) 423-25.

[5] Walker Percy, "Questions They Never Asked Me: So He Asked Them Himself" (1977), *Conversations with Walker Percy*, eds. Lewis A. Lawson and V. A. Kramer, Jackson, University Press of Mississippi, 1985, pp. 158-81.

Covington
February 8, 1988[1]

Dear Jan

Your letter quite floored me. Wow, as they say in the USA (yankee talk), or: Well, I be dog (Southern style).

In a word, I am honored – and grateful to you.

On the other hand, it is not altogether inappropriate. I know no other writer, living or dead, who owes more to "the great Danish philosopher and theologian," as Binx Bolling called him.[2] SK. [Søren Kierkegaard]

Thanks also for your invitation, but I doubt I want to get within a thousand miles of such a gathering. It would be like Banquo's ghost showing up at the feast.[3] I may not be dead by then, but I'd have sense enough to stay away – from both the positive and the negative critics. I don't [know] which is more embarrassing, praise or blame.

What am I up to? Doing my usual obscure semiotic number between making up stories. It may sell 200 copies. Tentative title: Thirdness. Or maybe The Delta Factor. Thesis: Descartes fucked things up royally with his res-cogitans-/res-extensa split, resulting in the present fuck-up of all the sciences of man (e.g. sociology, psychology etc), and how to unfuck them, using Charles Peirce's Firstness, Secondness and Thirdness, and SK and Heidegger for the source of the "existentialia" which can be arrayed on this new model.

It's not exactly humming along.

All best, and again my thanks and gratitude.

Cordially,
Walker

---

[1] Typed letter. U.S. Postal form.
[2] Binx Bolling is the main character of Walker Percy's first novel *The Moviegoer* (1961).
[3] The reference is to William Shakespeare's *Macbeth*, Act III. sc. iv.

The Existential South

Covington
Jan 29, 1989

Dear Jan –

Lovely to hear from you. How startling to see my name on your letter.[1]

I blush at the honor you do me.[2] Hope it works out. I know some folks who are going.

I'm feeling fine – Can't come, but I'll invoke the shade of the great Søren [Kierkegaard] –

All best,
Walker

---

[1] Heading on stationery using Percy's name in connection with planned symposium.
[2] The setting up of the symposium: "Walker Percy: Faith, Fiction, and Philosophy," at Sandbjerg Manor House, Jutland, Denmark, July 30-August 4, 1989.

Walker Percy: A Literary Correspondence

Odense
16 June, 1989

Dear Walker

I have just read your Jefferson Lecture,[1] the next best thing to being there. Louis Budd[2] was kind enough to send me a copy. And I hasten to congratulate you on a job well done. It is the challenge to science as "it is presently practiced by some scientists" that has made the deepest impression. I know that you have said this often in the past and most impressively in *The Thanatos Syndrome*, but it can't be said too often. Judging from the reaction of some journalists, notably in *The Washington Post*, it is still news to a lot of people.[3]

My son is still trying to draw a picture of an organism asserting a sentence. He claims it is *easy* because man is an organism. I am trying to convince myself that he missed something in the argument. My son's money is also on the homunculus. He claims that if this creature was accounted for, it would not be a homunculus! My son Glenn is twelve.

Congratulations on the fine Walker Percy issue of *Humanities*.[4] I am sure that the write-up will result in more attention to your novels. I always enjoy Cleanth Brooks' work, and though his sight is now impaired, he can still write better than most, as this essay clearly shows ... – Curt Richter's excellent photos make me speculate that, since you never got a chance to double for Henry Fonda in a western (p.8), your ambition is now to do Hamlet, or is it Marlowe's Dr. Faustus with Sweet Thing[5] as Helen, for the Royal Shakespeare Company.

The papers for our Walker Percy Symposium look fine. I enclose a program that I hope is the final one. As you can see, you could turn up at Sandbjerg and not a soul there would recognize you. Your presence could help stop such idle speculation as "Did Amy Carter Ghost-write *The Thanatos Syndrome*," which would, of course, explain a lot about mysterious policies.

....

Sincerely,
Jan

---

[1] Walker Percy, "The Fateful Rift: The San Andreas Fault of the Modern Mind," Eighteenth Jefferson Lecture in the Humanities, 3 May, 1989. Transcript from the National Endowment for the Humanities.
[2] Louis Budd, editor emeritus, *American Literature*, and Mark Twain scholar.
[3] See the reactions reported by Phil McCombs in "Partying and Pondering," *The Washington Post*, May 4, 1989, pp. B 1, B 16.
[4] National Endowment for the Humanities, *Humanities* 10/3 (May/June, 1989) pp. 1-34.
[5] "Sweet Thing" was the name for Percy's mini-collie.

The Existential South

Covington
June 26, 1989

Dear Jan –

I think your son Glenn understood that lecture better than most U. S. scientists. At least he paid attention.

Many thanks again for putting on the this symposium. I feel somewhat embarrassed to be the subject. If I could bear hearing a reading about me, I'd be there. However, I did get a look at a very able paper by Pat Poteat[1] about *The Thanatos System*.

But I'll be there in spirit with S. K. [Søren Kierkegaard] and my ghost writer Amy Carter.

All best,
Walker

---

[1] Pat Poteat is the author of *Walker Percy and the Old Modern Age*, Baton Rouge, Louisiana State University Press, 1985. Her essay, referred to, became "Pilgrim's Progress: or, A Few Night Thoughts on Tenderness and the Will to Power," *Walker Percy: Novelist and Philosopher*, eds. Jan Nordby Gretlund and Karl-Heinz Westarp, Jackson, University Press of Mississippi, 1991, pp. 210-24.

Odense
11 October, 1989

Dear Walker

I was in Meridian [Mississippi] on September 2, and since I was that close, ... , I took the liberty of calling your daughter (I must have been carrying her number ever since you and I first met in January 1981). She told me that you were in Minnesota, and I promised to write and explain why I was trying to reach you.

I was in the area to hand over to the University Press of Mississippi the essays from the Walker Percy Symposium in Denmark .... Our contact at the press is Ms Seetha Srinivasan, who is a delightful person. – Some of our mutual friends have probably mentioned the merry Sandbjerg days to you. Maybe you have even seen the poem on the symposium by Tjebbe Westendorp of the Netherlands.[1] It is a satire on Percy scholars, and it has some bite to it ....

I don't know how you are doing physically, and it is none of my business, though I worry about you. I mention this only as a preliminary to an old request. I had hoped that you would give me a couple of pages on you and your critics (often amusing or irritating relations, no doubt) that we could include in this volume. It seems to me that you have been polite and reticent on the subject, and I am sure that there are things that the Botherhood of Percy Scholars need to hear. The probable list of contents will give you an idea of what it is in your faith, fiction, and philosophy that has caught the eye of the critic. Is this the kind of attention you hoped for? Or, do you agree with Katherine Anne Porter's: "am I leaving my stuff to shit heads like you!" (marginalia by KAP in a book on her fiction).[2]

I wish you good health and happiness.

Sincerely,
Jan

---

[1] Tjebbe Westendorp, "Creation and Rotation: *Creatio ex nihilo*," unpublished.
[2] Katherine Anne Porter's marginalia in George Hendrick, *Katherine Anne Porter*, New York, Twayne, 1965. The copy is in the Katherine Anne Porter Room in the McKeldin Library, University of Maryland.

Covington
Oct 17, 1989

Dear Jan –

Many thanks for all the good stuff on the Odense conference. I confess that most of it made me uneasy. Praise makes me feel fraudulent, the best is Tjebbe Westendorp's poem which is a delight. (I like "Jan Gretlund – managed to come through stoically"). Mainly I could only imagine how sick you must have been of WP. Yet I've heard from some participants who enjoyed it very much ....

In a word, I am grateful to you.

Your intro to the collection is fine.

I'd be glad to give you a smart-alec paragraph for the U. of Miss Press book – if it works out. I don't feel like commenting on each of the contributions like Tjebbe.

I've not been well for past four months, but am better. I had a recurrence of a prostate cancer after prostatectomy a year and a half ago. Been going up to Mayo clinic for a new experimental treatment with two experimental drugs. It seems to be working pretty well. Cancer has not progressed. Lab tests show it's not as active.

Being an ordinary Catholic, I don't mind dying. But the rest is a pain in the ass – trouble, shots, horrendous side effects.

I'm feeling pretty good and am able to work a little –

Cordially
Walker

Odense
January 30, 1990

Dear Walker

Through the International Society for Keeping Walker Percy Constantly in the News (ISKWPCN) I get the impression that you are reasonably well. I have been informed that you visit your regular restaurants and seem to enjoy it. And I am pleased to hear it. But really, you should learn to behave like a sick man. Visiting restaurants, indeed!

We have a contract with U. P. of Mississippi for a book of twenty-one essays.[1] We had to take it, nobody would allow us to include all thirty-four essays. It has been the usual game, the reader cut the number to about half and we pressed in some essays we like .... The press wants the ms by March 1. So now I have to ask you for the "smart-alec paragraphs" you were careless enough to promise.

I am hoping for remarks on your critics, along the lines of "Me and My Shadows," or "Other Questions They Never Asked Me".... You do not have to know the essays that will go into the book. We just want you to whip, castigate, and mock critics and criticism. We are a masochistic lot. I hope you will dream up a couple of entertaining pages. (Warning: we already heard the one about the bottle of Two Natural.)[2]

I have just returned from a Southern Studies symposium in Genova ... I was to speak on "Southern Stoicism and Christianity: from William Alexander Percy to Walker Percy," but I changed it to "Central Heating and the Holy Grail," which in many ways is the same subject.[3] I managed to ingratiate myself with the Genovese, as they pride themselves on being first with central heating. And they claim to have the Holy Grail in St. Lorenzo. I tried to see it, but the cathedral was closed for lunch, and I missed the Holy Grail by fifteen minutes. But then I got a lot closer than some ....

My students request that you do *not* publish any more semiotic essays. You may enjoy writing them, but think for a minute of the poor student and critic afflicted with them – our bumper stickers read FICTION PLEASE! (Humor is a good ally, which is my excuse for the above.)

Sincerely,
Jan

---

[1] *Walker Percy: Novelist and Philosopher*, eds. Jan Nordby Gretlund and Karl-Heinz Westarp, Jackson, University Press of Mississippi, 1991.
[2] Walker Percy's amusing essay "Bourbon" [1975] collected in *Signposts in a Strange Land*, ed. Patrick Samway, S. J., 1991, pp. 102-107.
[3] Jan Nordby Gretlund, "Southern Stoicism and Christianity: From William Alexander Percy to Walker Percy," *The United States South: Regionalism and Identity*, eds. Valeria Gennaro Lerda and Tjebbe Westendorp, Rome, Bulzoni Editore, 1991, pp. 145-55.

The Existential South

Covington
Feb 9, 1990

Dear Jan –

Feel free to cut this, edit it, ad lib.[1]
   Sorry about the holograph – my typewriter gave out.

All best –
Walker

* * *

Odense
28 February, 1990

Dear Walker

Thank you for your letter of February 9 with your comments on our volume of essays. I am grateful to you for your pages, they will help us by boosting our credibility with Percy fans. As you can see, I have taken your advice and have edited your foreword. I hope you will o.k. the revisions or replace them by more lucid comments.

   We will submit the ms before I can receive your corrections, but I can fax an authorized version to the press. It always looks different when it is typed, ... , so please revise and add all sorts of wise-cracks. Do you like the headline? Or, should it be: "Looking at It Sideways," which was my original choice. I chose the present title[2] because it brings in your critics. I think your foreword gives a pretty good impression of "love and separateness" among "writing nuts."

   Thank you for taking time out to do this.

Sincerely,
Jan

---

[1] The four handwritten pages became Walker Percy's foreword: "Approving or Disapproving Eyes," *Walker Percy: Novelist and Philosopher*, eds. Jan Nordby Gretlund and Karl-Heinz Westarp, University Press of Mississippi, 1991, pp. vii-viii.

[2] "Approving or Disapproving Eyes."

Odense
8 May, 1990

Dear Walker

In the foreword you were kind enough to write for our collection, you ask, "Do Danes know that Søren Kierkegaard is the greatest philosopher – writer of the past two hundred years?" I realize with O'Connor that "for the almost-blind you draw large and startling figures,"[1] but the exaggeration aside, your question made me look for reminders of Kierkegaard in my everyday world.

There are references to Kierkegaard in Danish papers. The whole nation notices with pride that a dramatized version of *Forførerens Dagbog* [the seducer's diary] will be staged in Moscow. But it is not expected to lead to an increased sale of his books. A headline that I saw recently read: "Kierkegaards Sekretær Sælges" [Kierkegaard's Secretary for Sale]. Fortunately, this referred to the desk he wrote at, standing up. Significantly, it was sold at half the estimated price to a foreign dealer.

I was thrilled to see that Danish TV was going to air "The Søren Kierkegaard Road Show" (advertised in English). It turned out to be a program about two (imitation) truck drivers, who played country music, mainly the Highwaymen. But just what the relation was between the four elderly Nashville stars and the philosopher was never clear. I suspect the producers of the show had realized the PR potential of Søren Kierkegaard's name ....

In general the philosopher is highly regarded by his fellow countrymen, who know of his international reputation, but would not dream of reading a syllable by Kierkegaard ....

So who is a prophet in his own country? *You* are consulted on the dire problems of Louisiana in magazines and newspapers. You are a lot closer to the role of Shelley's poet-legislator-sage than Kierkegaard ever was.

Sincerely,
Jan

Walker Percy died on Thursday, May 10, 1990.

---

[1] Flannery O'Connor, "The Fiction Writer and His Country," *Mystery and Manners*, eds. Sally and Robert Fitzgerald, New York, Farrar, Straus, and Giroux, 1969, p. 34.

CHAPTER FOURTEEN

Josephine Humphreys's New Southerner

When I first read Josephine Humphreys's novels, I saw that she had been influenced by Walker Percy's existentialism. But in her fiction I sensed an even deeper relationship with Eudora Welty's work. When I heard that Reynolds Price, Miss Welty's worthiest disciple, had taught Humphreys at Duke University, I felt justified in supposing a connection. I gave a talk on Josephine Humphreys's "Citified Carolina" at a European Southern Studies Forum meeting at the University of South Carolina in November, 1993, where Humphreys was also present. An earlier version of chapter fourteen was published in Southern Landscapes, *eds. Tony Badger et al., Tübingen, Stauffenburg Verlag, 1996.*

Josephine Humphreys's New Southerner[1]

In his book on *Space and Place* Yi-Fu Tuan argues that place is different from space due to "locational qualities" associated with the contemplation of place.[2] From his mentioning of "the security and stability" of place it is clear that Yi-Fu Tuan endows place with values and complex emotions. "Place" is a more comprehensive word than "scene" or "landscape," it comprehends not only the natural physical characteristics, but also the sensory and imaginative experience of the setting. Place and sense of place both depend for their meaning on the human element, the presence of people and their feelings. We tend to measure ourselves against place and try to become a part of its more enduring identity. In this sense the psychological and existential ties that characterize a profound attachment to a place imply a universal desire to transcend the present. The critic must ask: what does consciousness of the landscape mean to the artist personally? And, how has it colored her description of the place and influenced its function in the particular story?

Like Donald Davidson's "autochthonous" Southern writer, described in his Lamar lectures, Josephine Humphreys is in a certain harmony with her social and cultural environment. But unlike Davidson's ideal writer, Humphreys *is* motivated by an urge to question, interpret, and explain the psychosocial situation in her Southern landscape. I will try to analyze the influence of the Southern landscape on Humphreys's fiction. What makes it a rewarding approach is her obvious identification with her town, her state, and its people.

It is both "natural and sensible" that our place of origin should also become the "primary proving ground" of our fiction, as Welty put it in "Place in Fiction."[3] Humphreys's fiction has come out of the particular landscape of her place of origin and is based on her long familiarity with its people, and her art is always bound to her Carolina. A sense of Charleston is "the whole foundation" on which her fiction rests, and she has devoted much time and space to it, but Humphreys never reduces her concept of her city to a simple definition.

Realism is above all what Humphreys has in common with Eudora Welty. Whatever they write, it is always wedded to place, they are "touched off by place," and place keeps them "responsible" for what they have put down for the truth. It would be difficult to find a writer who identifies with her community *more* than Humphreys does. Her favorite setting is without doubt Charleston. The city has a stubborn peculiarity of its own, and Humphreys has proved remarkably responsive to the past and present of her city. S. T. Coleridge was so taken up with German Idealism and so thoroughly convinced that the mind creates the world that he had only a limited sense of place. It is perhaps what primarily distinguishes Coleridge from his some-time friend William Wordsworth, who was totally convinced of the reality of what he saw about him, and whose sense of place is the heart of his poetry.

It was easy for Wordsworth to identify with the English landscape of his day. Today's creative artist in South Carolina has to look for the landscape behind a repetitive labyrinth of highways, motels, burger-places, gas stations, shopping malls etc. It is a modular world in which most of us are too easily at home because things are everywhere the same. What Humphreys has proved is that it is not merely pockets of virgin forests and overlooked (and therefore) unpolluted streams that awaken a feel for a place, but also cities. The city estranges us from the world *only* when it rapes and obliterates its site. Unfortunately, it has happened in Charleston and Mount Pleasant:

> Originally we had the city of Charleston, the town of Mount Pleasant, and then the country, but now they were jumbled, haphazard as a frontier settlement.... I was always impressed on this highway by the hordes of people stocking up on new shoes, blue jeans, groceries, hamsters, mini-vans, tomato plants, sheets of plywood, ice-cream cones. The level of shopping was an indicator, ... , of human trust in the future. I myself sometimes woke up in the middle of the night scared to death .... I had studied the town of Herculaneum, buried by hot mud in the year 79 A. D. My town had been similarly engulfed, not by mud but by overflow from the city of Charleston .... (*Rich in Love*, 3, 5, 11)

The identification of writer and home ground is unmistakable, and it is obvious from the fidelity to every detail that a special relationship exists between the writer and her place. Her town and state are not only the geographical and sociological settings of much of her fiction, they are parts of her interior landscape.

By studying her native place and expressing its essence in fiction, Humphreys studies her own self. She may satirize the people she sees about her in Charleston and elsewhere, but the purpose is always to amuse by displaying the folly of mankind and to offer laughter as a means of questioning our concept of "sanity." It is never to expose or ridicule her own community. The Faulknerian element of pity for the individual in his misfortune is always present. If we recognize flaws and elements of the grotesque in her characters, it is probably as reflections of our own limitations. Humphreys can negate her own emotions and enter all of her characters, give them life, and bring out their humanity in all their ways wherever they live; but it is extremely important just *where* they live. The strength of her sense of place is identification in her fictional territory, *both* with her native area and its people. Without trivializing the actual landscape, Humphreys's preoccupation with Charleston goes beyond the precise, identifiably local, and mimetic descriptions of life in that city to intimations of a universal landscape of timeless joys and sorrows. The art is that the cityscape of her novels encompasses everything that happens, has happened, and will happen for as long as landscape and memory exist. And the readers know they are a part of her map of that landscape.

The contemporary Southern novel has become increasingly city-oriented with novelists such as Ann Beattie, Doris Betts, Larry Brown, Clyde Edgerton, Shelby Foote, Kaye Gibbons, Barry Hannah, Madison Jones, Bobbie Ann Mason, Walker Percy, and Peter Taylor. Even when they set their plots in rural areas, the issues are mostly those of city-people, and the problems are those of moviegoers, kidnappers, college youths in jeans, city-doctors, and city-lawyers. A preoccupation with the city is nothing new in Southern fiction, novel after novel throughout the Southern Renaissance focused on the lives of young Southerners stranded in cities. Eugene Gant in Thomas Wolfe's *Of Time and the River*, Quentin Compson in William Faulkner's *The Sound and the Fury*, and Peyton Loftis in William Styron's *Lie Down in Darkness* are classic examples. In the impersonal crowds up North the young Southerners find themselves completely cut off from everybody, and for them the city becomes a nightmare experience.

But when they try to "go home," they find it impossible. If they attempt to function as members of their native communities, they are usually unable to accept the home community as found, for to their surprise the ways of the big cities have been imported there while they were away. So on their return they often fail to find any justification for their belief in the value of a life removed from metropolitan ways. They are forced to realize that their images of an agrarian South are images of the past, and that even at home the present offers no refuge from the placelessness of the city. So the return to the rural areas around Asheville, Nashville, Clarksville, Milledgeville, Charlottesville, Louisville, or Greenville never become real homecomings. Dreams of a traditional agrarian life-pattern are easily starved in the face of what John Shelton Reed called a reality of "instant grits and plastic-wrapped crackers."[4] Their fiction profited greatly, however, from the young writers' excursions to the Northern cities, and much of the best fiction of the Southern Renaissance was constructed on the foundation of those experiences. A young Southerner in search of city-experience today need not go North. The urbanization of the South and to some extent of its culture is *the* important sociological fact of the South after the Depression. Several Southern cities have developed rapidly from rural towns to modern industrial cities. Such urbanization is nothing new for the United States in general, where three fourths of the population already long has lived on about one percent of the land, but for the South it is a fairly recent development.

Fictional portraits of city life involve an obvious selective process, and the elements selected by Humphreys to represent life in cities make it impossible to overlook an implicit judgment. In her portrait of the city she is in tune with Thomas Jefferson, who wrote in his *Notes on the State of Virginia:* "The mobs of great cities add just so much to the support of pure government, as sores do to the strength of the human body."[5] And Humphreys is in tune with ideas about the development of American history going back at least to Frederick Jackson Turner: the city leaves its mark on mind and manners, and the impact on the individual of urban life is decidedly different from that of life in the country. This is usually mentioned *not* in praise of modern cities, but to remind us of American values and ideas associated with life on the frontier in the 18th and 19th centuries. These are values that have supposedly survived into our century among Americans living on and off the country.[6]

In the "citified world" a Humphreys character may feel "twined in" and insecure:

> If there were such a thing as a safe place, she knows it would have to be here in Charleston. It was for safety these houses were built, crowded together on the peninsula behind a wall to keep out Indians, Spaniards, outlaws. And now tourists come to see the place .... In the suburbs as shown on television, women drink coffee together in their kitchens and men borrow tools from each other. But here [in the city] people keep to themselves. (*Dreams of Sleep*, 6-7)

It is the woman's husband who wants to live where they do, which does not mean that he is not worried:

> Maybe he shouldn't leave his children alone in the house, even for the few minutes it will take him to walk to her car and back. Maybe he ought to lock the door. "Will they be safe by themselves?" Marcella [his mother] asks. "Of course," he says .... He could live in a safer place. He could live downtown near the Battery instead of in this ambiguous zone between rich and poor... but he won't move, he has set his family here. "Courting disaster," Alice [his wife] says. (*Dreams of Sleep*, 50-51)

The loss of a sense of security in the traditional place, Leonard Lutwack talks of "the pain of placelessness," is a characteristic that makes him a typical city-dweller.[7] Will Reese is moving in the stultifying atmosphere of an acquisitive and dehumanizing civilization. The impact on him of modern urbanized life is a profound sense of loss. As Blanche H. Gelfant describes the reactions of a man in the situation, Will feels he has failed somehow and that any course of action may involve him in "serious self-contradictions, if not indeed in self-destruction."[8]

Today most Southerners are not only citified, but also city-born, and their mental states are influenced by skyscrapers and shopping-malls in the urban sprawl. Is the citizen of the Southern urban industrial setting necessarily anonymous, rootless, insecure, alienated, and cut off from human relationships? Is he also enslaved by the media, paralyzed by traffic, and victimized because of caste and class, or by crimes and violence? Humphreys does not denounce the city-tied Southerner, instead she tells us with compassion how he lives in the citified world.

The emphasis in Humphreys's fiction is always on the individual character and his emotions. But by necessity the individual is in a place and in an interrelationship with the community of that place. With her accepted sense of place comes the acceptance of a whole body of thought founded on her situatedness in place and community. A sense of a particular landscape implies a sense of continuity, and both concepts presuppose and are based on the history of the place, are bound by the emotions of the individual, and indicate a sense of community with the generations of people who lived there. It is essential to understand this element in her art to grasp Humphreys's relationship with her community.

In one of her talks Flannery O'Connor said: "The novelist is required to open his eyes on the world around him and look. If what he sees is not highly edifying, he is still required to look."[9] Throughout the 70s and 80s Southern politicians have given emphasis to the interrelationship between place and community, and they have warned against the impact of change upon the values Southerners associate with their region. In 1975 Governor Reubin Askew of Florida said: "The economic development of the South need not result in the degradation of our land or the deprivation of our people.... We cannot allow what has happened in the North to happen here in the South."[10] The main reason for the concern in the midst of all the talk about growth was expressed by Gov. David Boren, who chaired the Southern Growth Policies Board in 1977. He asked: "How do we keep alive the values that make our system and our section so vital?"[11] The important question for these politicians and for Southern writers is whether it is possible to urbanize and yet keep basic Agrarian values. Is it possible to avoid creating polluted and devastated cities and alienated people by simply emphasizing the old values of a sense of place, a sense of community, and an awareness of the past? When she sees the importance of traditional values and virtues for individual and community even in the *urban* South, Humphreys is in the mainstream of Southern thinking of the last two decades.

Like everybody else Humphreys's characters learn that it is tough to be anybody. Living with yourself and others means that existential choices have to be made. The decisive factors for the choice are values with their origin in the community. The existential choice takes its point of departure in the individual's sense of place and community and has consequences for the ethics of the individual and for the community. This passage is from the opening of her third novel:

> It was only by chance that the general ruin, the wreckage of the mainland city and its islands, coincided with the specific ruin of himself. The two things simply happened together: the place ravaged by hurricane, the man by something more complicated .... Now was the time to do it. With the whole place thrown into confusion, one man's leap into a small personal chaos would be less noticeable .... He saw with the eyes of a boy again. There were possibilities afoot, even in the midst of ruin. (*Fireman's Fair*, 1, 11, 14)

Humphreys describes a place in detail because she writes about human beings, and to understand and define them, it is essential in her aesthetics of place to locate them. Their meaning always bears on what they came out of, and it is defined by it. In important respects we are products of our native place, its history, its atmosphere, i. e. its essence of place. It is, of course, also true of the artist who celebrates a place.

Humphreys's idea of place involves more than memories of times past, her "-place" is also time made visible. Charleston houses a tradition-oriented and class-conscious community. Originally the physical setting still shaped the social interaction in town, but the relationship between place and social place has weakened considerably in the town. For the young generation there is now a dissociation, so that their behavior is no longer determined or defined by their physical presence in the town. Humphreys seems to be implying that the next generation may grow up without the steadying point of place to focus their minds. As Joshua Meyrowitz has shown in his *No Sense of Place*, the physical location is hardly ever the social place in the new world of electronic media.[12] The community is changing rapidly, it is becoming fragmented, a sense of self is no longer necessarily ingrained with a sense of community, and in as far as a social order exists, it is becoming impersonal, technological, and increasingly disneyfied. In Humphreys's fiction some of the plans for Charleston's future include:

> "A theme park." "Theme park?" "Yes, you know, like Six Flags or Carowinds." "Disney World." "No, no, ... This will be much more low-key, more in tune with the environment and related to the historical traditions of the area" .... "What's the theme?" "Pirates. To tie in with the riverfront. We'll have a couple of pirate ships that actually go out, take people on the river, out to Drum Island, where we'll give them maps to dig for buried treasure. Everything will have the pirate theme. Our hotel, the restaurant, the villas. It's natural because there really were pirates here. One of them was hanged on the Battery. We plan to reenact it." .... "Oh God," Will says. "Let him have the goddamned thing .... We'd rather have you than those fuckers. Atlantans and Arabs! They're the same, except the Arabs are cleaner. Atlantans will mess with anything" .... "Oh, no. This is local money. Local people. In fact the initial idea came from them. (*Dreams of Sleep*, 178, 181)

Personal relations in the community are decaying, and a chance to make a good investment could easily matter more than any residue of reverence for the historic city – even for a true son of Charleston.

Humphreys's novels come from living in South Carolina – they are *part* of living in Charleston, of her long familiarity with the thoughts and feelings of those around her in that modern landscape. She *demonstrates* that the role of place in fiction is "to attach precise local values to feeling."[13] In "Place in Fiction" Welty wrote: "Location is the ground conductor of all the currents of emotion and belief and moral conviction that charge out from the story in its course." In the most recent version of the essay the point is elaborated in an added line, which reads: "From the dawn of man's imagination, place has enshrined the spirit." Humphreys's novels are "enshrined" in her place. Her Charlestonians seem located where they stand – part of their own map.

In important respects our minds are products of our native place, its history, its atmosphere, and its essence of place. Humphreys needs the self-definition of true attachment, a sense of continuity between her past and present, and accepts her relationship with Charleston. The city, she realizes, is an inextricable part of her identity. The community provides the necessary "set of standards to struggle within or against."[14] Like her fictional characters Humphreys has to see her life in context. She uses the identity of a place to measure herself. And she is finally measured against the enduring identity of her place, which means against all that has happened in Charleston and against all the human relationships that have been experienced there. The history of the city is an ever-present commentary on today's events. In this way the past of Charleston is integrated with its present, and contemporary Charlestonians participate in a drama of place that began before they were born and will end after they are dead. I believe that it is what C. Hugh Holman meant when in an essay on Ellen Glasgow he included "a sense of place as a dramatic dimension" among characteristics that set the best Southern writing apart from much American writing in this century.[15]

Place and writer have sustained each other, and it is obvious that "one is in a bad way without the other," as Walker Percy once put it.[16] As it reveals itself in Humphreys's changing attitude to her place, she continuously defines and redefines her own identity. In her novels she has continued her discovery and constant rediscovery of her place. For the critic it means that a study of Humphreys's idea of place, with a focus on place in fiction, becomes a way of describing her existential practices. It is the human life lived there, geographically and historically, which gives place its emotional impact in her fiction. Humphreys's characters are the place they live. Or better, their place is so much a part of them that their identity depends on the relation, whether it is the identity, present or past, of individual, family, community, city, state, or region.

What makes Humphreys's fiction art is not just the perfect evocation of a particular place, of a changing community, and a historical period, it is the analysis, discovery, and hopefully recognition of the existential landscape that is the result of the evocation of the particular place. Her hometown has changed beyond recognition. Her characters' growing disorientation and feeling of estrangement in Charleston are results of a general sense of malaise and displacement. When she writes about people as she knows them in the here and now, she is writing about everybody.[17] By seeing the particulars of her native place in time, she can successfully approach the universal.

The achievement of a national culture based on modern technology and spatial mobility, instead of a traditional culture based on a sense of place, does not necessarily appeal to Humphreys. She sees clearly what John Crowe Ransom meant when he explained that "what is called progress is often destruction."[18] Warren Odom of *Rich in Love* is Humphreys's representative of the carpeted and air-conditioned Southeast. Odom is a demolition expert, he removes the old buildings to clear the way for the new South:

> You want them to go down straight, ... , like a man shot in the knees, crumpling .... His last job was the old Wade Hampton Hotel in Columbia .... He stood in its portico, looking out past the spread of Columbia towards the sandhills, and he felt queerly lifted from his own life into a clean and quiet myth .... The Wade Hampton had gone down the way he had foreseen .... He could claim partial credit for the new look of the cities he loved: Columbia, Charlotte, Atlanta, Charleston. He had help clear the way for all their downtown Mariotts and Sheratons, office plazas and civic centers. Some of those hotels had indoor streams, and vines and trees genuinely growing in the lobby. Those buildings were proof that the Southeast had become nothing to be ashamed of. (*Rich in Love*, 80, 81, 82)

Other characters of Humphreys's novels look for a cultural continuity of traditional Agrarian ideas from their origin in the rural South to their presence in the urbanized South. Will Reese's and Rob Wyatt's mostly negative images of the city have their origin in their basically Agrarian ideas about place, identity, and a rewarding life. Lyle H. Lanier wrote in his contribution to *I'll Take My Stand* [19] that the real sense of community only exists in the agrarian community, whereas city life necessarily means a diminution of the communal experience and just serves to increase a sense of isolation. The patterns of conduct of city people are supposedly incompatible with the stability and integrity of family life. The good life is in an agrarian setting. Rob's brother Ernie is getting married to Rhonda: "Rhonda's got a little cabin and a horse pasture, horses .... I admit, marriage is a big step. I wasn't all for it right away. But I've thought it all out and made the decision." His brother reacts as could be expected, but he is thinking, "*a pasture, a cabin! Rhonda waiting at the cabin door in her faded jeans, the Florida greenery flashing, scrub jays in the piney woods ...*" (*Fireman's Fair*, 196). The hope for the future based on a life in harmony with nature has been in Humphreys's novels from the start. Will Reese speculates "on the length of time required for vegetation to retake an area the size of the Old South – building, pool, parking lot. If you jackhammered the concrete and asphalt just enough to bust it up, let the seedlings through ... With the help of kudzu the place could be green, even dense again, in two, three years" (*Dreams of Sleep*, 160). And in the same novel, Iris Moon is greatly relieved when she drives into the low marshland, down the coast of the state, and sees the still open land where Charleston does not yet touch Savannah – as she had feared. "Things are not as bad as you get to thinking they are," she said (*Dreams of Sleep*, 201). The opinion seems echoed in the most recent novel. Rob Wyatt glories in the "splendid sight" of what Hurricane Hugo had done to a golf course at the Sewee Club, he sees that nature has totally reclaimed the fairway, and he feels that "all was not lost" (*Fireman's Fair*, 79).

In his essay "Dodging Apples" Reynolds Price argues that all artists create because they believe in the "value and urgency" of what they see and attempt to understand. His point is that "all works of art came into existence to change something," "to cause some action," "in the hope of altering, literally causing movement" in the writer himself, his reader, and "the world at large."[20] Humphreys's creative principles reveal her moral principles, and her aesthetics of place is not finally distinguishable from the ethics of living in a place and finding one's identity in relation to it. She is not a sociologist trying to right social wrongs, she is not a psychologist trying to explain the origin of wrong, nor is she a preacher choosing between right and wrong. She is a novelist offering her vision of how it is with us now and how it has always been. A distinction between her moral and aesthetic values cannot be final. Like everybody else Humphreys's characters learn that living with yourself and others means that existential choices have to be made. The decisive factors for the existential choice are not abstract, but values with their origin in the community of the place, past and present. The existential choice takes its point of departure in the individual's imaginative sense of place and has consequences for the ethics of the individual and therefore for the community. Alice Reese's aesthetic impression of Charleston life on her way to the supermarket has existential implications for her, and her thoughts on "the project" become an ethical evaluation of herself, and of her time and place:

> The walk to the supermarket takes her through the black neighborhood of midtown. It is not the way she used to go; she used to detour around the project, sticking to the business streets .... People stared at her from windows and porches, from cars. Of course they'd stare. It is unheard of in any Southern city for a white person to walk through one of these places, the old colored town now gulped into the city and lost behind stores and hotels .... But this is not the worst of the city, it isn't Bayside, where old people don't leave their houses for months at a time, so frightened are

> they of what is on the street. No, this is just old colored town .... It is a pocket of slow, warm living in the middle of town, like a world coexistent with the rest but not visible from it, not from the ... places white people go .... What will happen to all these black people, now the movement is dead, their heroes tucked away in public offices? Was the whole civil rights movement nothing but a minor disturbance in the succession of years?.... Blacks and whites live farther apart than ever, like the double curve of a hyperbolic function, two human worlds of identical misery and passion but occupying opposite quadrants, nonintersecting. (*Dreams of Sleep*, 132, 133, 134)

Most of us approach the landscape focused on ourselves, looking for what agrees with our temperaments, and if we are artists, for what seems to embody our emotions, and what will suit us as setting for our creative efforts. Some people, such as Humphreys and Eudora Welty, have the good fortune to be born, and to remain, in country which is continuous with their personalities. When I see a correspondence between Josephine Humphreys's disposition and the scenery of Charleston, I am not implying an easy affinity between writer and city, or a superficial imposition of mood on a place. It is Humphreys's constant awareness of Charleston and South Carolina, and their presence in her mind as something powerfully Other to struggle with, which makes the relationship so valuable for her art.

The landscape as observed by Humphreys is a fusion of human and natural order, and the result may offer a peculiar window on the whole. The catalyst that converts the physical cityscape of Charleston into art is that Humphreys so obviously lays claim to it through her feelings for the city. The sounds and smells and sights and stories of Charleston haunt Humphreys, and it is against them that she measures the present. She responds with mind and body and claims her city and state, and out of her whole response comes her writing. When the nature of Charleston changes, Humphreys is influenced, her human values are affected, and her readers are subtly changed as well.

Josephine Humphreys is a Southern writer finding her place and defining herself in a landscape that is already crowded with talent and much-praised achievement. She is inspired by an innate historical perspective and seems to need the past to understand the present. And she is blessed by a keen sense of place and an obvious sectional pride. She is a great talent and exemplifies the continuity, change, and excellence of Southern fiction.

1. Josephine Humphreys novels were all first published by The Viking Press. Page references in this essay are to the Viking editions: *Dreams of Sleep* (1984), *Rich in Love* (1987), and *The Fireman's Fair* (1991).

2. Yi-Fu Tuan, *Space and Place: The Perspective of Experience*, Minneapolis, University of Minnesota Press, (1977) 1981, p. 6.

3. Eudora Welty, *The Eye of the Story: Selected Essays and Reviews*, New York, Random House, 1978, p. 129.

4. John Shelton Reed, "Instant Grits and Plastic-Wrapped Crackers: Southern Culture and Regional Development," *The American South: Portrait of a Culture*, ed. Louis D. Rubin, Jr., Washington, Forum, 1979, p. 25.

5. Thomas Jefferson, *Notes on the State of Virginia*, ed. William Peden, Chapel Hill, 1955, p. 165.

6. Frederick Jackson Turner, "The Significance of the Frontier in American History," *The Frontier in American History*, ed. Ray Allen Billington, New York, Holt, Rinehart & Winston, 1962 (1920), pp. 1-38.

7. Leonard Lutwack, *The Role of Place in Literature*, Syracuse, New York, Syracuse University Press, 1984, p. 226.

8. Blanche Housman Gelfant, *The American City Novel*, 2nd edition, Norman, University of Oklahoma Press, 1970, p. 23.

9. Flannery O'Connor, *Mystery and Manners*, eds. Sally & Robert Fitzgerald, New York, Farrar, Straus & Giroux, 1969, p. 177.

10. Reubin Askew, "Remarks of the New Chairman," Southern Growth Policies Board, Pinehurst, North Carolina, 13 November, 1975, p. 25. Quoted in Stephen A. Smith, *Myth, Media, and the Southern Mind*, Fayetteville, The University of Arkansas Press, 1985, p. 121.

11. "Governor Boren Pays Tribute to Askew for His Leadership," *Southern Growth: Problems & Promises*, 4 (1977) 2. Quoted in Stephen A. Smith, *Myth, Media, and the Southern Mind*, 1985, p. 121.

12. Joshua Meyrowitz, *No Sense of Place: The Impact of Electronic Media on Social Behavior*, New York, Oxford University Press, 1985.

13. Frederick J. Hoffman, *The Art of Southern Fiction*, Carbondale, Ill., Southern Illinois University Press, 1967, p. 61.

14. This is also a quotation from the original version of Welty's "Place in Fiction." New York, House of Books, Ltd., 1957 [p. 23].

15. C. Hugh Holman, "Ellen Glasgow and the Southern Literary Tradition," *Southern Writers: Appraisals in Our Time*, ed. R. C. Simonni, Jr., Plainview, New York, Books for Libraries Press, (1963) reprt. 1969, p. 123.

16. Walker Percy, "Eudora Welty in Jackson," *Signposts in a Strange Land*, New York, 1991, p. 223.

[17] Copy of Welty's untitled speech for the inauguration of Governor William Winter, Mississippi Department of Archives and History, Jackson, ms p. 5.

[18] John Crowe Ransom, "The Aesthetic of Regionalism," *American Review* 2 (January 1934) 310.

[19] *I'll Take My Stand: The South and the Agrarian Tradition*, by Twelve Southerners (1930), Gloucester, Mass., Peter Smith, 1976, pp. 122-54.

[20] Reynolds Price, "Dodging Apples," *Things Themselves: Essays & Scenes*, New York, Atheneum, 1972, pp. 7-12.

CHAPTER FIFTEEN

The Man by the Jukebox:
Larry Brown's Haunted Voices

Larry Brown is one of the many new writers in the South. I am not sure he is as talented as Barry Hannah or Mary Hood, but at his best he is very good. Although he lives in Faulkner's Oxford, Mississippi, he is perhaps more of the stoic Hemingway school of writing, but his worrying characters with existential problems are typical of much contemporary Southern fiction. I gave a talk on Larry Brown as a new Southern voice at the University of Warwick in September 1994. The talk inspired the present chapter.

The Man by the Jukebox

Southern writers of this century have always known that human beings are more important than ideas, and that any one idea, crazy or not, that we may be advocating is only one of our innumerable ideas and therefore cannot possibly do justice to our full potential. Southern fiction today does not look for the one idiosyncratic explanation that can account for the whole of reality. Philosophies of overriding ideas such as Marxism, Freudianism, and Existentialism seem, to no surprise to Southern writers, to have failed abjectly in helping us come to terms with the upheavals in our social, economic, and moral realities. And the contemporary Southern writers are making sure that their characters do *not* illustrate *an idea*. Southern writers are now, as always, looking for new ways of seeing and showing a world full of ancient human problems.

Larry Brown of Oxford, Mississippi, is one of the promising talents among the new writers of Southern fiction, but he is not always equally successful. He is a skilled writer and usually has something to say. His best fiction is so good that it enables us to talk of a continuity of distinctiveness in Southern literature. But Brown's fiction is also an important expression of the literary concerns and attainments of *his* generation of Southern writing. His fiction is often of the so-called K-Mart type: full of similar types of characters, all with flat diction and much pop syntax, who move in a social world stuffed with brand names and television. He believes that the human condition is very sad and very funny, and he dramatizes the lives of Southerners who are drugged by consumerism.[1]

Brown is a satirist who expresses the spiritual bankruptcy he encounters, and he raises his voice against the hypocrisy and phoniness he sees about him. He is a realist who tells the exact truth as he knows it, usually without sentimentality. He writes primarily of people who are down and out, often suicidal, and cut off from their own humanity. But they are people who try to regain their dignity and connect with the human race. His protagonists, who are often also the narrators, are distressed and almost defeated, but most eloquent. In several of the short stories collected in *Facing the Music* (1988) and *Big Bad Love* (1990) the tales Brown's characters tell us are absurd and graphic in the rendition of every menacing detail, but at their best they are humorous and reveal genuine emotion.

Due to his preoccupation with sex and violence, much of what Brown writes taxes our patience and may even be considered "disturbing." But his fiction usually goes well beyond his preoccupation with violence and sex. Its lasting value is not in the prevailing atmosphere of callousness, but in Brown's authentic compassion for our constant suffering in our bourgeois situations. He pities us because we are reduced to seeking satisfaction and redemption through the experience of sex and violence. He shows us our insane attempts at living "sane" lives and suggests ways of restoring our fragmented selves. In most of the stories and in the non-fiction we are both stylistically and thematically very much in the company of Ernest Hemingway and Barry Hannah; for example in this passage from his book of nonfiction, *On Fire*:

> You have to meet the thing is what it is. You have to do something in your life that is honorable and not cowardly if you are able to live in peace with yourself, and for the firefighter it is fire. It has to be faced and defeated so that you prove to yourself that you meet the measure of the job. You cannot turn your back on it, as much as you would like to be in cooler air, as much as you would like to breathe it. You have to stay huddled with the men you are with. (*On Fire*, 20)

Brown's characters get drunk in local bars, gamble, fight, hunt, have bad luck, are scared, shoot at each other, "womanize," live in bad marriages, try to speak the truth and use just the right phrase, and they try to do "the noble thing," whatever the dangers involved. And his men and women are as unerringly disgusted with mankind as most of Hemingway's characters. But Brown's knowledge of the mental states and motivations of his obsessive "no-counts," boozers, bar-room brawlers, and wife-beaters is singular in American literature. With uncompromising honesty Brown shows our bestiality and our hunger for affection.

All Brown's stories are narrated with wit and the saving grace of humor. But in some stories he demonstrates an unfortunate weakness for the sort of surprise-twist finish that may serve well to amuse friends in a bar when the storyteller tries for the biggest laugh. A rereading usually shows that these endings are uncalled for and too unrealistic to convince. The final story in the first volume of short stories is called "The End of Romance." The story details how an African American is brutally assaulted and shot in a convenience store by another African American. The police arrive on the scene. A man who happened to be in the store to buy beer ends the story by telling the police that his girlfriend did the shooting. Actually, she had never moved from their car and is terrified by what she has witnessed through the windscreen. But her friend ends their romance by being unable to resist a chance to deliver his punch-line: "She did it" (*Facing the Music*, 167). This remark certainly ends the romance, but it is a shallow ending to a story that starts as a truly provocative account of the last afternoon of a relationship.

Some of the stories of men and women and their lives together seem too private to be fully successful. They exist in situations so singular that readers may have trouble identifying with them. At times Brown's aesthetic distance is simply not there in the short stories. The justification for the title of the short story "Falling out of Love," which is the first story in the collection called *Big Bad Love*, turns out to be simply another joke. Inspired by two flat tires on the same side of the car a couple, who have slowly been falling out of love for some time, come back together and end up falling out of their car, naked and entwined, at the feet of some patrolling policemen.

Larry Brown shows that you do not have to be alone to be lonely. Some of his most moving stories show the sad persistence of the structures of relationships after their content is long decayed. In the title story of *Facing the Music* a husband admits to himself:

> I look at her and her shoulders are jerking under the little green gown. I'm always making her cry and I don't mean to. Here's the kind of bastard I am: my wife's crying because she wants me, and I'm lying here watching Ray Milland [on TV], and drinking whiskey, and thinking about putting another woman's breasts in my mouth. She was on top of me and they were hanging right over my face. It was so wonderful, but now it seems so awful I can hardly stand to think about it. (*Facing the Music*, 6)

Brown's characters live grim, menacing, and depressing lives that we recognize well enough, but their universe is not always convincingly universal. It is always difficult for readers to go in search of answers to existential questions with people they hardly know. And often Brown's characters in the short stories do not seem to grow as we turn the pages – their lives just go on. They appear to be static throwaway-characters living in a remote slightly uninteresting universe, yet their lives are obviously painful and sad, and we have to pity them. But it would be easier to share Brown's compassion for his suffering characters if he would give us just a little more of the background for their unhappiness. And this is precisely what Brown has done in his first two novels: *Dirty Work* (1989) and *Joe* (1991).

In his first novel Brown writes of two war veterans, one is Braiden Chaney, who is black and has no arms or legs, and the other is Walter James, who is white and has a displaced face. In this sense they are in a similar situation. And they also come from a similar background as they grew up in poverty in rural Mississippi. The stage is set for an interracial relationship. But even though Walter tells Braiden of his father's defense of a black family against a white landowner and of his own friendship with a black soldier in Vietnam, the two patients never quite overcome the traditional racial barrier. Braiden is not looking for a friend in a situation similar to his own. The black veteran from the Korean War simply does not care whether Walter's unsightly face now makes him as invisible as himself. Racial justice or injustice are far from Braiden's mind, after twenty-two years in a hospital bed he just wants to die. In Walter he hopes to have found the vehicle for his suicide. And Walter does help Braiden die at long last. But the author makes it clear that his motivation has nothing to do with a similar background, a similar fate in war, or a similar present situation. After Walter has listened to Braiden's stories about his hopeless situation, he pities him as one human being will pity another in a terrible situation, and the pity is Walter's true motivation for helping Braiden into the next world.

The main themes of the novel are love and pity. Brown works relentlessly towards the moment when he lets the lovers of *Dirty Work* come together. His unlikely heroes are a woman, whose legs have been badly chewed up by dogs, and Walter, the Vietnam returnee, whose face has been blown to the side of its natural position. The two outcasts come together in a first and final intercourse, which proves emblematic of their existence. Their truck is parked in Moore Creek, which was dry when they got there, but a rain storm soon floods the creek. At a climactic moment the man, who is very heavy, passes out, and the woman is locked in place beneath him. The woman demonstrates her humanity in a moment of truly unselfish compassion:

> The water rose onto the seat with her and her hair clung from the back of her head as she tried to keep her nose above it .... She pushed his head up and fought his dead weight like something caged or just released and sank back under the ponderous burden of his head and chest and legs. She fought him with everything she had. She tried to draw her legs out and tried to slide him sideways and the water rose over her cheeks, into her ears, into her nose until she strangled and lurched wildly up with it pouring over her head. She took his torn face and with every last ounce of strength she had, pushed it up and over and wedged it into the steering wheel. (*Dirty Work*, 233-34)

When they are found in the truck by a road crew, his head is just inches above, hers inches beneath the water.

There seems to be hope for a character like Joe Ransom, of the novel *Joe*, who despises life from the moment he wakes up, and yet does not commit suicide (or go bowling). Joe suffers periods of emotional instability, a qualified unhappiness, a constant pain, and a humiliating feeling of total inadequacy. He is drugged by alcohol, at times fighting it off, waking from the stupor of it, and mostly deeply conscious of what he has lost because of his drinking. Glamor, true eroticism, or obvious idealism are not in Joe's life. He is presented as the blue-collar loser that he is, and not with any implicit thematic emphasis. Without any hint of condescension in his voice Brown has placed Joe in a genuine social environment that allows him to take on substance in full complexity and depth through his relationships with the people who inhabit his environment. He comes to feel alienated from the world of shallow materialism in which he lives, and in this way he becomes a moral comment on that world. He is the foreman of a crew of blacks whose job it is to poison the woods for a lumber company, to make the trees easier to cut down later, so Joe is in a good position to assess the destructive potential of promiscuous consumerism.

Brown's male characters react in fundamentally male ways, by seeking solace in motion and putting confrontations on hold until the gasoline and the beer run out. Riding around in pickup trucks with a gun rack in the rear window, driving the back roads of Northern Mississippi, is a way of life for these men, and their travels become a sustained metaphor for the restlessness of their inner lives. As one of Brown's characters puts it: "If we'd get us a car I could get my driver's license" (*Joe*, 83).

Joe Ransom rides the roads in his pickup. He carries a pistol under his seat, along with an ever-present bottle of bourbon and enough beers in the Igloo cooler. Violence is never far away in his everyday life. His arrival at a local gambling house is described in these words: "They saw him bleeding from the four holes [pellets in his neck] and not a man asked the cause of his ills when he squatted with the money and the dice in the circle of light on the floor ... his eyes bright with pain and liquor. He won the money and nobody asked him to stay and try to lose some of it back" (*Joe*, 106). His former wife will not date, she is sure Joe will beat-up even a post-factum rival. Joe says he will not, but he does not really know himself. Yet, Joe is not quite crippled by his self-destructive life. He is a man who lives by old codes of ethics, and the whole county knows that. Just as Joe's own chances of a reasonable existence seem to be next to nothing, he acts with nobility to make sure that a young man gets a chance in life. The themes of the novel: good versus evil, temptation, sacrifice, and redemption are the themes of great fiction and echo William Faulkner's preoccupations.

Joe seems in several ways to be a literary cousin to the people populating Faulkner's Yoknapatawpha County. Like most of the new Southern writers Larry Brown sees a strong sense of place as his Southern inheritance. At a Southern Festival of Books in Nashville in the fall of 1991 he claimed it is his only tie to Faulkner: "I think the only similarities are some of the people who arrive out of that geography, out of that place where I live, that place where he lived. I think the landscape creates the people." Brown believes the poverty of the South has made a difference in its fiction. He said, "There's still an awful lot of poverty. I still see people who make their living getting aluminium cans out of the garbage cans."

In *Joe* some of his characters are beggars, delirious with hunger. Wade Jones is a poor white itinerant farm worker, who sells one of his sons to some rich people for a car. The youngest daughter of twelve or thirteen is rented out occasionally, for sex. The novel is Southern in reflecting the regional attitude to violence. It is full of fights, shootings, and killings that seem inevitable. In his 1971 study of Southern violence John Shelton Reed found that Southerners traditionally condone violence in certain situations and consider some homicides justifiable, especially when the unwritten cultural rules had not been observed.[2] But in the novel Wade Jones, "the breadwinner as Brown ironically calls him, goes far beyond what the Southerner will accept in his treatment of his family and others. Brown has given him no redeeming features. Wade will loot anybody around him, and he does not mind using violence to get what he wants. He knocks down his fourteen year old son Gary and steals the boy's hard earned money. He beats eight hidden dollars out of his wife, so he can get drunk. Later in a very realistic passage, he kills an old black man, totally unknown to him, striking him twice with an iron bolt. Apparently Wade's only motivation is his desire to possess the black man's liquor. His total booty is, as the narrator informs us in his usual detached way: "Thirteen dollars in cash, three U.S. Government food coupon booklets worth sixty dollars each. And the bottle of Fighting Cock" (*Joe*, 153). The old black man was in the act of passing the bottle to Wade Jones as he was struck on his forehead with a construction bolt.

It will be difficult for most readers to comprehend fully just how poor the Wade Jones family is. It is therefore a minor triumph for Brown's narrative style that when we get to the following passage, we are ready to accept it as an expression of the family's extreme poverty. A poor-white young man pays a visit to a prostitute and has an unexpected experience: ""Come in here," she said. He got up and set his beer down and staggered into the bathroom. She held up a blue implement that was foreign to him, made of plastic and with white bristles .... "Do me a favor and brush your teeth.... I ain't gonna fuck you if I can't even kiss you." "What am I supposed to do with it?" "You supposed to brush your teeth with it." "Well, how do you do it?" She glared at him. "Shit, do you not know nothin? Here." She showed him ..." I thought everybody knew how to brush teeth. Where you been all your life?" "Just around," he said" (*Joe*, 270-71). Brown manages to convince us that the boy has never even heard of a toothbrush before, even though he is now a young man.

These Mississippians and the place they live are "so vividly sketched you can all but mount it on your wall," as Leon Rooke wrote in an early review in the *New York Times Book Review*. Joe's world has all the trappings of a modern waste land:

> Tarpaper shacks and shabby mobile homes, actually no more than campers, lined the road, the yards full of junked autos and stacked firewood overgrown with weeds and pulpwood trucks with the windows smashed out and the rear ends jacked up and propped on oil drums. El Dorados with mud halfway up the sides parked before porches of rough sawmill lumber. Here and there were school buses fixed up with furniture and beds on the inside, the awnings made of splintered fiberglass, and new brick homes within sight of firetraps where carports were cluttered with dogs and three-wheelers and washing machines. (*Joe*, 73)

Brown expresses an almost Agrarian regret about the loss of the natural surroundings through the growth of the man-made environment. A sense of place involves a sense of the people who live in the place. If people in important respects are the place they live, and if their identity depends in any way on where they live, his characters are in serious existential, and by implication, moral trouble. Brown is a part of a community, and he finds his identity in relation to it by sharing in or rebelling against it. He certainly rebels against what his community is doing to its natural surroundings. But Joe knows how to detach himself from his community and its reduced landscape. If he turns onto a dirt road, he can leave the depressing modern scene behind. When he needs to, he can enter another part of his world, which is not an agrarian or pastoral place, but much more like a pocket of preserved primeval forest:

> After an hour or so they turned onto a dirt road, the entrance overhung with great leaning trees and vines, the shade deep and strong like a darker world within the outer, a place of cane thickets and coon dens and the lairs of bobcats, where the sun at its highest cast no light over the rotted stumps and stagnant sloughs. The trees that bordered the road and spread out across the land beside it had closed their tops together, so long had they stood there admitting neither light nor shadow of hawk nor the blue smoke of chain saws. (*Joe*, 90-91)

Joe is not proud of his job, which is to poison the trees in preparation for the cutting and destruction of the last leftover woods: "He surveyed his domain and the dominion he held over them not lightly, his eyes half-lidded and sleepy under the dying forest. He didn't feel good about being the one to kill it. He guessed it never occurred to any of them what they were doing. But it had occurred to him" (*Joe*, 203). *Joe* is a more mature effort than Brown's earlier fiction on the same themes. The novel is amusing, as is always the case with his fiction, but it is also realism of the uncompromising and unblinking kind, and with an almost Faulknerian touch Larry Brown makes Mississippi of today come to life as a world full of ancient human problems.

By exposing the surprising narrowness of his range, the novel *Father and Son* (1996) brings out some of Larry Brown's limitations. One of the main characters, Glen Davis, is somewhat deranged. It is clear from the moment he is introduced that the author intends to kill him off eventually. But the novel is long, and it takes Brown too long to let him die, even though only his death can offer release for him, and for the reader. It is possible that the author wants us to see Glen as a tragic figure. But he has not created a tragic figure.

It is true that Glen kills his younger brother Theron by accident and in a car with bad breaks runs over another child, and his mother takes her own life, but a sense of the tragic is not created. The streak of bad luck is too much for any one family, and it is certainly too much for any one reader to accept. It is equally difficult to stomach the lesson at the end of the novel, which sets some sort of record for faked sentimentalizing in modern Southern fiction:

> But now she [his mother] was dead and nothing was going to bring her back and now he couldn't tell her again that he didn't mean to shoot his brother or that he didn't mean to run over that little boy. It all rose up in him and choked him and he fell against a stall with hot tears blinding him, knowing full well about love and the pull of it and the way of flesh and how weak it was, how it could turn you away from the path of what was right and good." (*Father and Son*, 323)

The passage is liable to make a few readers cry, as well, but not necessarily for the reason Brown intended. *Publisher's Weekly* called the novel "humane and haunting." It is certainly haunting.

Glen Davis is far from being a victim of circumstance. And he is not a good man paying for one fatal flaw in his mental make-up. He is not a thinking man, he has only weak traces of reasoning: "He wondered when people would learn not to mess with him. Somebody always had to be messing with him and he was tired of it. He was sick of it. You couldn't just let people run over you. They'd get to thinking they could do it all the time and they'd keep on doing it if you didn't do something about it. And he'd had about enough...." (*Father and Son*, 318). With an unquestioning finality he hates his father and does not in the least care about his own son. His five-days rape and murder spree demonstrates an egotism so overpowering that Glen finnally appears as a singularly unfortunate choice as vehicle for an insight into relations between fathers and sons. In spite of the title the focus is never really on David, Glen's son, who must grow up without a father in the house. The boy remains unimportant in the novel. From the moment we first see him Glen is too psychologically damaged to be able to qualify as tragic father, or son. He is simply not yearning for what could have been. Glen Davis is a character that demonstrates Madison Jones's acknowledged influence on Larry Brown. But Jones would have used Glen Davis as the inexplicably evil figure that he is; and unlike Brown he would not have sentimentalized the character.

As Glen Davis is not normal enough for most readers to identify with, and as his existential worrying is simplified to the level of brute animals, Brown ends up with a story that is *not* the tragic story of epic proportions that it was clearly his intention to write. It is obvious that Glen would only be able to survive if he lived alone in the woods. He will never be able to fit into the community. The inefficient sheriff, Bobby Blanchard, is offered as a positive counterpoint to the stunted Glen Davis. We see the sheriff in several subplot situations, but Brown never succeeds in making Blanchard a convincing figure.

The novel seems to have been written for the movies, it has the obligatory number of sex scenes and the scenes of inexplicable violence, and it will no doubt make Larry Brown some money. What is really troubling about the novel is what it implies about writing for Hollywood; it seems that a writer has to ignore the human condition to be successful. Instead the emphasis must be wholly on gratuitous exotic scenes. The novel sports an impaled monkey:

"Sometime during the night somebody had pinned the monkey to the bar with an ice pick through the thorax and it lay there atrophied with its palms upward like Christ in His final agony. Several people had put out cigarettes on it. Somebody had bought it a drink. Somebody had cut off its tail" (*Father & Son*, 37). The dead monkey certainly comes alive, if you will excuse the expression. The passage shows what Brown is capable of as a writer, but the good writing cannot obscure that the Barlow plot, with the killing of Barlow and his monkey, is added melodrama and superfluous in the novel.

In *Father and Son* Brown attempts to see North Mississippians of the early 1960s as figures in the tapestry of human history, but the implied invitation to compare with Faulkner's intricately woven *As I Lay Dying* only brings out the extent of Brown's failure. With suspense-creating phrases such as "the clock ticked its slow minutes and the afternoon crept on by," *Father and Son* is at best a psycho-thriller that rivals Stephen King's achievement in that field. Unlike *Joe*, which does deal with the way we live now, *Father and Son* is not likely to be remembered in literary history as another great novel from Mississippi.

Larry Brown is a Southern writer finding his place and defining himself in a landscape that is already crowded with talent and achievement. He is a talent that exemplifies the continuity and change of Southern fiction. It can only be hoped that after his detour with *Father and Son* he will find his way back to the control of style and subject characteristic of *Joe*.

---

[1] Larry Brown's books were published by Algonquin Books of Chapel Hill, North Carolina: *Facing the Music* (stories), 1988; *Dirty Work* (novel), 1989; *Big Bad Love* (stories), 1990; *Joe* (novel), 1992; *On Fire* (non-fiction), 1994; *Father and Son* (novel), 1996.

[2] John Shelton Reed, *The Enduring South: Subcultural Persistence in Mass Society*, Lexington, Mass., D. C. Heath, 1972.

The Lagniappe

CHAPTER SIXTEEN

New Frames of Southern Mind

To celebrate the publication in September, 1989, of an edition of William Faulkner's Spotted Horses, *with original litographs by Boyd Saunders, I was invited to give the keynote address at the University of South Carolina. It surprised a good many in the audience that I did not speak on William Faulkner but on "Southern Fiction in the 1980s," but I felt it was a topic that needed more attention. An early version of chapter sixteen was published by the Danish Association for American Studies in 1991.*

New Frames of Southern Mind

Southern fiction of the 1980s was concerned with loneliness and the disintegration of minds, lives, marriages, families, relationships, community, and tradition. In a sense the object of the early Renaissance had not been abandoned, for the existential search was not necessarily divorced from the attempt at arresting the disintegration of memory and history. The heritage of Kaye Gibbons, Barry Hannah, Josephine Humphreys, Madison Jones, Larry Brown, Mary Hood, Clyde Edgerton, and Dori Sanders could not be disowned in the creative process.

The virtues of Southern fiction provide clues to its faults. If Southern writers are inspired by an innate historical perspective and blessed by a sense of place, they are also more likely to fall prey to mannerism. If it is true that they need the past to understand the present, it is also true that they can be trapped by it, like Mark Twain's river boat which got locked forever in a bayou when the Mississippi changed its course overnight. In the same way "a sense of place" can decay to the merely bizarre, and "a sense of person" may be pushed to caricature so the whole region seem populated with eccentrics created by Lewis Grizzard. It is what happened to much Southern fiction in the 50s and 60s. But it does not mean that the great tradition is dead; the only true death is in lack of change and development, and there is plenty of change in today's Southern fiction. A great deal of good writing is being done in the South, much of it by young women who realize that to be Southern is more than sectional pride, it is also to be aware of the merits of fiction.

At least a dozen women writers of the front rank were writing fiction in the old Confederacy in the 1980s. Some of these are Ann Beattie (Virginia), Mary Ward Brown (Alabama), Pam Durban (South Carolina), Ellen Gilchrist (Mississippi), Shirley Ann Grau (Louisiana), Rebecca Hill (Tennessee), Mary Hood (Georgia), Beverly Lowry (Texas), Bobbie Ann Mason (Kentucky), Ruth Moose (North Carolina), and a host of others that could and should be mentioned as *new* writers of the decade (i.e. they published promising fiction in the 80s). At their best they transcended their Southern origin. They are *Southern* in that they spent their childhood in the South and conceive of themselves as Southern, even if they now reside in New York or Los Angeles. With an emphasis on the mundane the Southern tradition of excellence in fiction continued.

The subjects of the Southern fiction of the 1980s were often what we heard about in the lyrics of country music; in reviews these topics are collectively referred to as K-Mart realism. It was rejected by some as parochial and therefore unworthy of the attention of the serious reader (which was also the criticism that greeted Faulkner's initial efforts). But the worst kind of parochialism is, after all, of the abstract parish. It would be easy for writers to concentrate on the totally abstract entity in order to escape the disorderly nature of life in their own backyard, but fortunately it has not been the choice of Southern writers of this century. The unacceptable regionalism is that of the abstract region, which is a demonstration of ignorance of one's own neighborhood and its people. In the awareness of the importance of a localized and individualized framework and in choice of subject there is little difference between country lyrics by, for example, Kenny Rogers or Willie Nelson and the fiction of say Mary Hood or Bobbie Ann Mason. The emphasis on the everyday problems of the way we live was the strength of Southern fiction in the 1980s, and its weakness.

Universal appeal is built into texts about problems on the job, heart trouble, cheating on your partner, drinking, loneliness, etc. The job facing the fiction writer is to write something about the way we live on our particular postage stamp that is not only universally appealing, but also memorable and of a lasting quality, so the fiction can survive longer than the hit songs of country music. What was the lasting quality William Faulkner wanted to distil from his fiction? If it were easily said, he would not have written so extensively, but we can refer to his own attempt to sum up the purpose of his fiction. In a letter to Warren Beck, a literary critic, Faulkner wrote: "I have been writing all the time about honor, truth, pity, consideration, the capacity to endure well grief and misfortune and injustice and then endure again in terms of individuals who observed and adhered to them not for reward but for virtue's own sake, not even merely because they are admirable in themselves, but in order to live with oneself and die peacefully with oneself when the time comes" (6 July 1941).[1] How does Faulkner's stoic resolve compare in determination and achievement with the writers of the 80s?

What haunts us in our day, as Marion Montgomery put it, "is the recognition that increasingly we can tolerate life only when it is made safe from examination, when it is reduced to goods and conveniences."[2] Does the recognition apply to fiction? Is fiction simply an object to be consumed, a convenience that protects us from examination? The Southern writers work in a tradition which opposes a life that destroys the individual by cutting him off from his community and its past, and from his aesthetic and spiritual needs. Fortunately the function and purpose of fiction is still to show human endurance and possibility. In the permanent ideological battle between "progressive," "scientific," "industrial" values and "aesthetic," "humanistic," "agrarian" values, writers discover and demonstrate their regional bias. Implied in their vision there is the message: enjoy the gift that life is, for to live and experience fully is crucial.

I have mentioned the importance of "a sense of place" in the traditional sense of the phrase. We may also, with Charles East, use the expression about the generation of writers who were trying to find their place in a tradition that is already crowded with achievement. The new writers face a critical consensus that "everything had ended with Faulkner, or would end with Welty: they were not merely a part of something, but the tail end of it."[3] Since the 1980s we have been able to see that there is no reason to be pessimistic about the writers who are now seeking their identities through fiction. At no other time in Southern history, not even in the period between 1920 and 1955, has the Southern prose writer provided more divergent themes, treated evocatively and convincingly, than at present. A whole generation of new writers in the South deserve to be read. Even Walker Percy, who was not known for his optimism, was optimistic about the trend of Southern literature: "Writers-in-residence, as well as local poets who for years have been writing two-word sentences like the chimp Washoe and during readings uttering exclamations, howls, and routinely exposing themselves, have begun writing understandable novels and genuine poetry in the style of Robert Penn Warren ...." (*The Thanatos Syndrome*, 349).

There is little agreement among writers or critics on maximum length for a short story. Traditional attempts at defining the distinction between short story and novel do not seem to apply to the fiction of Anton Chekhov, nor to Southern classics by Katherine Anne Porter, Eudora Welty, Peter Taylor, and others. Even when they allow themselves many pages, they do not necessarily supply the large context, situation and scope are not necessarily developed, and everything is not always resolved or accounted for. On the other hand it does not mean that their fiction observes established criteria for the short story. This is also true of many contemporary Southern writers, they are rarely satisfied with the Jamesian slice of life or the achievement of Poe's single effect, nor do they always look for the compact structure customarily assigned to the short story. Often they try to combine novel and short story in the short story cycle, a form successfully exploited by Faulkner, Welty, and Madison Jones. In other words, it is not always helpful to see modern Southern fiction as developments in the established genres of novel or short story; it is too limiting. Some Southern writers refuse to impose an artificial form on the formlessness of the lives they describe, and their fiction is a reflection of the formlessness.

"*If the South would've won/ we'd had it made,*" sang Hank Williams, Jr. In his much praised short stories Peter Taylor, a Tennessean, often warned us not to believe too much in the plastic present. He and many other contemporary Southern writers gave warning that "the past is still real and present somehow and is demanding something of all men." (*A Summons to Memphis*, 24). What is needed, and what is recognized as desperate need, is a sense of history. "Without it, the highway from Selma to Montgomery becomes just another road, ... and the greatest Southern experience ... is reduced to the banality and triviality of the TV mini-series *North and South*, beside which *Gone with the Wind* seems like Shakespeare next to Neil Simon," as Charles East put it.[4]

Superficiality is always the true enemy, and the main reason fiction writers and their humor are needed so badly. The past provides perspective not just as a period of rather sentimental devotion but as a treasure house of permanent values, which offers comments on our own times.

Surprisingly many of the new writers such as Josephine Humphreys and Pam Durban, both of South Carolina, love the place they come from and count on a strong sense of place in their daily lives and return there daily even when they live far away. It does not mean that they feel their relations with the Southern past are simple. But they *want* to remember, and it hurts to forget. Humphreys realizes that it is possible to forget anything, so she tries to remember everything. What good is a life if you cannot remember its "milestones and themes"? So Humphreys tries to become "the official human memory" by getting life down on paper for "memory is all we've got over collies," as she puts it in *Rich in Love* (52). What is the lesson that history teaches? It shows us the decay of the present and demonstrates that nothing sticks together for very long without immense effort. Our house is in a constant process of disintegration, our work has no permanence, and we are for ever "patching, gluing, temporizing, begging for time." "Is this noble activity" for our generation? (Humphreys, *Dreams of Sleep*, 112).

"Feeling nearly faded as my jeans," sang Kris Kristofferson in his "Bobby McGee." Some of the Southern writers from the 1980s, like Barry Hannah from Mississippi, felt oppressed by the past, even if it is fading, and rebelled against the tradition through a dialogue with it. Hannah wrote, "All the generations of wonderful dead guys behind us. All the Confederate dead and the Union dead planted in the soil near us. All of Faulkner the great. Christ, there's barely room for the living down here" (*Boomerang*, 137). In his rebellion against the Southern tradition in a book which is both autobiography and fiction, short story and a novel all in one, Hannah invented Mona Neary, "a legend of world literature." Although Hannah for once used a fictitious name, the writer in question is without a doubt Eudora Welty, his fellow-Mississippian, who has been writing wonderful fiction since 1936. In *Boomerang*, he lets Mona Neary the sensitive and blameless "genius of American literature" fall over in some tomato plants, where she "farted violently over and over." And in an old chapel he drinks vodka with her, kicks her down the aisle, and shouts, "Die, die!" But when he sobers up, he drives her home, puts her to bed, and kisses her forehead, "knowing she was a national treasure" (113-14). So even the most radical of the writers in the South admitted the presence and the necessity of a living tradition. They may have felt severely restricted by past achievement and wanted to rebel against it in their writings, but eventually they had to find their self-definition in relation to it.

Bobbie Ann Mason, a Kentucky writer of international repute, was also preoccupied with the past in the light of the changing present. In her most successful short story "Shiloh," she demonstrated that the old world of the pioneers had disappeared; it is not even possible to build a log-cabin in the subdivisions of modern Southern cities. The neighbors would not allow it. Leroy, who is out of work, tries to be king of his household in the old patriarchal way. He takes his wife Norma Jean and his mother-in-law on a trip to the Civil War battlefield of Shiloh, Tennessee, presumably to bring to life the old clash between Southern Agrarian values and Northern commercial values. But he is forced to admit to himself that just like the inner workings of marriage, the real inner workings of history have escaped him. The battleground is now taken up by a gender battle. Norma Jean is at Shiloh rebelling against the likes of Leroy. She does not want to wake up one day to find that she is a total housewife. At a distance Leroy notices with joy that his wife is waving her arms beckoning him; as it turns out Norma Jean is simply doing exercises for her chest muscles.

"*Home Is Where You're Happy,*" *sang Willie Nelson.*
"If there is such a thing as a Southern way of life, part of it has to do with not speaking of it," as Walker Percy put it in his last novel. But talking about the way Southerners live now was what Southern writers did all the time in the 1980s. If we judge by Southern fiction, the record of how people have behaved through the years is not impressive. Barry Hannah's version of history is short and to the point: "Before us there were tribes of people wandering around deciding what to eat or fuck or own .... Then came religion and all the long-winded phony bastards like Plato .... The Europeans occurred with tea and gunpowder. Some of the afternoons were tedious and so they began killing thousands of each other to own shit" (*Boomerang,* 67). In Hannah's brief history of mankind there is no mentioning of the family, but otherwise it is obvious in Southern fiction that first there is the family. And much Southern attention is devoted to life in the family: some of the fiction from the 80s has fine observations on the family, as in Gail Godwin's *A Southern Family,* and some of it is boring because of our overfamiliarity with the topic. But the sense of family is pervasive, both the pride in it and the disgust with it. In general the new Southern writers regret that the traditional family pattern is coming undone at the seams. Humphreys describes the Frobiness family of Charleston, a family whose unity became diluted by hobbies and pleasure pursuits such as a fitness center, a plastic surgeons' supper club, a book club, and a wind-surfing group. She concludes: "No family can stick together under the strain of so many outside interests. The human heart needs to be confined, not royally entertained" (*Rich in Love,* 15). According to the fiction, the Southern family was not doing well in the 1980s; it was slowly disintegrating or simply collapsing.

"*I beg your pardon/ I never promised you a rose garden,*" *sang Lynn Anderson.*
For most Southerners there is no rose garden. With the changing family patterns, the children increasingly depend on their teachers for guidance. Traditionally the high school teachers of the South have been instrumental in finding and encouraging promising literary talent. Many writers owe their choice of career to these guardians of culture who have decided that writing is

important. How are the idealistic and helpful teachers treated in the fiction of their "grateful" former students? Josephine Humphreys' Lucille Odom finds that her teachers are "morose because of their jobs," and she reveals that her good grades came with the realization that teachers are tired and hungry for love, and besides "their cars broke down constantly." Schools are particularly dangerous for well-intentioned men; they will be ruined by teaching, as Lucille sees it "men teachers are the sorriest spectacles in the world" (*Rich in Love*, 170). Mark Steadman, a South Carolina writer with roots in Georgia, wrote about Miss Fulmer, a troubled teacher, in *Angel Child*. She is not cruel or distracted by nature, "it was only that she had enough sadness of her own to occupy her attention." Every evening the small distraught-looking teacher of thirty-eight would retire to her room to smoke Avalon cigarettes and sip bourbon. She would then listen to out-of-town stations, on her bed with the lights out, and – unloved and alone she would cry with unbearable longing. It is tough to confront spinsterhood in a society that ranks fecundity "the first duties among many, and the last joys among few." "The misery of her own life kept her from paying much attention to the problems of others, especially her students, since they were young, they had futures before them. That alone made her hate them a little" (p. 10).

"*I'm so Lonely I Could Cry,*" *sang B. J. Thomas.*
After our initial life with our families and after our first encounter with our teachers, many are lonely and have to get professional help. In her first short novel Kaye Gibbons, who forces us to focus on contemporary problems, sent young Ellen Forster, who has had to grow up too quickly, to a psychiatrist. The girl has good sense, and also obvious psychological problems, but characteristic of contemporary Southern fiction, the analysis does no good. Ellen goes to the therapy sessions because she knows the psychiatrist gets good money for his efforts to find what ails her, but she would rather be digging a ditch. The primary object of the sessions seems to be to make the therapist feel pleased with himself, which he manages by bending and stretching what the girl says into exactly what he wants her to say. When Ellen gives an unfriendly answer to a question, the psychiatrist pretends to be less than pleased. But Ellen knows that such a reply makes him very happy, as it means that he has his job cut out for him, "If everybody was friendly and sweet he would not have a job" (p. 88). The girl will never tell him he is wrong, as she knows that it took him a long time to make up his ideas, and what is worse he believes them. When he questions her on her newly assumed identity as Ellen Forster, she finally tells the psychiatrist that he is the one who is mixed up. And after he has written this down really fast and says he plans to discuss it, Ellen announces that she does not plan "to discuss chickenshit" with him and leaves then and there.

In *Hey Jack!*, where the fiction is as fragmented as the lives depicted, Barry Hannah's dentist character wants to talk to a young psychiatrist in Meridian about the possibility of expanding the range of subjects for discussion beyond the accepted in the state: money, blacks, women, religion, and Elvis Presley. When the psychiatrist asks him to undress, the dentist decides not to come back (p. 13). In her story "Love" Bobbie Ann Mason introduces a young married woman who seeks help from a psychologist at a free mental clinic. But the therapist, or "the rapist" as she thinks of the word, wants her to talk about herself although it is her husband who has nightmares about crawling through tall grass pursued by memories of Vietnam. Whenever she brings her husband into the conversation, the therapist looks bored. Finally Jeannette tells him, "I came to you to get advice about Donald, and you're acting like I'm the one who's crazy. I'm not crazy. But I'm lonely" (*Love Life*, 122-23). In Southern fiction of the 1980s little help was found in psychotherapy against the psychological scars and isolation of childhood, family life, school years, and early marriage.

"Talking about you and me and the games people play," sang Joe South.
The 1980s were a confused decade, Southerners played confused games like everybody else, and tended to try to overcome their disorientation through rampant materialism. At times the characters who people the fiction of the time have to go out of their everyday way to make money. Langston James of *Angel Child* by Mark Steadman is a fine representative of the materialism of our age. Accidentally he gets run down by a car and gets paid $10 by the driver who is relieved that Langston is all right. In his greed the boy suggests to his mother that he begin jumping in front of cars professionally. His mother's reaction is finally surprising: "It's sweet of you to think about it, Langston James, but you needn't go to jumping. We'll make do." "Couldn't we live off no twenty dollars a week?" "Son, I hate to tell you, but we're living off twenty dollars a *month* this minute" .... "You got better coming to you is what I mean." She stared at her hands folded in her lap for a minute. "Once a week would do it, son," she said at last. "No need to run it in the ground. It ain't worth your getting hurt over" (p. 15). When he makes the mistake of jumping the same car twice, the boy does get hurt. The driver decides to get his money's worth, puts the car in reverse, and runs him over on purpose. As his tires thump over Langston James the driver shouts, "Once is enough, Jumper."

"When his corporate day comes to an end/ he rides away in his Mercedes Benz/ soon he is lost beneath the neon sky," sang Waylon Jennings and the other Highway Men in "Angels Love Bad Men."
If we have made the money, we have to find something to do with it and with our leisure time. Harry Crews lets his characters in the story "The Wonderful World of Winnebagos" play golf. Two of them drive down the Skyline Drive hitting golfballs off every overlook in the park. At a height of four thousand feet they hit the golf balls into the valley below so that each drive is of a record length. When they are asked why they do it, they can only show what they are doing; they do not seem to have thought about a reason for it. But if they were not doing this they would probably be even more bored in their affluence. Another way of avoiding a recognition of the boredom of our lives by spending

some money is to buy a plot of land in Florida. In her story "He Holds a Black Umbrella" the talented Ruth Moose describes, in her own gritty style, how a middle-aged couple resists the invitation of the Great American Land Developers Association to buy a "Piece of Paradise." An attack on their sales resistance armor is made by an eager young salesman, called "the cheerleader": "During dinner they talk golf. Mr. Cheerleader asks if we play. No, my husband says. Sail? No again. Swim? Boat? Fish? Three more nos. Then he asks exactly what my husband does do. He reads, I say. Reads ! Cheerleader is astonished. Reads he repeats. Reads. He meets all kinds of nuts in this business but this is a new one" (*Dreaming in Color*, 143). Later the salesman wants to know their religion, claiming that all faiths have a chapel on the Florida estate, a different door for each. When they tell him they are Waldenites, followers of Henry David Thoreau, the Cheerleader says, "We have that too."

If we cannot afford to buy land in Florida, we can always try to leave our boredom behind by going there to visit a theme park. What could be more life affirming than spending one's savings in Disney World. It is considered a prize to be zapped in Disney World; it is a part of the way we live now. In Walker Percy' s *The Thanatos Syndrome* Tom More goes there to relax and to find himself. He finds he could have made a better choice for his vacation: "Disney World is indeed splendid – though I could not stand more than one hour of it. After one day of the Magic Kingdom, Tomorrowland, Adventureland, Mickey and Goofy, Spaceship Earth, the World of Motion, the living Seas, I take to the woods." The Mores stay a week, and with retired Canadians and Ohioans, they stand around nodding and smiling in the sunshine and at something of a loss. Percy questioned whether it is the final reward for these amiable people, who have finally escaped children and grandchildren, after a life of work, to stand under the minaret of Cinderella's Castle in Disney World? Or is it just emblematic of the way we always live our lives? Walker Percy told us that we live as if we were "stunned, knocked in the head, like dreamwalkers in a moonscape": "Tomorrowland! – We don't even know what Todayland is!"

"*I love You Because You Understand Me,*" sang *Johnny Cash*.

But did the man mean it? – "The immediate, natural and necessary relation of one human being to another is that of man to woman," as the young Karl Marx already noticed. He felt it his duty to inform the world that "From the character of this relationship, it can be seen how far man has developed," but then he felt obliged to inform of us of so many thoughts he had had.[5] The relationship between the sexes was no doubt the most popular topic in Southern fiction of the 1980s, and it still is. The state of Southern society in general is gauged through evaluations of gender relations. Some gender differences are obvious even to young people; this is particularly true as regards the topic of sex. Josephine Humphreys explores the politics of acceptance and rejection in her fiction. She gives us insight into the mind of a modern boy of seventeen through the thoughts of a girl of the same age: "Wayne's idea about sex was that it was still a healthy, fun thing for people in love to do, especially us because we were new at it. He said this whenever I held back .... Sex, he said, was dying out, and we ought to take advantage of it while it was still available.... I advised him to see Laura Migo, who I thought most likely shared his sense of urgency in the matter" (*Rich in Love*, 12-13). The young woman realizes that she cares for Wayne the way she cares for Huck Finn: she has an affection for him because he is so innocent, so good and American. But as a woman she knows that "this kid has a long way to go." Huck is so happy with his Jim, his raft, and his old river. Clearly *Huckleberry Finn* was not written by a woman. And women are not necessarily looking for somebody good, innocent, and American. They probably never were.

Some of our ideas about sex and gender roles never change. In the fiction of the 1980s they are often reflected in conversations between parents and children. Ruth Moose's "King of the Comics" contains a standard exchange between mother and daughter. The girl explains that a boy has tried to pull off her clothes. The mother wants to know where it happened and what her daughter was doing in the boy's room. The girl explains that it is where the comic books were, but it does no good, her mother is mad *at her*. The scene ends when the mother announces: "If you had been wearing a bra, this would not have happened" (*Dreaming in Color*, 119). But whatever the traditional ways of raising boys and girls, the result seems unavoidable – in the end they marry.

Southern writers of both sexes often describe marriage as a trap. In *A Summons to Memphis* Peter Taylor tells a story in the tall-story tradition of a soldier in Chattanooga, who wakes up one morning after a long night and knows instinctively and immediately that his good life is over. After all the liquor of the night before he remembers nothing, but he knows instantly "by the way a strange young woman ... was humming to herself as she brushed her hair that she and he had got married before the past evening was over" (p. 90). What could be going through the mind of such a man occurs to a Larry Brown character in "Night Life," "Here's the one thing I don't need: to get hooked up with somebody who has more problems than I do" (*Facing the Music*, 107). Brown, a Mississippian, writes realism of the uncompromising and unblinking kind. You have to be awfully careful in your choice of partner; but the characters who people Southern fiction of the 1980s were mostly unlucky in their choice. Marital relations are confused and at times destructive, so married life is often unhappy, but it is nobody's fault. The husband has to be careful, because for just one second of anger a woman can "make you pay with your house, and your car, and your money and self-respect," as Brown puts it in the same story. A husband has to be equally careful not to say the wrong thing, if he does not want his wife to wind up crying in the bathroom. Brown knows that marriage is "having to live with a woman. That's what marriage is."

At times marriage reduces us to "animals who can talk," as in Mary Hood's

"Something Good for Ginnie." But mostly marriage becomes a habit that controls our lives. In "Private Lies" Bobbie Ann Mason's Mickey "sometimes felt that marriage to Tina was like riding a bus. She was the driver and he was the passenger. She made all the decisions – food, furniture, Kelly's braces, his socks .... With her, life had a regularity that was almost dogmatic" (*Love Life*, 148). One of Barry Hannah's characters tries to break out of the pattern of regularity. He and his wife live in a gray house hating each other. Every night like most couples they quietly and desperately face the TV, until they go into a coma when the station from Memphis takes over. When he is sure his wife is asleep, the husband slips out trying to "get next to strange nooky." But his wife always wakes up and in her bedroom slippers she tracks him down and screams in the alley "like a fishwife" and it is over (*Boomerang*, 127). It is obvious that he wants her to come and get him, and their love is reawakened by his attempt to snap out of the marital coma.

"Sometimes it is hard to be a woman," sang *Tammy Wynette.*
But the title of the song is "Stand by Your Man." – According to Ann Beattie, who lives in Virginia, many modern men develop peculiar ideas about what people actually do in the afternoon. Hildon of *Love Always* seriously believes that "all day, people were pretending to be Tinkerbell or Mr. T. or marine sergeants or Godzilla and being hung by their thumbs and checking into motels with their lovers to put on diapers and play patty-cake .... Wives were told their husbands were in a meeting would never know that they were off at nude archery practice" (pp. 70-71). Beattie builds up the male character to the point where "Platonic love was about as probable as the last game of the World Series being televised without Instant Replay." The great comic fall that Beattie sets up for Hildon comes when he is asked to speculate about the whereabouts of his own wife, "Sleeping," he replies. It is in response to such unimaginative chauvinism that women writers rebel in modern Southern fiction.

Although we have to erase most of Ann Beattie's world of imitation identity in order to enter Josephine Humphreys' universe, there are obvious parallels in the treatment of gender relations. In *Rich in Love* a girl learns that certain roles have to be lived up to, whether you are a man or a woman. In a comic vein Humphreys describes a father figure who loses his driver's license after a speeding offense. The daughter sees that "a man without a car is a miserable creature...especially a Southern businessman" (p.10). The father refuses to ride the bus, so he ends up being driven everywhere by his wife. But he sits with his head lowered, embarrassed to the bone, feeling like "a pansy," because he has to sit on the passenger side. In a more serious vein the stereotype woman's role becomes abundantly clear to the seventeen-year-old girl when her mother rebels and vanishes. The daughter's life is now swallowed up by household worries: "There were not only laundry and food, but also wiring, bills, termite treatment, moths, Jehovah's Witnesses, telephone calls saying that the lady of the household had won a microwave if she...I was unprepared to be the lady of a house" (p. 32). The same complaint of being settled with all household worries characterized Southern fiction by women writers throughout the 1980s. In Mary Hood's story "After Moore" it is a question of who should do the everyday cooking. The husband does not think much of his wife's cooking and complains that "if she ever lose the can opener she'll starve to death," and he buys her *The Joy of Cooking* (*And Venus Is Blue*, 27). He does not say a word about what *he* would do if his wife lost the can opener.

"Please release me, let me go," sang Dolly Parton.
And many women echoed the refrain. – In the modern South with its changing pattern of gender roles, it may now be a question who should bring home the paycheck, and it leads to ugly domestic confrontations. In Ruth Moose's appropriately titled story "The Vinegar Jug" we witness the rebellion of a modern Mrs. Armstid. Sharon complains when her husband turns down a job of teaching at a junior high. He argues that it would not have been a job but a sentence of hard labor. Sharon wants him to do something–anything. She wants him out of the house. All he does is read the sports section of the paper, drink beer, watch TV, and gain weight. His behavior is that of the prototype male of the decade as seen in the fiction by Southern women writers. For a long time Sharon has been silent on the subject, but one day when he is talking about getting a job: "I'll dig ditches, if that's what ... I'll .... " Sharon quietly stops him, by saying, "Do it, dig ditches, do something. I'm tired of all this" (*The Wreath Ribbon Quilt*, 32). But Sharon's rebellion is not as simple as it first appears, for as it turns out, it is something else that bothers her. She thoroughly dislikes leaving a mess behind in the morning, as she knows her husband will have cleaned it up when she returns home. She is also a product of her background and training, and she does not consider house-cleaning a job for the man she married.

In the fiction of the 1980s Southern women were fighting a battle among themselves on the issue of women's liberation. Ann Beattie described a clash between women in a small Southern town. A woman store-owner, who has left the hysterical Upper West Side for a life of peace in a town in Virginia, has two women customers who ask for useful things for the contemporary woman: "thermal underwear, body building devices, hiking boots, and Mace." "Women must provide for women," one of the women said. "The day of the damsel is gone," etc .... "Oh, shit," the saleswoman said" (*Love Always*, 195). When the two customers loudly and insistently advise another customer, who is pregnant, to wear "extra large camouflage shirts as nightgowns" in order to communicate more power to the unborn child, the owner decides to call the police. Ann Beattie's own divided loyalties in the scene are revealed through her description of the dialing itself: "Her nails were so long that she dialed the phone with the back of a pencil" (p. 196).

In real life it was not always easy to convince women of the necessity of sisterhood and women's solidarity. In Mary Hood's story with the ironic title

"Inexorable Progress" a woman is campaigning against ERA and in favor of the traditional family. She hands out pamphlets "ERA – The Trojan Horse," repeating that her subject is "vital to the survival of the American home." The results are truly mixed. She tries to convince women to write their congressmen, but she is immediately associated with various religious denominations such as Jehovah's Witnesses and also with "Mormon fellers" (*How Far She Went*, 121). The irony is that it would not have made any difference whether she had canvassed *in favor* of ERA, her reception would have been much the same.

"You picked a fine time to leave me Lucille," sang Kenny Rogers.
And the Lucilles of the South were not the only women to leave their men in the 1980s. The desire for independence, the longing for the right to the private experience, and the jealousy in defense of the memory of it became more and more obvious in Southern women's fiction. In "Even the Bees in Denmark" Ruth Moose describes a moment of rebellion, which is an attack on men who try to hold on to their normality so hard that they appear insane: On a lawn in the center of Copenhagen an American housewife sees a beautiful woman on a blanket, completely naked in the sun. She lures her husband away so he does not see the woman, for she knows he would destroy the natural beauty of the scene, by staring too much and talking about it for ever. "Later when he talked on and on of the nude beaches, she smiled, said nothing" (*Dreaming in Color*, 186-87). But the kind of retreat into the inner fortress of thought is not always enough to overcome the rough scenes in a marriage. After many years the main character in Mary Hood's story "The Goodwife Hawkins" wants to divorce her husband because of his physical cruelty to her. He makes her strip and crawl, drags her by her hair, gives her cold showers, makes her change places with the dog at night, and he rapes her. The male doctor prescribes Valium. "She wanted to ask, For me, or Hawk? She wanted to ask, Have you ever raped your wife?" (*And Venus Is Blue*, 130). She does not ask these questions, but Mary Hood does

In spite of all the wrong treatment of women, it is often men who want a divorce. In "Solomon's Seal," an early Mary Hood story, husband and wife live together for forty years in a perpetual but inexplicable rage with each other. He is preoccupied with his rabbits, dogs, and TV, she with her plants and trees. They either do not speak or speak both at once without listening. They never hear "the one thing they were each listening their whole life for." Finally he wants a divorce. She looks at herself in the mirror before she goes down to the courthouse and is surprised by how much her face looks like his. In court he winds up with the house and she gets the lot. And he has to move the house without stepping on her plants (*How Far She Went*, 27-29).

"You gotta walk that lonesome valley," sang Johnny Cash as "The Reverend Mr. Black."
For most Southern writers the world is still a place where the whole is myster-

iously greater than the analyzable parts. But was the South in the 1980s still Christ-haunted in the way Flannery O'Connor defined it in her time? Religion is not an important issue or element in most Southern fiction of the decade. Surprisingly Southern fiction writers paid little attention to religion. It is not that it was rejected, it was simply ignored or taken for granted. Poetic and powerful religious passages may, of course, still be found, as in Ruth Moose's "He Holds a Black Umbrella." In the story a woman opens her door late in the evening to a child who has rung the doorbell. A wet and soiled girl of nine or ten stands before the door holding "a used paper bag both hands tight around its neck as though it is alive.... She reaches inside her bag, hands me a torn slip of paper. My Father, she says, wants you to read this. Against the rain and Johnny Cash, her voice is a whisper." The woman unfolds the slip of paper and reads the pencil scrawl: "For God so loved the world, He gave His only begotten Son." She invites the girl in, but she will not enter the house, her "Father" would not like it. The girl snatches the paper bag and runs down the street. Under a street light the puzzled woman sees a man, "He holds a black umbrella" (*Dreaming in Color*, 139-40). But in fiction of the decade the image of faith is rarely this poetic and hauntingly convincing.

Mostly people are not interested in religion. For Sam in Bobbie Ann Mason's story "Wish" the supposed mainstay in our lives is so boring that he falls asleep: "The sermon was about pollution of the soul and started with a news item about an oil spill. Sam drifted into a dream about a flock of chickens scratching up a bed of petunias. His sister Damson, beside him, knifed him in the ribs with her bony elbow. Snoring, she said with her eyes" (*Love Life*, 233). In Larry Brown's story "Old Frank and Jesus" one of Mr. P's problems is that he used to be able to talk to Jesus all the time and everything would be all right. Now he has stopped talking to Jesus. Things were better then. – Josephine Humphreys tells us tongue in cheek of a young woman who did not go to church because her mother did not believe in "laundry or carpools or God" (*Rich in Love*, 33). Instead the girl has to patch together her own religious education through TV preachers and radio gospel programs. In school she is embarrassed because she does not know the basic Bible stories. Her classmates have been saved at an early age and have been speaking in tongues since they were thirteen. But even when it is present, religion is not necessarily a day-today mainstay in life.

The old fundamentalism gained a new, but less impressive concreteness in the 1980s. In "Airwaves" Bobbie Ann Mason describes Joe's new church "the Foremost Evangelical Assembly": "The church is a converted house trailer, with a perpendicular extension. There is a Coke machine in the corridor. People sit around drinking Cokes and 7-Ups. No one is dressed up" (*Love Life*, 188). The service itself has changed, too. Individual testimonials come randomly and interrupt the "sermon." The young preacher opens his Bible and reads from what he calls "the Philippines." A young couple brings up a child to be healed; the child is walleyed. The preacher is astonished and cries, "Who me? I can't heal nobody!" (p. 189). Apart from the expected story of how bad the preacher was before he found Christ, the "sermon" is focused on gender relations. He claims that it was his wife's infidelity that made him turn to the Lord. And to impress his congregation he brags that he has given his wife "a beautiful house with a custom-built kitchen and a two-car garage." Actually they live in a dumpy old house that they rent. In the story religion is clearly seen as a ridiculous charade which does little to solve the real problems in our lives.

In "The Retreat," an early story by Bobbie Ann Mason, the topic is Christian marriage. Two ministers' wives argue on the subject of their husbands. One of them declares, "A man is born of God – and just think, you get to live with him" (*Shiloh*, 143). But the other woman asks a question that remains unanswered: "What do you do if the man you're married to ... say he's the cream of creation and all, and he's sweet as can be, but he turns out to be the wrong one for you?" Most Christian denominations would not provide an answer to the question from the pulpit. If we judge by most Southern fiction of the time, it was, however, women who held on to the fundamentalist beliefs, at times much to the dislike of their worldly husbands. Barry Hannah wrote, "It is terrible to see a woman become religious. Jesus on the telephone, etc. Jesus sleeps with her. Jesus is asking her to *join* him. There is no record of Jesus making love with anybody. But he is the eternal lover...." (*Boomerang*, 47). It seems that in Southern fiction religion and religious thoughts tended to get mixed up with sex and gender roles.

"Try a Little Tenderness" sang Billie Jo Spears.
Although most Southerners did not take the advice, violence, which is another all-American topic, is accorded far less attention in the fiction than one would expect. But some Southern writers who took up the subject. Mark Steadman exposed religious hypocrisy by associating a religious figure called Brother Moates with the American belief in the right to bear arms. The preacher believes in defending himself, so when a young man comes to his house for religious comfort and help, he is offered a twenty-five caliber Baretta for ten dollars. And the following revealing exchange occurs: "Is it better than prayer?" "What?" Brother Moates looked surprised. "I pray every night the Lord will keep me safe." Brother Moates looked at him thoughtfully. "Well, yes. Of course".... "Prayer is, you know, good *basic* protection, but you can't always count on it to handle the specific case." "You can't count on it?".... " You can't leave *everything* up to the Lord. He got a right to expect you going to do your part too." "And my part is to carry a gun?" (*Angel Child*, 74-75). It is, of course, a humorous narrative, but the inclination to violence, individual or public, is real enough. In his story "Midnight and I'm Not Famous Yet" Barry Hannah

tells us of a young man who seems to have served in both the Civil War and the Vietnam War. His fate reflects the life of many young Americans from the 1960s. The young man sums up his life in these words: "It seemed to me my life had gone straight from teenage giggling to horror. I had never had time to be but two things, a giggler and a killer" (*Airships*, 114).

"*Oh! What Could I Do Without God*" sang the Oak Ridge Boys.

But religion is only used in the fiction to bring out much humor; otherwise it is ignored. There is an unbroken tradition of humor in Southern fiction going back to the 1830s and 1840s, and humor is also the main strength of the writers of the 1980s, as demonstrated in the quotations above. One of the best of the new writers is Clyde Edgerton, whose fiction is absurd and graphic in the rendition of every detail, and it has humor and genuine emotion. In humor very close to William Faulkner's achievement in "Spotted Horses," he manages to combine the sense of the elemental with a sense of the ornamental and a sense of the concrete with a sense of religious mystery. (See e.g. the section called "The Vine" about the burial of a leg in Edgerton's *The Floatplane Notebooks*.)

Religion was not taken seriously by most Southern writers in the 1980s. Only racial integration seems to have been a more completely outdated topic than religion. Nevertheless, it is to religious faith that one of the best Southern writers of the 1980s turned for help in his struggle with the greatest threat to us. Walker Percy's adversary was clearly rampant scientism. With *The Thanatos Syndrome* it became clear that Percy polarized abstract scientism and Christianity. The true enemy is revealed in the section called "Father Smith's Confession." What Tom More, the main character, should do to stop the scientists from experimenting on the people of Feliciana is implied in Father Smith's account of what he did not do (or understand) in Germany in the 1930s. This is why Father Smith talks of "The Louisiana Weimar psychiatrists" (p. 252).

As the fiction of these writers substantiates, there can be no doubt that the Southern Literary Renaissance perpetuated itself with unchecked vitality in the 1980s. The way we live now is the topic of the fiction. The Southern writers of the 1980s described our lives of possibility in the family and in school, they focused on our parents, teachers and psychiatrists, they demonstrated the importance of the past in our present, they exposed our materialism and loneliness, they pried into our marriages and divorces, revealed our sexual and violent behavior, and unmasked our hypocritical attitude to religion. Faulkner's celebrated work on how we endure and attempt to live so we can stand our own selves was not wasted on the present generation of Southern authors. The writers referred to in this chapter exemplify the continuity, change, and excellence of Southern fiction in the 1980s, and their output was impressive.

1. *Selected Letters of William Faulkner*, ed. Joseph Blotner, New York, Vintage Books, 1978, p. 142.
2. *Possum. and Other Receits for the Recovery of "Southern" Being*, University of Georgia Press, 1987, p. 53.
3. "Introduction," *The New Writers of the South: A Fiction Anthology*, ed. Charles East, University of Georgia Press, 1987, p. xix.
4. *The New Writers of the South*, p. xxx.
5. Quoted by Kenneth Muir, *The Comedy of Manners*, London, Hutchinson University Library, p. 26.

Bibliography

Ann Beattie	*Love Always*	Vintage	1986 (85)
Ann Beattie	*The Burning House*	Random	1982
Larry Brown	*Facing the Music*	Algonquin	1988
Harry Crews	*All We Need of Hell*	Harper	1987
Pam Durban	*All Set about with Fever Trees*	Godine	1985
Clyde Edgerton	*The Floatplane Notebooks*	Algonquin	1988
Kaye Gibbons	*Ellen Foster*	Vintage	1988 (87)
Kaye Gibbons	*A Virtuous Woman*	Algonquin	1989
Shirley Ann Grau	*Nine Women*	Avon	1987 (85)
Barry Hannah	*Hey Jack!*	Dutton	1987
Barry Hannah	*Boomerang*	Mifflin	1989
Mary Hood	*How Far She Went*	Avon	1986 (84)
Mary Hood	*And Venus Is Blue*	Ticknor	1986
Josephine Humphreys	*Dreams of Sleep*	Viking	1984
Josephine Humphreys	*Rich in Love*	Viking	1987
Madison Jones	*Season of a Strangler*	Doubleday	1982
Madison Jones	*Last Things*	L.S.U.P.	1989
Bobbie Ann Mason	*Shiloh & Other Stories*	Harper	1982
Bobbie Ann Mason	*Love Life*	Harper	1989
Ruth Moose	*The Wreath Ribbon Ouilt*	St. Andrews	1987
Ruth Moose	*Dreaming in Color*	August	1989
Walker Percy	*The Thanatos Syndrome*	F&S&G	1987
Mark Steadman	*Angel Child*	Peachtree	1987
Peter Taylor	*The Old Forest*	Dial Press	1985
Peter Taylor	*A Summons to Memphis*	Knopf	1986

CHAPTER SEVENTEEN

Frames of Southern History, Biography, and Fiction: A Provocation

In 1995-96 I was back at the Institute for Southern Studies at the University of South Carolina, this time as a Fulbright Fellow. I was invited to participate in the conference "Southern Writers of Fact and Fiction" at Coastal Carolina University. My talk "Fact and Fiction in Three Easy Provocations" was an interesting experience because Josephine Humphreys, Elizabeth Spencer, Ellen Douglas, Dori Sanders, William Styron, C. Vann Woodward, and most of the historians I mention in this chapter were in the audience.

Frames of Southern History, Biography, and Fiction

My first miry trace of thought has led me to the conclusion that *history, as written by contemporary historians, is really fiction*. History supposedly deals in the verifiable time past, and fiction enjoys a certain timelessness, transcending history. Some historians are not willing to admit that their recreation of history makes them close cousins of the fiction writer. Are they worried about the status of history as an objective science? Some fiction writers are proud that they are not limited to facts, that they deal in not only *what was*, but also in a Faulknerian *what might have been* that is supposedly more true than truth. The fiction writers may think that by employing historical data they challenge the reader to distinguish between fiction and history. Good fiction can certainly encourage us to question the absoluteness of "historical verities" and help us raise the question of just whose truth it is that we are now voicing. Fiction writers therefore see a definite value in *recreating* the past. They insist on the freedom to communicate and improvise the emotions, the ambiguity, and the mystery of a character, whether historically documented in act or fact, or not. But in spite of blood-chilling claims by both parties, it often seems impossible to distinguish between history and fiction.

The confusion between history and fiction is due to the very nature of narrative. And we have to accept that this is what history is: it is a text, a narrative text. Except in our own brief lives we do not experience history, we read about it; and what we read is not history but historiography. It is a construct, written and rewritten, and the result can be defined as a historical reconstruction of a fictive nature. Even when we have primary sources, we have no personal knowledge of events in earlier centuries, we cannot observe history, so we have to rely on narratives written by historians. For us the Battle of Waterloo exists as a textual phenomenon and not as objective or scientific fact.[1] And when we read a narrative about it, we read *a story* of the battle, and our interpretation of the text before us is just as subjective as our interpretation of fiction. Both types of narrative *are produced* in the same way. The purpose for the historian is supposedly to inform man of his history, and literature is often thought of as a way of informing man about himself, so *the objective* at least seems to be the same. It is customary to talk about a difference based on a distinction between the real and the invented, maybe even between truth and imagination. But is fiction limited to the realm of the imagination? And is history limited to the recording of the actual? I am asking, in other words: is history ever simply a mirror of historical reality?

In the American South the question has been considered troublesome ever since the first novels and histories. No matter how exhaustive the history, a grey mass of facts not written about will always remain. And it is, in theory, in the use of the grey area that the fiction writer differs from the historian. William Alexander Caruthers, the 18th-century Virginia novelist, was aware that in his role as a writer of historical fiction, he had at times to replace what was, with what could have been. By employing historical data in his fiction he challenged the reader to distinguish between fiction and history, and he encouraged us to question the absoluteness of historical verities. Some historians are not willing to admit that the selection of material and recreation of history make them close cousins of the fiction writer. But antebellum Southern writers of the historical novel, such as Caruthers, John Pendleton Kennedy, and William Gilmore Simms, thought it just as important to give their readers knowledge of man through history, as it is to inform man of the past.[2]

What Caruthers shared with Kennedy and Simms was an ability to combine memory, tradition, and formal history in a matrix we can call fiction. All three insisted on the freedom of the novelist to speculate on and communicate the sensations, desires, hopes, frustrations, and reactions of their characters, whether the emotions could be historically documented, or not. It is obvious that Caruthers had his doubts about the capacity of the ruling Southern gentry and *The Cavaliers of Virginia, or the Recluse of Jamestown*, (published in 1835, the first golden year of Southern literature) reveals his democratic sympathies. Caruthers' cavaliers appear as the necessary antidote to Kennedy's ideal image of Virginia aristocrats in *Swallow Barn, or A Sojourn in the Old Dominion* (1832). In Caruthers' novel the aristocratic group under Governor Berkeley seems to arrogate all privileges to themselves. As he portrays them their manners are flawless, but their judgment is often limited and inadequate.

Even a die-hard historian would not deny that he has to limit himself to certain data, and that, in short, he cannot know the whole truth. As some historical information is excluded, his is a carefully selected truth. At times historians are like paleontologists who reconstruct whole dinosaurs from the evidence of a few fossilized bones. No matter how exhaustive the history, facts will always remain that he chose *not* to write about. By deciding what is insignificant enough to be excluded, and therefore sentenced to sink into oblivion, the historian *creates* history. – As Bertram Wyatt-Brown had to in his two books on the Percy family (*The Literary Percys*[3] and *The House of Percy*[4]) – As Dan Carter had to do in writing on Governor Wallace in *The Politics of Rage*.[5] But when Carter has described George Wallace's dramatic stand in the schoolhouse door in Tuscaloosa and the showdown with Assistant Attorney General Nick Katzenbach on June 11, 1963, the historian takes time out before the ensuing confrontation with General Creighton Abrams of the, for the occasion, federalized National Guard of Alabama. The trained historian as story-teller takes time out to show the governor at lunch: "A relieved Wallace wolfed a steak, hash brown potatoes, and fried onion rings, all doused with ketchup and washed down with three glasses of iced tea and a glass of milk." As we see, the effect of the factual is not always limited strictly to the facts. The enumerated menu is probably exactly what Wallace had for lunch that day, and the factual information is impeccably correct. But surely, unless we ascribe a historical role to fried Alabama onion rings with ketchup, the function of such a passage is literary: it helps to the author characterize the protagonist of the narrative.

It could be argued that the detailed mentioning of the lunch serves to bring out Wallace's unwillingness to change his everyday routine, that it shows his calmness in spite of the circumstances, and that his appetite indicates that he was actually enjoying himself. But Dan Carter, the historian, makes no such claims for his inclusion of the lunch details. The report of Governor Wallace's lunch potentially includes the responses of different readers to the governor, the situation, and fried onion rings. That is the way fiction works, and as it would seem history, too. The human interest element in the writing of history is as old as history itself. In some of the early sections of his history it is immediately apparent that Herodotus enjoyed telling us how Candaules, King of Sardis, forced his servant Gyges to hide behind a door and watch the queen "gradually disrobe herself," so he could fully appreciate her beauty. In revenge the queen has Gyges kill the king, and she marries the former servant. Although Gyges went on to rule for thirty-eight years, the historian devoted almost all his attention to the watching-behind-the-door scene.[6] Edward Gibbon also liked the story and told it with a variation about Rosamond, queen of the Lombards, in *The History of the Decline and Fall of the Roman Empire*.[7]

Even if a historian reports again and again on the same subject and the same period, his interpretation of the past will remain just that: an interpretation, based on selection. As David Cowart puts it: "History cannot escape imprecision because source material, frequently incomplete and slanted, must undergo interpretation by historians who, unlike physicists or chemists, can never neutralize or obviate the effects of their own subjectivity."[8] It seems that the historian must accept that his perspective is a part of a social construction that shapes allegiances, words interpretations, and that it is a perspective that it is hard to rid yourself of. And in this sense, whether he likes it or not, the historian is not only the cousin, but the twin of the writer of fiction. The claim was already made by Hayden White, who in his classic study *Metahistory*,[9] wrote of work by major historians in terms of their commitment to the tropes of classical rhetoric. White insisted that this element in their writing is more fundamental than the historians' ideas about their topics.

It is worth noting that the "facts" that a historian finds sound enough to rely on do not exist independently of language, except archaeological evidence, and still have to be expressed in something as elusive and inexact as language. Shelby Foote's career as fiction writer followed by twenty years as a historian of the Civil War offers an interesting case in point. The three novels that he wrote from 1949 to 1951 were influenced by his background as a professional soldier and as a journalist, but they did not reveal that a great historian was in the making.[10] But in 1952 he published the novel *Shiloh* about the 1862 Civil War battle of that name. It is fiction that only with difficulty can be distinguished from history, and it prompted Random House to ask Foote to write a "brief history" of the Civil War. As it turned out Foote wrote it in three volumes that appeared in 1958, 1963, and 1974. It is an interesting task to read *Shiloh* the novel and then proceed to the chapter on the Battle of Shiloh in the Civil War history.[11] In the novel there is more emphasis on the individual soldiers and their thoughts, but the battle and its history dominate the narrative. The historical results matter more, also in the novel, than the fates of the individualized soldiers. In the history all the tricks and techniques of the novelist are put to good use, and that account is as exciting as in the novel.

After the publication of the final volume of the Civil War history, Foote tried his hand at fiction again. On the bases of the civil rights battles in Little Rock during the administration of Gov. Orval Faubus and the surprisingly calm situation in Memphis, in 1957, Foote wrote *September September* (1978). When I had a chance to talk briefly to him in May of that year, he stressed that his career as a historian was over. But he was still very much the historian in his return to fiction. Time and place are so important in *September September* that plot and characters are dwarfed in comparison. The reader quickly suspects that the characters only exist to illustrate a historical period. The history of the month of that September *is* the structure of the novel, and it also becomes the only theme. In the so-called novel Foote was not satisfied just to deal in human beings and ideas. He could not, it seems, escape the great number of facts that he had gathered.

Some historians of today, such as Winthrop D. Jordan[12] and William S. McFeely[13] do not seem to mind the relationship with fiction, have the courage to admit they do not know the whole truth, and do not shun literary techniques in their recent books of history. Winthrop Jordan, who is usually a very precise and fact-oriented historian, ends his *Tumult and Silence at Second Creek* with a delightfully poetic chapter called "A Separate Peace." Theodore Rosengarten, the historian and author of *Tombee: Portrait of a Cotton Planter*,[14] notes that his main character Thomas B. Chaplain was "confused and ashamed" as the result of a case of racial injustice and murder on a neighboring St. Helena Island plantation. But the wording of Chaplain's own journal for February 19, 1849, reveals that Rosengarten's reading is open to question. I would argue that Chaplain seems more *furious and disgusted* than anything else. In his reasoning about why the owner and murderer of the slave is *not* made to stand trial, Rosengarten speculates wildly. According to the historian himself, he has now begun writing a novel about other events. And there are rumors of forthcoming books by historians patterned on Faulkner's narrative technique in *The Sound and the Fury* and on the structure of modern plays. – If historians are beginning to admit to and be proud of their writing of fiction, is it because they realize that in the history of the West, culture has been recorded and defined better by artists than by historians? After all, in defining their civilization Herodotus, Plutarch, and Francis Parkman were no match for Homer, Virgil, and Walt Whitman.

My argument should not be seen as a desperate attempt to aestheticize history, or to de-historicize history. I have no intention of consigning it all to the realm of the imagination, but it is a fact that history is always fictive, whereas fiction is almost always historical as regards the use of time and place. Great imaginative works by Homer, Virgil, Dante, Shakespeare, and Tolstoy depend on and have their origin in histories and historical data. The truth is that the writing of history and the writing of fiction depend on each other, even need each other. Both try to understand past experience in order to come to terms with the present. Finally, both the historian and the fiction writer try to inform the self by describing its origin and situation. And the historian is, of course, as interested in the result of his inquiry, the knowledge gained, the message, if you will, as the fiction writer. Although the reader may come to each with different expectations, there is not much difference between the methods of writing. Both the fiction writer and the historian are *authors* writing for their readers. The question: "who is the author of this book?" is equally important for readers of history and fiction. Both authors want, as a rule, to deal in the real and hope the facts will reveal a deeper meaning. But raw facts mean nothing in themselves, the author must process them, make the facts cohere, and make sense of events by relating them through the structuring of the book. Just how the author does this depends upon his or her background, knowledge, and time. But in the selection and the structuring *is* the interpretation for the historian, and this is when he makes judgments.

The writer of history needs the fictional mode to make past events come alive through narrative. The historian dramatizes by evoking both people and fried onion rings. To convince, his account must have concrete human beings as actors in the plot he details. The fiction writer on the other hand needs the historical mode to convince the reader of the reality of the fiction by placing it in a concrete setting. In view of so much common ground and so much overlapping, the virtue of maintaining a division into component parts may be questioned. Nevertheless, we hypocritically insist on a hard and fast distinction between history and fiction. So when a writer of fiction, or a historian, takes the consequence of our vague distinction between fiction and history, he will hear about it. As John Jakes did from historians and literary critics, after the publication of the highly popular *North and South*,[15] and as William Styron can testify, after the reception, especially by African-American and Jewish representatives, of the historical novels *The Confessions of Nat Turner* (1967) and *Sophie's Choice* (1979).

The second miry road that I want to walk is called "biography," but is it really biography in the sense of "personal history," or *is (auto)biography, at least by novelists, really fiction?* We are curious about the author who wrote the text, because we believe that knowledge of her will help us demystify her writings. More than sixty years of New Criticism, or for that matter decades of structuralism, semiotics, hermeneutics, and deconstruction of everything have not succeeded in killing off our interest in the author. Writers, teachers, and critics keep telling us that what we read is *fiction*, "a pure product of the imagination," – and "pure" means untainted by the facts of our private lives. – So *Biography* has been officially banished from the literary classroom, but has anybody been convinced? Even critics read biographies. Impervious to all abstract reasoning, our interest in biography endures. Perhaps because we still suspect that literature is in essence autobiographical.

Our reading of fiction is doubly oriented, we read it as a discourse which invokes another. Our focus is often on the fiction *and* on the author's involvement in her own fiction. We *want to know* more about the person who wrote the fiction, and we are curious about the life that produced the published thoughts. To what extent, we ask, does her life translate into fiction? If we are honest, we must admit that we ask the question quite frequently. What I ask is a related, but rarely voiced question: does fiction translate into a life? In other words, instead of reading biography in the fiction, I suggest that we see the fiction in the biography; e.g. in Eudora Welty's best-selling autobiography, *One Writer's Beginnings*.[16] If we read, speak of, and teach fiction in terms of biography, is it because we sense, in the face of all opposition, that there is *no difference in kind* between fiction and biography? – We are likely to get the notion when we read *contemporary fiction*, which is drifting towards biography, and also when we read *contemporary biography*, which looks more and more like fiction. We have been conditioned to think of the difference between fact and fiction as fundamental, and we come to autobiography with the specific expectation of learning about the autobiographer's life and background; but the dividing line between fact and fiction is now often obscured in autobiography, and in some instances it is invisible – Should we not expect to find not only the life in the art, but also the use of the art in the life?

Autobiography is as thematic as any novel. The former is as heavily emplotted as the latter, i.e. facts are also "bent and shaped to specific ends" in autobiography. Fiction and autobiography employ the same literary strategies to transform a chosen experience into art. – Welty's autobiographical writing never becomes fiction, but it certainly stretches the boundaries of autobiography. In this respect *One Writer's Beginnings* is not unlike the autobiographical books by William Alexander Percy, Richard Wright, William Styron, and Maya Angelou. There is a pronounced out-of-life-into-fiction tendency in

Welty's work, and her realism about family ties is nowhere more obvious than in the portrait of the Weltys at home. But to what extent have the Weltys we met been *fictionalized* in her autobiography? Welty has always considered the distinction between "private" and "personal" to be essential for the creative artist.[17] If "art" is simply raw experience, it reveals the artist's lack of detachment. If the perspective remains private, it probably remains too subjective to offer anything of universal significance and will therefore remain uninteresting to anybody but the artist. Good writing, like all good art, presupposes the work of the imagination on private history. If detachment from the private facts can be achieved, it will still be the artist's experience. But with the gained distance to the experience, it is now *personal* rather than private.

In *One Writer's Beginnings* Welty remembers through a finely honed narrative consciousness, belabors her private experience, and creates a great work of art. In her biography Welty employed her knowledge of the artifices of fiction, so that the end product became a readable and lively narrative. An example is a remembered dialogue between the father Christian Welty and his daughter from when they were on a car ferry operated by a single man pulling on a frazzled rope made from cornshucks: "I watched the frayed rope running through his hands. I thought it would break before we could reach the other side. "No, it's not going to break," said my father. "It's never broken before, has it?" he asked the ferry man. "No sirree." "You see? If it never broke before, it's not going to break this time.""[18] It is a good story, dramatized with actual dialogue, and it is both convincing and lively. But is it autobiography or fiction? Both are the results of omissions and selection, and both are more tidily patterned than the reality actually lived.

There is, however, a difference between *living a life* and *detaching yourself* in order to view it as autobiography. In *writing* it, you have to be able to create yourself and determine your own personality, for yourself and for the reader. For that reason Welty sat down to select from memory, to reject parts of her experience, to single out specific events, to skip long periods for various reasons, and to focus on characters that seemed all-important to her. Welty did this *deliberately*, and it was one of the ways in which she became her own inventor and the emplotter of her own past. She wanted to try to make her record of her life mean something. The germ of the whole of *One Writer's Beginnings* is in the italicized opening note, which is on the whistling up and down the stairs in the Welty home during the writer's childhood. It marks her last step in a long journey towards independence from her mother. It is a text that brings out what it was the writer "feared realizing" about her mother (p. 102). It is about a child's earliest relationships, and it is about the successful writer "matching family faces" (p. 58). As she feared, she found that "the faces" of mother and daughter do not match in most respects.

In an autobiography emphasis is expected to be given to the autobiographer herself. But Welty's autobiographical book is not about Eudora Welty. *One*

Writer's Beginnings is not the traditional tale of a white girl growing up in the South and her search for self-discovery. It does not live up to V.S. Pritchett's "favored, if limited, definition of autobiography," which reads: "It is myself I portray."[19] And it is not a book where the author sees herself as a member of a group, such as women or the middle-classes, nor does she write as a representative of a "minority," such as white Southern liberals – or Southern writers. Welty is clearly anxious to discover the continuities of her own experiences and the legacies conferred on her. She tries to limit herself to the events of her life as a young woman that seem to have formed her as a writer. But that is, of course, an impossible limitation to observe in practice. Welty is definitely not the protagonist of her autobiography. But she is the central consciousness and has to recreate herself as such a literary device. The process of her autobiography is that of an explorative statement. And the exploration volunteers little about the emotional life of Eudora Alice Welty.

The subject of *One Writer's Beginnings* picked Welty, so to speak. It is obviously private concerns that surface and ask to be written. Telling it is her way of confronting the memories. The main characters of the book are her parents. It is their lives she makes into a narrative. No reason exists to assume that they are not exactly what Welty wanted them to be in the book. The artist recreates them for a narrative purpose, and they are just as much created characters, as the characters in Welty's undisputed fiction. Through her characters, primarily the character of her mother, Welty seeks to master a troubling past. The story she tells us of her mother is finally a type of psychoanalysis, but so is most storytelling. The uncharacteristic glimpses into her private life that Welty offers in the book are there for a reason. She is not trying to tell "the whole story," only what is necessary for her. The true narrative purpose seems only to have been revealed fully to her as she wrote down the private details. And used narratively they become instruments of explanation. Like fiction the book is structured on certain moments. *If* it has a beating pulse, "it isn't steady" (p. 9). It is true that "the events in our lives happen in a sequence in time, but in their significance to ourselves," Welty wrote, "they find their own order, a timetable not necessarily – perhaps not possibly – chronological" (pp. 68-69). The autobiographer, or the novelist, may, of course, stumble upon an unexpected cause and effect sequence in her own life (p. 90). The book shows clearly that what Eudora stumbled upon was the memory of Mrs. Welty. Her dominant presence in the memoir offers essential information for our understanding of the daughter.

From the middle of page four, the mother is easily the most interesting character in this postmodern novel. She is shown as a woman who is mostly preoccupied with herself. She *will* be the main character and runs away with the narrative. We are told in no uncertain terms what to think of the character with her impatience and self-satisfaction. Technically it is done by leaving the mother standing apart "scoffing at caution as a character failing" (p. 4). The presence of the mother is nevertheless what unifies the disjointed narrative. Many paragraphs have the word "mother" in the first sentence, and many focus entirely on the character. In enumerating these traits of "a character" from the book *One Writer's Beginnings*, I am not at all interested in the real life of Mrs. Welty or that of any other character in the book. My interest is not in whether *One Writer's Beginnings* is true to life. Statements such as "that is not the way it was" or "that is terribly unfair to Mrs. Welty" are totally irrelevant for my attempt to read the book as pure fiction. When I consider the number of times, critics have read pure fiction as autobiography, I feel justified in ignoring Mrs. Welty's "real story" in my attempt to see her as the creation of the novelist's secondary imagination.

I have no interest whatsoever in evaluating the ethics of anybody, but only in the characteristics of the main characters *as they are described* in the text. *One Writer's Beginnings* is finally not so much an autobiography, but more of a postmodern narrative analyzing "my mother's component parts" (p. 56). It is hard not to be fascinated by a character who is proud to be a pessimist, almost never gives in to her pleasure, finds it impossible to forgive, cannot be consoled, always blames herself, and "would remember" only the worst from her past (pp. 46-49). The explanations in the narrative for the extraordinary behavior are that she grew up in West Virginia, that mentally she always remained there, and that she lost her first baby boy (whom Eudora was supposed to replace) (p. 53). Why the character is allowed so much space is not explained. Even on the few pages, such as the opening of the third part, where she is not mentioned, she is there, as an absent presence.

The obvious difficulty for the fiction writer as autobiographer is to combine the literal transcription of her life with her accustomed creative freedom of the imagination. In short, how to write autobiography as fiction without actually making it fiction. And Welty's autobiography is fictional not only in form. When everything is seen from the present, the Welty remembering is, of course, different from the young Welty remembered. She wrote of another person in another time, which left ample space for her imagination to contribute to the narrative, and which must have served as an invitation to fictionalize the memoir. The distinction between the genre of fiction and that of autobiography blurs in our reading of *The Optimist's Daughter*[20] and *One Writer's Beginnings*, as Sally Wolff has pointed out.[21] The recurrent formal features in these books are those of fiction. This is true whether we talk of narrative voice, control of the unstable narrator (with authorial intervention and suppression), characterization, choice of setting, use of family history, imagery, plot-delineation, scene by scene development, dramatization, use of dialogue, the revelation of theme, and the need for the participating narrator to come to an ending.

By remembering and through the act of writing it, call it fiction or autobiography, Welty hopes to be able to understand, alleviate, and perhaps to preserve her memories against the diminishment of time. As Welty defines it on the last page of the book: "The memory is a living thing – it too is in transit. But during its moment, all that is remembered joins, and lives – the old and the young, the past and the present, the living and the dead" (p. 104). For Welty memory is the very basis of identity. Her need is, of course, to understand, to be liberated from, and enriched by her family history and the origin of her identity. Toward this end she tells it as she believes it was. Finally, *One Writer's Beginnings* is not a private biography, it is a fictionalized memoir that always remains personal. We have to accept that like all autobiographers, Welty is an unreliable informant about her life, and fully as imaginative in compensating and distorting as any other writer of fiction. The autobiographer's intention of telling "the truth" may differ rather obviously from the intention of the fiction writer, but they are both engaged in asking questions of how we can invest our world with comprehensible life. The good autobiography is also an attempt to probe the depths of the human condition, which matters more than any historical accuracy. And in that sense, there is no difference between autobiography and fiction.

My third and final "miry" subject is fiction. And without pleasure, I have found that *modern fiction is (auto)biography*. The main trouble with fiction today is that much of it is based exclusively on memories of family members. The problem is that it is not really *fiction*. Hence the true emotional development of characters is at best simply indicated, and mostly just not there. It is not a part of the family lore. So we read accounts that recreate a part of reality only. One reason for it is the immediate success that many young writers are experiencing with their initiation stories. They are always told in a wonderfully catching, convincing, and humorous first person voice. Nobody does it with more genuine conviction than Kaye Gibbons, as in this passage from *Sights Unseen* :

> She told the arresting officer what she fully perceived to be the truth: She was on her way to the shoe store because the radio announcer had told her to come downtown right away, and then she saw this woman on the sidewalk wearing her clothes, trying to look just like her, and she despised it when people tried to mimic her, and she thought she would just knock the woman with the car and teach her a lesson and see if she came downtown dressed in clothes that she had no business wearing because only Maggie Barnes wore a red swing coat with a black collar and if somebody had to be arrested then what about locking up that bitch who was in there sniveling about her bruised, fat hips that could stand a clip off either side anyway .... The report makes my mother say she ran the woman down because she had fat hips, when what Mother had really meant was that the woman, by her dress and haughty gait, was trying to steal her soul. When she was sick, the theft of her soul by strangers was a topic she dwelt upon. Long after she recovered, she said she had been afraid of being left a shell of a person, a husk.[22]

This is impressive writing by any standard. In the middle of high comedy, the passage even manages to bring out the seriousness of mental illness. But even here, where a universal problem *is* brought up, a negative capability is not demonstrated. Unlike Dori Sanders, who does become Mae Lee Barnes in her novel *Her Own Place*,[23] Kaye Gibbons does not in any place in the book, not even for a moment, *become* Maggie Barnes. That character is and remains, we are always aware, a creation of the narrative voice we listen to. And that voice is always more alive than the characters it tells us about.

Is it then enough just to repeat the success of slipping into the right tone and voice, or should the author be able to negate her own person and world? I suggest that the author has to overcome her natural hesitance of rendering, inventing, and imagining emotions and innermost thoughts of somebody close to her. What happens in some recent novels, is that good characters are left as stunted growth – lost and subsisting in the enumeration of the "amusing" episodes we use about family members to ward off questions, such as "who was my grandmother, now dying?" or "what did the woman do and *feel* in life?" But to create art those are the questions we must ask. A confession of intimate family history exists for the writer's own peace of mind. The confession may be a boast, but mostly it is a cry for pity. The confessional mode is the true civilizing and embalming of Southern fiction. The ideal storyteller does not tell stories because she is eager to confess. She talks to us because she is genuinely concerned about the human condition. She tries to describe human identity, to outline how it was shaped, and to indicate the meaning of its history.

Knowing your history is important in contemporary fiction, as Clyde Edgerton proves in *Redeye*, his most recent novel, in which he deals in ancient mummified Indians of the caves in the American West:

> "Let's get a electric wire and hook her up and shock her," said Zack. "See if she comes back to life. I bet something like that ain't ever been tried. Ask her anything you want to."
> "That's ridiculous," said Mr. Copeland.
> "No, it's not," said Mr. Blankenship. "You could use sign language."
> "Not ridiculous *that* way. I mean ridiculous to think you can bring her back to life."
> "I bet it *ain't* been tried," said Mr. Blankenship. "Lightening kills you if you're alive. Maybe it works the opposite, too. Can you arrange it?" he asked Zack.
> "Well, they got that generator," said Zack. "All we need do is take her in there and get them to hook her up."
> "That's crazy," said Mr. Copeland.
> "They said Newton was crazy," said Mr. Blankenship.
> "Newton who?" said Mr. Copeland.
> "Newton. Sir *Isaac* Newton."

"Oh yeah, the one discovered electricity."
"That ain't ... Newton didn't discover electricity."
"What'd he discover then ?"
"He discovered *gravity.*"
"You planning to drop her off a building or something?"
"No. No. I said, "They said Newton was crazy." That's all I said."
"I'm saying 'Stay on the subject.' "
"You're saying you didn't know who the hell Sir Isaac Newton was," said Mr. Blankenship, "and I'm saying you ought to know your American history."[24]

The Southern grotesque lives. Even Shakespearian gravedigger comedy surfaces in the traditional Southern attack on book learning. And it is placed in the American West at a time when Twain himself was still alive. – As I am looking not only for wisdom, knowledge, and at least glimpses of insight, but also for a message, i.e. a desire to communicate something to me about the human condition, I must add that I do not believe the object of storytelling can be just to entertain. In contemporary Southern fiction the object often seems to be simply to make the reader laugh. But in the middle of the laughing, a thought emerges: Yes, it *is* hilarious, and then? Does the passage exceed in any way the situation described? Edgerton has continued in the trend toward situation comedy in *Where Trouble Sleeps* (1997), in which he has included several full length anecdotes. The difference that made Twain outlive the reputation of any of his competitors among the "Southwestern humorists" was his didactic nature. He always spoke of the human condition and spent his life confronting age-old human nature with its lasting problems.

Reading contemporary writers I would at times settle even for the simplified propagandistic message: "men are really ridiculous," if it is a choice between that refrain and no message at all. But I hope for a message on a slightly higher level. What I look for is best described as a confluence and a departure. First there is recognition in reading good fiction, then hopefully insight. Recognition of the social (family) situation, the comedy, the desperateness, the drama, the history, the biography, the politics, the poetry, the technique, yes, all of this and more, flowing together. But then, hopefully insight into the human condition, insight that will depart from the fiction and transcend the private and public history, insight that matters more than any historical or biographical accuracy.

We have now walked the miry road three times, the road "where pleasure never dies." We have found that historians, autobiographers, and writers of fiction select, arrange a pattern, unify, and emplot certain significant moments *for effect*, and they use memory and imagination in an interplay of fact and fiction. I must conclude that history is now fiction, (auto)biography is fiction, and, if it is not situation comedy, fiction is autobiography. Are our categories defunct?

1. This passage was inspired by Steven Lynn, *Texts & Contexts*, New York, Harper Collins College Publishers, 1994, p. 128.

2. For the Southern frame of mind in the year 1835, see my essay "1835: The First *Annus Mirabilis* of Southern Fiction," *Rewriting the South: History and Fiction*, eds. Lothar Hönnighausen & Valeria Gennaro Lerda, Tübingen, Francke Verlag, 1993, pp. 121-30.

3. Bertram Wyatt-Brown, *The Literary Percys: Family History, Gender and the Southern Imagination*, Athens, Ga., University of Georgia Press, 1994.

4. Bertram Wyatt-Brown, *The House of Percy: Honor, Melancholy and Imagination in a Southern Family*, Oxford University Press, 1994.

5. Dan T. Carter, *The Politics of Rage: George Wallace, the Origins of the New Conservatism, and the Transformation of American Politics*, New York, Simon & Schuster, 1995, for the lunch see p. 150.

6. *The History of Herodotus*, trans. William Beloe, London, Leigh and Sotheby, 1791. I, 9-19. Sections vii-xiv.

7. Edward Gibbon, *The History of the Decline and Fall of the Roman Empire*, London, J. M. Dent & Sons, Ltd., 1954, IV 454-56.

8. David Cowart, *History and the Contemporary Novel*, Carbondale, Southern Illinois Press, 1989, p. 14.

9. Hayden White, *Metahistory: The Historical Imagination in Nineteenth-Century Europe*, Baltimore, Johns Hopkins University Press, 1973. See also Paul Ricoeur, *Hermeneutics and the Human Sciences*, ed. and Trans. John B. Thompson, Cambridge University Press, 1981.

10. Shelby Foote: *Tournament* 1949, *Follow Me Down* 1950, and *Love in a Dry Season* 1951.

11. Shelby Foote, *Shiloh: A Novel*, New York, Random House, 1952,. & *The Civil War Narrative: Fort Sumter to Perryville*, New York, Random House, 1958, I: 314-51.

12. Winthrop D. Jordan, *Tumult and Silence at Second Creek: An Inquiry into a Civil War Slave Conspiracy*, Baton Rouge, Louisiana State University Press, 1993.

13. William S. McFeely, *Sapelo's People: A Long Walk into Freedom*, New York, W.W. Norton & Company, 1995.

14. Theodore Rosengarten, *Tombee: Portrait of a Cotton Planter*, New York, McGraw-Hill, 1987, pp. 121-24. Chaplain's plantation journal is reprinted in this volume, for the incident in question see pp. 456-58.

15. John Jakes, *North and South*, New York, Harcourt Brace Jovanovich, 1982.

16. Eudora Welty, *One Writer's Beginnings*, Cambridge, Mass., Harvard University Press, 1984.

[17] *Conversations with Eudora Welty*, ed. Peggy W. Prenshaw, Jackson, University Press of Mississippi, 1984, p. 214.

[18] Eudora Welty, *One Writer's Beginnings*, p. 45.

[19] V. S. Pritchett, "Autobiography," *The Sewanee Review*, 13/1 (January-March, 1995) 15.

[20] Eudora Welty, *The Optimist's Daughter*, New York, Random House, 1972.

[21] Sally Wolff, "Eudora Welty's Autobiographical Duet," *Located Lives*, ed. J. Bill Berry, 1990, p. 80.

[22] Kaye Gibbons, *Sights Unseen*, New York, G. P. Putnam's Sons, 1995, pp. 12-14.

[23] Dori Sanders, *Her Own Place*, Chapel Hill, Algonquin, 1993.

[24] Clyde Edgerton, *Redeye*, Chapel Hill, Algonquin, 1995, pp. 160-61.

INDEX

A Modern Southern Reader, 11
Abolitionists, 152
Abrams, Creighton, 266-67
Algonquin Books of Chapel Hill, 12
American Literature Association, the, 125
Amin, Idi, 81
Ammons, A. R., 9, 167
    "Hardweed Path Going," 167-68
    "Tape for the Turn of the Year," 167
    "Unsaid," 168
    "Visit," 168
Anderson, Lynn, 251
Anderson, Sherwood
    Winesburg, Ohio, 53
Angelou, Maya, 149, 270
Antietam, 25
Argonne, the, 78
Army of Northern Virginia, the, 29
Askew, Reubin, 223
Atlanta, Georgia, 117
Atlantic Monthly, 35
Auburn University, Alabama, 45
Aurelius, Antoninus Marcus, 41, 75, 80, 83, 176, 201, 203
    Meditations, 75-76
Austen, Jane, 173, 174
Austin, Texas, 42
Ayer, A. J.
Language, Truth and Logic, 131

Bachelard, Gaston, 185
Baker, Houston A., Jr., 103
Baldwin, James, 65, 113
Balzac, Honoré de, 131
Baptists, 119
Barksdale, William, 23
Barnett, Ross, 129, 137
Barthelme, Donald, 200
Beattie, Ann, 221, 247
    Love Always, 256
Beatty, Jack, 196
Beck, Warren, 248

Beckett, Samuel, 168
Beckwith, Byron De La, 129-30, 151
Benson, Robert, 154
Betts, Doris, 221
Boone Nathaniel, 33
Boren, David, 223
Bradbury, John M., 39
    Renaissance in the South, 49
Bradford, Richard, 165
Brady, Matthew, 23
Brinkmeyer, Robert H., Jr., 184
Brooks, Cleanth, 11, 180-81, 191, 209
Brooks, Edith Ann, 39
Brown, James, 155
Brown, Larry, 9, 12, 221, 231-41, 247
    Big Bad Love, 233, 235
    Dirty Work, 235-36
    "Facing the Music," 235
    Facing the Music, 233-35, 255
    "Falling out of Love," 235
    Father and Son, 239-41
    Joe, 235, 236-39
    "Night Life," 255
    "Old Frank and Jesus," 259
    On Fire, 234
    "The End of Romance," 234
Brown, Mary Ward, 149, 247
Bull Run, 25
Byrd II, William, 75

Cairo, Illinois, 188
Candaules, King of Sardis, 267
Carter, Amy, 209, 210
Carter, Billy, 155
Carter, Dan T.
    The Politics of Rage, 266-67
Carter, Hodding, III, 142n 12
Carter, Jimmy, 118, 155
Caruthers, William Alexander
    The Cavaliers of Virginia, 266
Cash, Johnny, 254, 258
Chancellorsville, 24, 26, 78

INDEX

Chaplain, Thomas B., 268
Charleston, South Carolina, 147-48, 219-28
Chekhov, Anton, 130, 131, 168, 201, 249
Cheney, Fanny and Brainard, 65, 79
Chicago, 173, 175, 176, 185
Church of England, 205
Citizens' Council, 129
Civil War, the, 21-29, 121, 261
Coastal Carolina University, 263
Coleridge, S. T., 23, 190n 20, 205, 220
   Biographia Literaria, 186
   "Ode to Dejection," 29
   "The Rime of the Ancient Mariner," 113
Conrad, Joseph
   Lord Jim, 80
CORE, 128
Covington, Louisiana, 191
Cowart, David
   History and the Contemporary Novel, 267
Cowper, William, 22
Crane, Hart, 29n. 7
Crane, Stephen, 22
Crews, Harry
   "The Wonderful World of Winnebagos," 253
Cunningham, John, 191

Danish Association for American Studies, the, 245
Dante, Alighieri, 269
Davidson, Donald, 22, 24, 29, 47
   Southern Writers in the Modern World, 219
Degler, Carl
   Place over Time, 10
Denmark, 200, 201, 258
Descartes, René, 207
Desmond, John F., 206
Dickens, Charles, 201
   Nicholas Nickleby, 180
Dickey, James, 9, 163-67
   "Deliverance" (film), 51-52
   "The Performance," 163-65
Dickinson, Emily, 22, 167
Disney World, 254
Dollard, John, 136

Donahue Show, 82
Doob, Leonard W., 135
Dostoievski, Feodor, 204, 205
Douglas, Ellen, 80, 149, 263
Doyle, Arthur Conan, 180
Dryden, John, 27
Duke University, 149, 217
Durban, Pam, 247, 250

East Germany, 201
East, Charles, 249
Ebenezer Baptist Church, Atlanta, Ga., 117-19, 122-23
Ebrecht, Ann, 198
Edgerton, Clyde, 12, 221
   In Memory of Junior, 149
   Killer Diller, 149
   Redeye, 275-76
   The Floatplane Notebooks, 261
   Where Trouble Sleeps, 276

Eliot, T. S.
   "The Waste Land," 21
Ellison, Ralph, 9, 103-14
   "And Hickman Arrives," 107-14
   Invisible Man, 105, 106, 109, 112
   "It Always Breaks Out," 108
   "King of the Bingo Game," 106-107
   Shadow and Act, 105
   "The World and the Jug," 105
Epictetus, 80, 83
   The Enchiridion, 75-76
Erskine, Jr., Albert, 38
Etheridge, Jack, 118, 123
European Southern Studies Forum, the, 217
Evers, Medgar, 125, 128-31, 137, 151
Falstaff, John, 79
Faubus, Orval, 268
Faulkner, William, 12, 38, 92, 99, 108, 149, 186-87, 188, 201, 204, 205, 220, 239, 248, 249, 250, 261, 265
   "A Rose for Emily," 39
   Absalom, Absalom!, 39
   As I Lay Dying, 241
   Go Down, Moses, 53
   "Raid," 39
   "Spotted Horses," 39, 245, 257, 261
   "That Evening Sun," 39

"The Bear," 39
The Sound and the Fury, 39, 221, 269
Yoknapatawpha County, 108
Fitzgerald, Sally, 57, 72n 3, 72n 4, 72n 14
Flaubert, Gustave, 200
Fonda, Henry, 209
Foote, Shelby, 150, 221
   September September, 268
   Shiloh, 268
   The Civil War Narrative, 268
Forkner, Ben, 11
Forrest, Nathan Bedford, 133, 134
Frankenheimer, John, 51
Fredricksburg, 23
Freeman, Douglas
   R. E. Lee, 79
Fugitive Poets, the, 21, 22, 47
Fulton Court House, Georgia, 121

Gelfant, Blanche H., 222
Gettysburg, 25
Gibbon, Edward
   Decline and Fall of the Roman Empire, 180, 267
Gibbons, Kaye, 12, 221, 247
   Ellen Foster, 148, 252
   Sights Unseen, 148, 274-75
Gibson, Donald B., 115n 11
Gilchrist, Ellen, 271
Givner, Joan, 33, 35, 93, 102n 3
   Katherine Anne Porter: A Life, 33
Glasgow, Ellen, 132, 225
Godwin, Gail
   A Southern Family, 251
Gossett, Louise, 35, 36, 42n 5
Grabher, Gudrun, 159
Grau, Shirley Ann, 67
Gray, Francine du Plessix, 196
Greenville, Mississippi, 200
Gretlund, Glenn Nordby, 209, 210
Grizzard, Lewis, 247
Gulledge, Jo, 200

Haley, Alex, 120
Handy, William J., 42
Hannah, Barry, 45, 221, 231, 234, 247
   Boomerang, 250, 251, 256, 260
   Hey Jack!, 252-53
   High Lonesome, 148
   "Midnight and I'm Not Famous Yet," 261
Hardy, John Edward, 180, 181
   Katherine Anne Porter, 206
   The Fiction of Walker Percy, 206
Harper's, 199
Hawthorne, Nathaniel
   The Scarlet Letter, 151
Heidegger, Martin, 207
Hemingway, Ernest, 231, 234
   The Garden of Eden, 101
Hendrick, George, 34, 37, 40, 42
   Katherine Anne Porter, 34
Herion-Sarafidis, Elisabeth, 219
Herman, Wladimir, 195
Herodotus, 267, 269
Highway Men, the, 215, 253
Hill, Rebecca, 247
Hitler, Adolf, 81
Hobson, Fred
   The Southern Writer in the Postmodern World, 13
Hobson, Linda, 83
   Understanding Walker Percy, 81
Holloway, Gay Porter (sister), 102n 6
Hollywood, 240
Holman, C. Hugh, 132, 225
Holmgren, Staffan, 197
Homer, 269
   The Illiad, 22
Hood, J. B., 152
Hood, Mary, 231, 247, 248
   "After Moore," 257
   "Inexorable Progress," 257-58
   "Solomon's Seal," 258
   "Something Good for Ginnie," 255-56
   "The Goodwife Hawkins," 258
Houston, Texas, 191
Howorth, Richard, 201
Hubbell, Jay B.
   The South in American Literature, 5
Humphreys, Josephine, 9, 12, 147-48, 217-28, 247, 263
   Dreams of Sleep, 222, 224-25, 227-28
   Rich in Love, 220, 226, 252, 254-55, 256-57, 259

The Fireman's Fair, 149, 223-24, 226-27
Humphries, Jefferson, 11, 13
I'll Take My Stand, 226

Indian Creek, Texas, 34
Iser, Wolfgang, 164
Jackson, Jesse, 155
Jackson, Mississippi, 128-33
 Department of Archives and History, 140
Jackson, Thomas J. "Stonewall," 25, 198
Jakes, John
 North and South, 249-50, 269
James, Henry, 75, 249
Jefferson, Thomas, 10, 41, 48, 75
 Notes on the State of Virginia, 222
Jessner, Ulrike, 159
Jones, Madison, 9, 45-56, 151-55, 221, 247, 249
 A Buried Land, 50-51, 53
 A Cry of Absence, 52-53
 "A Modern Case," 51, 56n 1
 An Exile , 51-52
 Forest of the Night , 49-50
 "Home Is Where the Heart Is," 51, 56n 1
 "I Walk the Line" (film), 51
 Nashville 1864, 54, 151-55
 Passage through Gehenna, 43, 53, 55
 Season of the Strangler, 53-55
 "Tales of Dixie," 51
 The Innocent , 48-49
 "The Red Bird," 47
 To the Winds, 51
Jordan, Winthrop D.
 Tumult and Silence at Second Creek, 268
Joyce, James
 "The Dead," 40
Justice, Donald, 9, 165-67
 "First Death," 165-67
 "Fragment: To a Mirror," 166
 "The Missing Person," 166-67
 "The Telephone Number of the Muse," 165
 "Unflushed Urinals," 165

Kant, Immanuel, 205
Kaplan, Justin, 150
Katzenbach, Nick, 266
Kaunda, Kenneth, 118
Kazin, Alfred, 205
Kelly, Gene, 63
Kennedy, John F., 128, 137
Kennedy, John Pendleton
 Swallow Barn, 266
Kieft, Ruth Vande, 138-39, 181, 182
Kierkegaard, Søren, 9, 194, 195, 200, 207, 208, 210, 215
King, Coretta Scott, 117
King, Jr., Martin Luther, 118, 119, 122, 174
 "I have a dream," 117
King, Richard
 A Southern Renaissance, 11
King, Sr., Martin Luther, 9, 117-23
King, Stephen, 204, 205, 241
Kirkus Review, 153
Koontz, John Henry, 37
Kreyling, Michael, 11, 12, 13
Kristoffersen, Kris, 250
Ku Klux Klan, 134
Kyle, Texas, 35, 36, 40, 42n 4, 93

L'Amour, Louis, 204, 205
Lanier, Lyle H., 226
Lawson, Lewis A., 31, 191, 195, 206
Lee, Robert E., 24, 41, 75, 81
Lewis, Jerry Lee, 155
Lincoln, Abraham, 152
Little Rock, Arkansas, 130, 268
Lopez, Enrique Hank
 Conversations with Katherine Anne Porter, 34
Los Angeles Times, 80
Louisiana, 203, 215
Lowell, Robert
 "Ode to the Union Dead," 28
Lowry, Beverly, 247
Lund, Peter Wilhelm, 194
Lytle, Andrew, 47, 98

Malvern Hill, 25
Marlowe, Christopher
 Dr. Faustus, 209

INDEX

Mason, Bobbie Ann, 221, 247, 248
    "Airwaves," 259
    "Love," 253
    "Private Lies," 256
    "Shiloh," 250-51
    "The Retreat," 260
    "Wish," 259
McCorkle, Jill, 12
McFeely, William S., 268
Melville, Herman
    Billy Budd, 151
Meredith, John Howard, 129, 137
Mérimée, Prosper
    Carmen, 51
Methodists, 119
Meyrowitz, Joshua
    No Sense of Place, 177, 224
Miami University, Ohio, 47
Milton, John
    "Lycidas," 25
    Paradise Lost, 150
Mississippi Quarterly, 31
Mississippi State University, 151
Mitchell, Margaret
    Gone with the Wind, 82, 249
    Modern Language Association, the, 191
Montgomery, Marion, 248
    "Solzhenitsyn as Southerner," 162
Moose, Ruth, 247
    "Even the Bees in Denmark," 258
    "He Holds a Black Umbrella," 254, 259
    "King of the Comics," 255
    "The Vinegar Jug," 257
Morrison, Toni, 149

NAACP, 117, 121, 123, 128, 129
Nashville Scene, 12
Nashville, Tennessee, 197, 237
Natchez Trace, 49
National Review, The, 204
Nelson, Willie, 248, 251
New Criticism, 11
New England Transcendentalists, 109
New Orleans, 36, 38, 173, 191
    Elysian Fields, 41
    Vieux Carré, 100
New Republic, The, 196

New York Review of Books, 204, 205
New York Times Book Review, 196, 238
New Yorker, The, 132, 174
North Carolina State University, 73

O'Connor, Flannery, 9, 12, 31, 50, 57-71, 98, 203, 205, 215, 223, 259
    "A Circle in the Fire, " 63
    A Good Man Is Hard to Find, 64
    "A Good Man Is Hard to Find," 61
    "A Stroke of Good Fortune," 60
    "A View of the Woods," 60
    "An Exile in the East," 57, 64-66
    "Everything That Rises Must Converge," 60, 66
    "Good Country People," 60, 68
    "Judgement Day," 64-65
    Mystery and Manners, 59, 59-60, 61, 63, 65, 66, 67, 71
    "Parker's Back," 60
    "The Artificial Nigger," 60, 63, 64
    "The Barber," 60
    "The Crop," 60
    "The Displaced Person," 59, 64, 66-71"
    "The Geranium," 64-65
    The Habit of Being, 67
    "The Life You Save May Be Your Own," 61, 62
    "The River," 63
    "The Shiftlet Fragment," 57, 61-63
    The Violent Bear It Away, 64
    Wise Blood, 62, 64
O'Connor, Regina Cline, 57
Oak Ridge Boys, the, 261
Odense University Press, 19
Old Salem College, North Carolina, 171
Oxford, Mississippi, 231, 233

Paris Review, 33, 81
Parkman, Francis, 269
Parks, Rosa, 163
Parmenides of Elea, 24
Parton, Dolly, 197, 257
Peck, Gregory, 51, 52
Peirce, Charles, 204, 205, 207
Pelham, John, 82
Percy, Walker, 9, 12, 45, 73-84, 138, 191-215, 217, 221, 225

"Approving or Disapproving Eyes," 191, 214
Biografgængeren, 206
"Bourbon," 213
Conversations, 81, 193
"If I Were King," 78
Lancelot, 81-82
Lost in the Cosmos, 82, 191, 194, 196, 197
Love in the Ruins, 82-83
More Conversations, 78, 198
Signposts in a Strange Land, 204n 3
"Stoicism in the South," 78
"The Diagnostic Novel," 191, 199
"The Failure and the Hope," 78
"The Fateful Rift," 191, 209-10
The Last Gentleman, 79-80
The Message in the Bottle, 196, 205
The Moviegoer, 76, 79, 80, 207
The Second Coming, 80, 82
The Thanatos Syndrome, 82-83, 191, 199, 200, 201, 202, 203, 204, 206, 209, 210, 249, 251, 254, 261
Percy, William Alexander, 76-78, 81, 83-84, 205, 213, 270
"Enzio's Kingdom," 77
Lanterns on the Levee, 76-78, 79, 177
Pitavy-Souques, Danièle, 187-88
Plutarch, 269
Poe, Edgar Allan, 21, 168, 249
"Al Aaraaf," 161
"Silence—A Fable," 161
Poinsot, John (John of St. Thomas), 204
Porter, Catherine Anne (grandmother), 34, 35, 36
Porter, Harrison Boone (father), 34, 36, 37, 38
Porter, Katherine Anne, 9, 31-42, 89-101, 130, 211, 249
"All the Evidence," 97
"Audubon's Happy Land," 39
Mexico, 37
Miranda stories, 40
"No Safe Harbor," 41
"Noon Wine," 39
"Notes on the Texas I Remember," 35
"Rope," 40
Ship of Fools, 41-42, 98

"Texas: By the Gulf of Mexico," 37-38
"The Fig Tree," 41
"The Man in the Tree," 89-101
"The Never-Ending Wrong," 95
The Old Order, 93
"The Southern Story," 93
Porter, Mary Alice Jones (mother), 34
Porter, Paul (nephew), 31
Poteat, Patricia Lewis, 210
Prenshaw, Peggy, 134, 138
Presbyterians, 119
Presley, Elvis, 155
Price, Leontyne, 155
Price, Reynolds, 173-74, 187, 217
"Dodging Apples," 131, 227
Pritchett, V. S., 272
Publisher's Weekly, 153, 240

Ransom, John Crowe, 47, 226
Reagan, Ronald, 63
Reed, Ishmael
Mumbo Jumbo, 109
Reed, John Shelton, 221, 237
Revue Francaise d'Etudes Americaines, 45
Richard, Claude, 103
Richter, Curt, 209
Roberts, Philip Davies, 161
Rogers, Kenny, 248, 258
Rooke, Leon, 238
Rosengarten, Theodore
Tombee: Portrait of a Cotton Planter, 268-69
Rousseau, Jean Jacques, 48
Rubin, Louis D., Jr., 11, 13, 41
Rushdie, Salman, 150
Russell, Diarmuid, 130
Russia, 201

Samway, Patrick, 11, 206
San Antonio, Texas, 36
Sanders, Dori, 12, 247, 263
Her Own Place, 149, 275
Santayana, George
The Sense of Beauty, 131
Sauerberg, Lars Ole, 19
SCLC, 117
Scott, Walter
Ivanhoe, 80

INDEX

Seneca, Lucius Annaeus, 77, 176
Sewanee Review, 47, 79, 154
Shakespeare, William, 202, 249, 269, 276
   Macbeth, 207
   Othello, 150
Shelley, Percy Bysshe, 215
Shiloh, 25
Silver, James W., 142n 13
Simms, William Gilmore, 266
Simon, Neil, 249
Simpson, Lewis P., 10-11
Singal, Daniel
   The War Within, 11
SNCC, 128
South Carolina, 220-28, 250
South Carolina Review, 45
South, Joe, 253
Southern Growth Policies Board, 223
Southern Literary Renaissance, 12, 163, 221, 233, 247, 261
Southern Quarterly, The, 89
Southern Review, The, 45, 200
Southwestern Humorists, 276
Spears, Billie Jo, 260
Spears, Monroe K., 52
Spencer, Elizabeth, 263
Spinoza, Baruch de
   Ethica, 131
Squires, Radcliffe, 27
Srinivasan, Seetha, 211
St. Helena Island, South Carolina, 268
Stangerup, Henrik
   The Road to Lagoa Santa, 194
Steadman, Mark
   Angel Child, 252, 253, 260-61
Steiner, George, 162
Stengel, Marc K., 12
Straumann, Heinrich, 142n 19
Stuart, J.E.B., 82
Styron, William, 12, 150, 263, 269-70
   Lie Down in Darkness, 221
   Sophie's Choice, 270
   The Confessions of Nat Turner, 270
Sullivan, Walter, 186-87
Swaggart, Jimmy, 155

Tarleton, Banastre, 94
Tate, Allen, 9, 21-29, 47, 168, 187
   "Narcissus as Narcissus," 21, 26
   "Ode to the Confederate Dead," 21-29, 161, 171, 173, 176, 184, 187
   Poems: 1922-1947, 21
   Selected Poems, 21
Taylor, Peter, 12, 221, 249
   A Summons to Memphis, 249, 255
Tennessee Valley Authority, 50
The History of Southern Literature, 11
Thomas, B. J., 252
Thomas, Dylan, 201
Thompson, James J., Jr., 155n 1
Till, Emmett Louis, 129
Time Magazine, 150
Tocqueville, Alexis de, 198
Tolstoy, Leo, 269
Toomer, Jean
   Cane, 105
Travis, Randy, 148
Tuan, Yi-Fu
   Space and Place, 219
Turner, Frederick Jackson, 222
Tuscaloosa, Alabama, 266
Twain, Mark, 99, 247
   Adventures of Huckleberry Finn, 150, 154, 255

University of Alabama, 128
University of Florida, Gainesville, 47
University of Maryland at College Park, 31, 89
   McKeldin Library, 34, 39, 89
University of Mississippi, 129
   Center for the Study of Southern Culture, 14, 125
University of South Carolina, 73, 245
   Institute for Southern Studies, 19, 217, 263
University of South Carolina Press, 125
University of Southern Mississippi, 89
University of Tennessee, Knoxville, 47
University of Virginia, 103
University of Warwick, 231
University Press of Mississippi, 73, 212, 213
Unrue, Darlene Harbour
   Katherine Anne Porter's Poetry, 37
   Truth and Vision in K. A. Porter's Fiction, 37

Index

Vanderbilt University, Nashville, Tennessee, 21, 47, 73, 191
Vietnam War, 163, 174, 261
Virgil, 269
　The Aeneid, 27

Wake Forest University, North Carolina, 73
Walker, Alice, 149
Wallace, George, 128, 266-67
Warren, Robert Penn, 11, 12, 26, 38-39, 47, 49, 55, 92, 137, 163, 249
Washington Post, The, 153
Waterloo, 265
Watkins, Floyd C.
　The Death of Art, 163
Wellek, René, 45
Welty, Chestina Andrews (mother), 272
Welty, Christian (father), 271
Welty, Eudora, 9, 14, 31, 38, 125-41, 171-88, 196, 201, 217, 228, 249, 250, 270-74
　Collected Stories, 130-31
　Conversations, 133
　"Death of a Traveling Salesman," 19
　Delta Wedding, 127, 179
　Eye of the Story, 134, 187
　Losing Battles, 127, 179
　"Must the Novelist Crusade?" 130
　One Writer's Beginnings, 270-74
　Photographs, 134
　"Place in Fiction," 127, 174, 187, 219, 225
　"Some Notes on Time in Fiction," 186
　"The Demonstrators," 127
　The Golden Apples, 53, 127, 174, 179, 186
　The Optimist's Daughter, 127, 171, 273

The Ponder Heart, 174, 180
"The Winds," 127
"Tribute to Walker Percy, A," 138
"Where Is the Voice Coming From?" 127-41, 151, 154
West Virginia, 177, 183
Westarp, Karl-Heinz, 57, 73, 205
Westendorp, Tjebbe, 211, 212
Wheeler, Monroe, 43n 21
White, Hayden
　Metahistory, 267
Whitman, Walt, 167, 201, 269
　"Out of the Cradle Endlessly Rocking," 40-41
Wilderness, the, 26
Wilkins, Roy, 129
Williams, Jr., Hank, 249
Williams, Tennessee
　A Streetcar Named Desire, 206
Wingate University, North Carolina, 9, 13-14
Winter, William, 140
Wittgenstein, Ludwig, 204
Wolfe, Thomas
　Of Time and the River, 221
Woodward, C. Vann, 149, 263
Woolf, Virginia
　"An Unwritten Novel," 93
Wordsworth, William, 220
Wright, Richard, 112, 270
Wyatt-Brown, Bertram, 139
　The House of Percy, 266
　The Literary Percys, 266
Wynette, Tammy, 256

Yardley, Jonathan, 153

Zeno of Elea, 24